District Administration in India

About the Editor

Professor S.S. Chahar is Director of the Centre for Haryana Studies and Chairman of Local Centre, Indian Institute of Public Administration, New Delhi. After doing M. Phill and Ph.D. in Political Science, he started his teaching career in 1986 at Kurukshetra University. In 1989, he joined Maharshi Dayanand University, Rohtak, as a faculty in Public Administration.

Besides 48 research papers published in national and international journals of repute, Prof. Chahar has to his credit many books, including *Dynamics of Electoral Politics in Haryana, Pattern of Legislative Leadership in India, Governance at Grass-roots Level in India*, and the *Challenges of Consumer Protection in India*. Moreover, his two major projects Roles and Capacities of Panchayati Raj Institutions in the Maintenance of Health System: A Study of Haryana; and Consumer Protection: A Study of Awareness level in Haryana are in progress.

District Administration in India

In the Era of Globalization

Edited by

S.S. Chahar

Prof. Department of Public Administration
and Director, Centre for Haryana Studies,
M.D. University, Roahtak

CONCEPT PUBLISHING COMPANY, NEW DELHI-110059

Cataloging in Publication Data—DK
Courtesy: D.K. Agencies (P) Ltd. <docinfo@dkagencies.com>

District administration in India : in the era of globalization / edited by S.S. Chahar.
p. cm.
Contributed articles.
Includes bibliographical references.
Includes index.
ISBN 13: 9788180695629
ISBN 10: 818069562X

1. Local government—India. 2. Internet in public administration—India. I. Chahar, S. S. (Satvir Singh), 1955-

DDC 320.809 54 22

ISBN-13: 978-81-8069-562-9
ISBN-10: 81-8069-562-X

First Published 2009

Published and Printed by
Ashok Kumar Mittal
Concept Publishing Company
A/15-16, Commercial Block, Mohan Garden
New Delhi-110059 (India)

Phones : 25351460, 25351794
Fax : 091-11-25357109
Email : publishing@conceptpub.com

Dedicated

To

My Mother

Smt. Bishni Devi

Foreword

The Indian Administrative system rests on division of the entire national territorial jurisdiction into different units, called districts. Essentially, it is rooted in what we call district administration, which is a legacy of the colonial rule. It proved handy in smoothening administrative delivery particularly after independence by a model on which new reforms could for administrative viability. It was expected to transform itself into an instrument of social change, economic development, and political reconstructon. Ever since, it has served to work as the hub of all activities of the government.

With multiplication in the developmental functions of government, the role and work responsibility of district administration has increased tremendously, with high expection for facilitating active public participation in the formulation and implementation of governmental development policies and programmes. It has however, failed to perform to the level of popular expectations because of a number of problems. More important among these are bureaucratic mindset, eroded credibility of civil services, self-serving attitude of servants, long and cumbersome procedures, undue political interference, increasing urbanization, pollution and environmental threats, etc.

In view of these problems, work structure and role performance of district administration has come to be a subject of increasing debate and discussion, often in the backdrop of criticism on the delivery front. Whatever be the nuances of such debate, a serious effort currently goes on in search of alternative strategies and supplementary approaches for speedy mitigation of grievances of the common man and providing enhanced facilities for a better life to the public at large.

To adequately respond to the challenges posed by globalization, district administration needs new methods and techniques of developmental governance. Also urgently required is a whole network of administrative institution to work as necessary checks and balances in the governance mechanisms at the grassroot level. A greater degree of flexibility in policy formulations and impelementation deserves to be accompanied by effective delivery systems in order to achieve the desired developmental goals more effectively and in a time-bound manner.

For the said purpose, the existing administrtive set-up need to be reviewed, renewed, and revamped in tune with the New Public Management and Public Choice Theory. As specifically reiterated therein, it has to be made more effective, open, responsive, and citizen-friendly. This would, in fact, require a complete overhauling of distirct administration both in terms of its structures and functions.

Thus, the work undertaken by Prof. S.S. Chahar in the light of the above, is certainly a very bold attempt inasmuch as it throws light on some of the important aspects of the working of district administration in general, as also in relation to its existing structures, problematic areas, role restructuring, required administrative changes evolving corrective mechanisms, etc. The effort is, indeed, very timely. It would go a long way in benefiting academicians and administrators equally well.

I congratulate the author for bringing out this work of great contemporary relevance.

R.P. Hooda
Vice-Chancellor
M.D. University
Rohtak, Haryana

Preface and Acknowledgements

The district administration – a colonial legacy – was expected to be an instrument of economic development, social transformation and political reconstruction. However, it failed to perform these functions on expected lines because of inefficient and unresponsive bureaucracy, rigidities, complex and cumbersome procedures, corruption etc. Moreover, the advent of public choice Theory and New Public Management has challenged the monopolistic role of district administration and a research for alternative ways of problem solving and delivery of services began. In the present scenario, a need is to explore new methods and techniques, ways and means, a network of administrative institutions at grassroots level was felt. Now we should expedite administrative reforms including socio-economic and take steps for overhauling institutional and infrastructural tail backs innate in the system.

The present work is an attempt to discuss the inadequacy and incapability of the existing district administration in the supply of goods and delivery of services to the people in an effective, transparent, responsive manner and how to modernize and restructure it in the wake of liberalized and globalized world.

It includes 22 well researched papers presenting an in-depth, comprehensive and cogent discussion on modernizing, restructing the district administration in the era of globalization. In their contribution, the scholars have not only been candid in sharing their concerns on the issue of reforming the district administration but provide some remarkable suggestions on the scope, strategy and approach for the modernization and reformation exercise.

The work appropriately opens with an article by the editor himself, based on his experience and expertise. He has made a critical presentation of the existing set up of district administration and provided a frame for making it an effective and efficient means of redressing the public grievances. He is being assisted by Rajesh Kundu in the venture. The article by P.L. Sanjeeva Reddy is a wonderful description of traditional set-up of district administration and the ways and means to make it SMART. Similarly, N.C. Wadhwa and Vikas Gupta have pointed out the perception and attitude of civil servants (which matter the most) posted at district level. The way the red tape and favourtism prevail in their functioning is really an issue of serious concern and this requires drastic changes in conventional set-up of district administration along with some radical civil-service reforms to devise strategy for effective delivery and citizen satisfaction. S.L. Goel and Shalini Rajneesh have discussed the various reforms taking place in the district administration of Karataka. Mohinder Singh has raised the critical issue of MPLAD vis-à-vis DRDA and favoured the abolition of the former.

Suresh Mishra, Chaitali Pal, Raj Kumar Siwach, Navneet Kaur have reviwed the effectiveness of e-governance and IT as strategic reform approach with far-reaching effects on district administration. They have evaluated the impact of some of the ongoing e-governance and IT projects in lubricating the administrative machinery as well as combating corruption.

V.B. Singh and B.L. Sah have discussed the vitals of district administration in globalized society of 21st century. Shri Krishan has provided an excellent description of governance during the colonial rule to suppress and repress the ploughmen and wild tribes and tried to show its reflections in the present administrative set-up.

Manjusha Sharma, Rajesh Kumar and Ram Avtar have highlighted the significance of good governance at the district level and suggested the measures to put it in place. S.S. Rana and Anita Kharab have presented a critical picture of working of Food and Supply Department, Haryana w.s.r. to ills and problems prevalent in the procurement, storage and distribution of food-grains. At the same time they have offered very candid suggestions to the government for making the department functioning more responsive and transparent.

Lalneihzovi has flashed light on the working of district administration in Mizoram w.s.r. to Aizawl district and suggested the urgent need of democratic decentralization along with the adequate administrative machinery for its effective functioning. R.S. Gulia and Neera have pointed out the cultural problem of rural institutional credit w.s.r. to cooperatives and recommended the measures to make it accessible to more and more rural poor. Jagbir Narwal and Neelam have stressed the need of reforming the police in order to provide efficient service to the people. Finally, Satyawan and Anju have overviewed the drought management in Sirsa district of Haryana.

Therefore, I am highly grateful to all these scholars for contributing their articles. Moreover, I express my sincere thanks to all those who have helped me in numerous ways in bringing out the present work.

At the same time I am thankful to all of my colleagues in the department for providing their constructive suggestions during the completion of this work. I am also thankful to all my friends.

I shall be failing in my duty if I do not express my deep sense of affection to my brothers, sisters and children including Dabbu who have provided me the emotional succour when I needed it most.

The prime mover behind the work is my Mother who has always inspired me work hard and it was my father who really encouraged me to go for higher education and be a teacher.

I am also grateful to Shri Ashok Kumar Mittal of Concept Publication to bring out the work after a vigorous editorial exercise.

I am highly grateful to Prof. R.P. Hooda, Vice-Chancellor, for commending and forwarding the book.

Editor

Contents

1 Modernizing and Restructuring of District Administration in India

A Frame

*S.S. Chahar** and *Rajesh Kundu***

Indian administration has been divided into different territorial units called district for better development and effective supervision. District administration, being a legacy of colonial rule, proved handy in smoothening the transactions after independence by providing a model on which the new reforms could lean for administrative viability. It was expected to transform itself into an instrument of social change, economic development and political reconstruction. With the increase in the development functions of the government, the operational area of district administration has increased significantly and it is expected to ensure greater people's participation in the process of formulation, implementation and evaluation of all development policies and programmes. While incorporating all the agencies of government, the individual officials, functionaries and public servants, district administration assumes the total functioning of government[1].

The prominent functions of district administration include the maintenance of law and order, administration of criminal and civil justice, public safety, assessment and collection of various taxes and duties, recovery of loans, land reforms, land management, land record, irrigations,

* Professor, Department of Public Administration and Director, Centre for Haryana Studies, M.D. University, Rohtak

** Lecturer, Department of Public Administration, M.D. University, Rohtak

community development, industrial progress, co-operatives, public health, education, social welfare, panchayat raj, food and supply, disaster management and many others.[2]

India's development experience is embodied in a highly expanded role of state as envisaged by Nehru's model. It occupied commanding heights in the economy producing goods and services and the public sector began to acquire a larger role in development process. The colonial services being the beneficiaries, became great supporters of Nehruvian model. Indira Gandhi also expanded the role of state by nationalizing the banks, hotels and many other services and bureaucracy became all pervasive in the society. However, bureaucracy was unwillingly to change its ethics, elitist character, development perceptions and orientations and it came under heavy attack for not being able to perform and keeping the people deprived of basic amenities. Moreover, the problems like complex and cumbersome procedures, political interference, luxurious and expensive and inaccessible civil services, poverty, increasing urbanization, pollution and environmental threats, etc. brought district administration under heavy public criticism for its utter failures. Furthermore, for quality of service being poor, misutilization of public resources, declining credibility of public institutions, weak implementing machinery etc, aggravated the problem.

We have failed to deal with the problems of poverty and providing at least the basic necessities of life such as food, safe drinking water, sanitation and access to health facilities, minimum education and simplest kind of social security. Caste, communal, ethnic and secretarian division have assumed serious dimensions. Thus, we have transformed democracy into mere electoralism. There is a crisis of characterized values in politics and administration. Rajni Kothari has expressed his serious concerns about the crisis of institutions where much stress is on leadership and little on institutions, their integrity and autonomy. There is a tendency to treat power as a personal aggrandisment and administration as an instrument of patronage and profile.[3]

There is considerable frustration and dissatisfaction among the people about the apathy and lack of accountability of public servants. There is increasing anxiety about giving instances of corruption and criminalization in the public life. The deterioration in the performance of law and order and investigative agencies is also a cause of concern.

In view of such problems, growing public unrest took the form of movement and the government resorted to repressive tactics in order to deal with them instead of responding to their changing needs. This resulted into more movements[4] for civil liberties and democratic rights. Actually, the government undertook the transformative task but lacked the will to set up institution, involve people and sustain public spirit. This led to half-hearted attempts of mobilization, giving rise to more problems than solving them while giving repressive and coercive indication of crisis of governance.

Changed Indian Scenario

The New Public Management and Public Choice Theory paved the way for reshaping the administrative system in order to cope with the emerging problems in the era of globalization. For this purpose, many commissions and committees were set-up to suggest changes in the structure and working of administrative system at different levels. In order to decentralize the administration, 73rd and 74th Amendment Acts were passed. Moreover, the government of India organized a conference of Chief Secretaries of states in November 1996 and May 1997 to discuss the issues of accountable government, open, responsive and citizen friendly governance. It also talked of citizen charter, more people participation, review rules, regulations and procedures, transparency and right to information, code of ethics of civil services, etc.

The Information Technology Act was passed in 2000 for arranging citizen-centric services online. Furthermore, Right to Information Act was enacted in 2005 in order to bring the element of transparency and accountability in the administrative system. At the same time the Second Administrative Reform Commission has been constituted in 2005 to suggest ways and means to deal with the needs emerging in the wake of market economy.

Despite all such attempts, the desired improvements and changes have not taken place and much remain to be done in the field of right-sizing the government, use of information and technology, delegation of authority, more peoples participation, adherence to ethical standard etc. So, there is a need to reshape the system very drastically.

Responding to challenges posed by globalization, district administration started to find out new methods and techniques as well as a widespread and interrelated administrative network at local level. The main challenge is to percolate the benefits of development policies and programmes to the beneficiaries.

From New Public Management (NPM) to Governance

The NPM model, 1980s is all out to reshape the administrative system[5] to cope with the emerging problems in the 21st century. It advocates the spatial decentralization of management and production of services, need to improve service quality, greater attention to be given to the individual service user.

The basic tenets for reinventing the government are:

- Steering rather than rowing.
- Empowering rather than serving.
- Transforming rule-driven organization.
- Funding outcome.
- Meeting needs of the customer.
- Central issue in the Public Choice Theory is also to limit the government and to check the natural tendency for over government.

- Competition in delivery of public service.
- Dissemination of more information for public benefit.
- The hegemony of state and power of bureaucracy is to be challenged.
- Opening up possibilities of non-bureaucratic citizen friendly organization option.
- How to make the state more democratic and citizen friendly.

Development as Freedom : A Framework, 1999

Amartya Sen has advocated a theory that development takes place where a free environment is made available to citizens. In India - crossing of legitimacy, retarted development and curtailment in freedom are common problems.

- Development through people's participation.
- Governance and people participation.
- Governance and public meeting.

With the advent of concept of governance, a need to redefine and reinvent the government is felt by the scholars. The focus is to be shifted to serving the people. For this purpose, it is necessary to converge the efforts of various administrative agencies for delivery of basic services in rural and urban areas and for single-level dealings with the public. This calls for steps to reorganize work procedures, delegation down the line and an effective management information system accessible to all. Simultaneous steps to address the right-sizing of public services, value for money on public expenditure, effective audit, monitoring and evaluation good financial management system, etc. are required.

Action Plan for Modernizing and Restructuring the District Administration

Now time has come for a strong message to be conveyed that administration is meant for the people and not for public servants themselves. So, all necessary steps must be taken to arrest the present drift in government and public service and to the urgent measures to restore faith of the people in the fairness and capacity of administration. There is an increasing emphasis on well-defined mechanism for redressal of citizen grievances.

Restructuring of District Administration can be affected by :

- Strengthening and empowering the machinery of general administration.
- Integration of activities of various developmental departments in the district and a provision of a common expansion organization.

In other words it can be affected in two ways —

- Restructuring of administrative net-work
- Restructuring the procedures and methods of functioning.

The first pertains to inadequacy of administrative machinery and needs modernizing the existing ones and creating some more new structures and institutions. The second pertains to the operational part of the system whereby it is expected to deliver public service more promptly. For this purpose, certain steps are required to be undertaken such as—

Developing an Indigenous Model of Civil Services

The egoistic bureaucrats are not serious and substantive towards the basic needs of the people. Instead they employ all means to protect and promote their own interests as well as to please their political bosses. They cling more to the form than the essence of administrative rules just to delay the matters, but they flout rules or intercept them as per their personal convenience.

But now the changed situations warrant a drastic change in their behaviour and working style such as :

- They are supposed to be simple, accessible, transparent, purposeful, challenging, informal, moral, etc.
- To develop a focus on employees in an organization.
- There must a provision as performance related incentives to the employees.
- Emphasis on outcome rather than rules and procedures.
- De-emphasis hierarchical differentiations.
- Task-based organizations rather than power-focused structure.
- Quality developers, quantity maintainer, quality enhancer organizations be promoted.
- Establishment of client based organization.

In order to re-engineering the bureaucratic set up, we should undertake some major steps[6] like :

- Administrative engineering through in-service training in order to enhance the skills of civil servants.
- Strengthening the institutions of CVC, Ombudsman in order to deal with the issues of corruption and insentivity in civil services.
- Downsizing the bureaucracy and a law to this effect may be enacted on the lines of Japan.
- Colonial attitude may be replaced by managerial courtesy and helpfulness.

Code of Ethics for Public Service[7]

Public servants should adhere to ethical standards and the basic principles of the Constitution, such as, secularism, racial justice, protection to weaker and vulnerable groups, equality and rule of law. Moreover, the code of conduct should incorporate the positive statement of values and beliefs that should govern the public and private conduct of civil servants. Moreover—

- How to make the public feels that the decisions taken by civil servants are objective, transparent and don't calculate to promote improper gains for the party in power, bureaucrats themselves and third party.
- How to inculcate a sense of accountability and responsiveness, concern for value of public assets and funds, proper use of official position, profession and team work.
- In order to eradicate the evil of corruption, rules and legal provisions should be amended to enable immediate and exemplary prosecution and removal of corrupt officials having political protection.
- The investigating agencies and vigilance machinery should be strengthened by the provision of adequate staff, power, resources and autonomy accompanied by proper accountability for results.
- In order to deal with the issue of corruption, Section 197 of Code of Criminal Procedure may be restructured which provides that the public servants, in no way, be investigated by an agency like CBI without prior sanction of his superiors.[8]
- Areas of discretion available to public servants at various levels of administration should be curtailed to the minimum along with steps to prevent their arbitrary use.

Moreover, the civil services should have ethical consideration like: —

- Purpose — hopes and vision to determine the goal.
- Pride — proud of themselves and their organization.
- Patience — long term strategy.

- Persistence — action consistent with the set purpose.
- Perspective — a mechanism of control, monitoring and evaluation.[9]

Review of Laws, Regulations and Procedures[10]

In the age of economic reform and liberalization, the administrative red-tape, requirement of multiple-approvals and cumbersome rules and regulations causing delays and cost escalation stand in the way of efficient and effective working of administration. So, the old and overlapping laws, rules and regulations should be done away with and citizen friendly rules should be put in place like —

- All public offices should publish handouts in simple local language, the procedures to be followed, the methods of filling forms, fees and other requirements, and make them available to the public on demand.
- There is a need to simplify procedures based on the feedback received from beneficiaries and stake-holders.
- Various forms used by public can be standardized at district and state levels.
- Pilot modules for simplified procedures and processes can be developed on identified services and circulated for application.
- A shift from hierarchy to participation and team work on the pattern of 'Public Comes First' in U.K., Performance Evaluation in USA, Administrative Responsibility in Australia and Decentralization and Privatization in Israel,[11] may be made promptly.

Public Service Delivery and Grievance Redressal

It is essential that the services should be responsive to voters needs. Willy McCourt points out that service delivery should focus on three important points[12] :

- Ensuring performance.
- Developing competition.
- Responsive service.

In order to have efficient delivery of public services, reengineering of administrative system[13] is required in terms of :

- Making administration accountable and citizen friendly.
- Ensuring transparency and right to information.
- Taking steps to cleanse and motivate the civil services.
- Effective and speedy public grievance redressal system.

It is noticed that many of government departments and their subordinate offices at local level, having substantial public interface, do not entertain them properly and even the basic facilities like seating arrangement, drinking water, sanitation, etc. are not made available. Therefore, some urgent steps are required to be undertaken in this regard like:

- Such offices should be located under one roof i.e. district mini secretariat so that information pertaining to various issues may be provided through a window-service.
- There should be display-boards pointing out the information generally desired by the public on location of offices, facilities, various procedures involved, fee, submission of forms, time taken in disposal etc.
- Grievances from citizens should be received through all modes of communication like integrated voice, response systems, verbal, application forms, SMS, phone and website.
- Importantly, the language and tone of various application forms should be user-friendly and all sorts of forms should be available at a place.

- For effective grievance redressal, governance may be taken to the door steps through some programmes like *Sarkar Aap Ke Dwar* in Haryana, *Jan Sunvai* in Delhi and Rajasthan. The senior officers like Deputy Commissioner, Superintendent of Police, Director, Social Welfare, DDPO, ADO, DEO, Civil Surgeon, etc. should be present for prompt response in such programmes.

Such provisions may be made separately or women, Dalit and other weaker sections, senior citizens, disabled, etc.

- Every public office should have well defined mission-statement spelling out the standard of service to be provided to public such as garbage removal, water supply, power supply, etc.
- For redressing the petty grievances of common people at grassroots level like matrimonial, domestic violence, clashes relating to agricultural land and *lal-dora* land, social and religious matters, etc. a provision of concilation councils may be made which can be helpful in settling such disputes at the pre-litigation stage.
- Creation of village/area 'yahoo' group to address specific problems.
- Grievance should be monitored through computers and programmes like 'administration to the people' on the lines of Andhra Pradesh and Tripura.
- For prompt redressal of public grievances, independent grievance committees, consisting of eminent citizens be constituted. Such committees should be authorized to inspect the adequacy and functioning of grievance redressal system in various public offices and to suggest firm steps to be taken against negligent officers.
- Watch-dog committees may be constituted at the

district, block and village/town levels on the pattern of Mizorum to deal with routine problems of public at the grassroots.

- The district officials are required to visit the blocks and villages periodically in order to listen to the frequencies of people and their redressal on the spot on the lines of Tripura.[14]
- A district grievance board may be constituted having its units at block level and all public utility departments be brought under its jurisdiction.
- Giving one-life-time certificate to the people on the lines of Andhra Pradesh by incorporating birth, domicile, caste, etc. to avoid unnecessary red-tapism and delay on the part of the various agencies involving in issuing these at present.
- There is a need to develop a 'citizen satisfaction index for the core-services provided by various district offices and a third party quality assurance may be made mandatory.
- There must be an effective grievance tracking system to ensure redressal in a time-bound manner.
- There is a need to bring about a total change in the attitude of public servants towards redressal of public grievances at all levels and to pin-point responsibility for action on grievances of the people.

Introduction of E-Governance

Information technology helps in reinvigorating the government by enhancing the administrative capacity and organizational efficiency. It has the potential of improving people's access to government information and use of information pertaining to development and welfare activities. It also provides an opportunity to government to improve policy formulation and execution, widening opportunities and institutionalized innovations.

In order to implement of IT project we should :

- Identify the departments which have public interaction.
- Identify the existing functional modes in each department.
- Identify the existing manpower as well as required skill levels for proper public interface.
- Identify the models required for smooth interface.[15]

Resources in a district may be mapped and district information system may be created incorporating 'general information system'. For this purpose :

- Formats may be restructured to enable easy flow of information to the people.
- Dissemination of information should be done proactively through news-bulletins, websites and other forms of information, education and communication.
- Computerized City Civic Center should be established on the pattern of Sankaryam Project in Visakhapatnam Municipal Corporation[16] which can perform the following —

  (i) Online filing and settlement of complaints and grievances.
  (ii) Online tracking of building plan status.
  (iii) Online registration of births and deaths.
  (iv) Instant issuance of birth and death certificates.
  (v) Online tracking of garbage lifting.
  (vi) Infrastructural works online.
  (vii) Online citizen forum for furthering democracy.

- Land record should be computerized.
- Local area network providing information to citizen

about the status of their files and number of days to be taken for their clearance at various stages.

- Online payment of pension to the aged, widows and handicapped.
- The project like FRIENDS (Fast, Reliable, Instant, Efficient, Network for Disbursement of Services, in Kerala)[17] should be started in all districts of India where citizens can remit taxes, pay bills, access commonly required government services and obtain the latest information on various government programs.
- Community Internet Centers be established on the lines of Tamil Nadu[18] to enable the local population to use e-mail facilities in local language, to seek and obtain essential market-related information about commodity prices and agricultural inputs, medical and educational facilities, to procure print-outs of various application forms for different services offered by government departments, educational institutions, financial institutions, etc.

In Haryana, government has instituted an Information Technology Institute Fund (ITIF) with an initial corpus of Rs. 10 crore for e-governance and to promote IT in the state. For this purpose, 'Drishtee Project' is established at Sirsa which offers e-governance, education and health services through a software package which facilitates communication and information interchange within a localized internet between villages and a district center. The objective of the project has been to establish community owned, innovative and sustainable IT projects in the most poverty stricken areas.

Similar projects namely Bhoomi to computerize land record in Karnataka, Gyandoot Project in MP, etc.[19] should be undertaken.

The project like Gramsat Pilot in Orissa[20], must also be started in other states providing for —

- A hub-center at state's capital.
- Sub-centers at the district and block headquarters level.
- Direct reception system at gram panchayats level for providing live communication between the state capital, districts and blocks by creating a Master Data Base on land information such as land use, ground water, soils, village and forest boundaries, rail/road network, river, power distribution network etc. Besides, data on amenities and infrastructure such as markets, banks, co-operatives, industries, schools and colleges, health-care centers, service center, drinking water sources, fertilizer departments, seed distribution centers, bus stand etc. is made available. Data on demographic parameters, house-holds data, disaster-management is also be flashed.

Responsive Administration

Responsive administration[21] calls for morality and accountability of public functionaries directly to the people. Thus, citizen empowerment constitutes the single most crucial element of responsive administration. It focuses on the following—

- *Service standard*: Citizens should be told what level and quality public services, they will receive so that they are aware of what to expect.
- *Access:* All citizens should have equal access to the services which they are entitled, for example, increasing access of public services for those who have not previously received them. Many people who live in remoter areas can be reached by setting up mobile units and deploying facilities and resources closer to those in greatest need.

- *Remedying mistake and failures (redress):* If the promised standard of service is not delivered, citizens should be offered an apology, a full explanation and a speedy and effective remedy and when complaints are made, citizens should receive a sympathetic, positive response.
- *Getting the best possible value for money:* Public services should be provided economically and efficiently in order to give citizens the best possible value of money.
- *Consolation:* Citizens should be consulted about the level and quality of the public services they receive and whereas possible, should be given a chance about the services that are offered. It is important that consolations not only cover aspects about services currently provided but also about the new basic services to those who lack them. In that way, consolation can help to foster a more participative and cooperative relationship between the providers and receivers of public service.

Thus, policy making should show sensitiveness to citizen's problems and must not be influenced by extra-national interests.

Transparency and Right to Information[22]

It is increasingly realized that more the effort at secrecy, the greater the chances of abuse of authority by the public functionaries. Therefore, there must be a greater degree of transparency in the functioning of public bodies and widespread and easy access of people to all information relating to their operations and decisions as well as their performance :

- With the enactment of Right to Information Act, 2005,

there must be greater openness in working of public agencies. Adequate information on procedures for various statutory approvals, details of allotment of land and property, criteria for assessment and levy of taxes, criteria for award of work tenders and procurement of goods and services, selecting the beneficiaries under various government schemes, building approval, development expenditure and works, etc., should be made available to the public.

- Counters could be set-up in public offices for easy and prompt availability of such information to the public.
- Vigilance and monitoring committees at block level should be constituted to maintain transparency in the execution of rural development programmes on the pattern of Assam.
- Information should be provided in easy, understandable language.
- The employees at local levels should be directed to be courteous and open in dealing with the public.

Citizen's Charter : Bureaucracy-Client Interface

Citizen charter[23] is a technique for total quality management in public bureaucracies as well as ensuring accountability and transparency in the agencies engaged in providing services to the people or enforcing laws and regulation etc. Therefore,

- In India also such charters should be formulated involving District Collector, Superintendent of Police, Municipality, Zila Parishad, transport department, electricity offices, water supply, sanitary service, etc.
- There must be citizens' entitlement to easy, unhassled access to public services with stipulated quality and specifications, in an efficient and courteous manner

and transparent conduct on the part of service provider.

- The requisite procedures involving in obtaining the available services, structure for obtaining user feedback, procedure of making complaints and mechanism for their redressal, machinery for system audit, performance monitoring and evaluation should be displayed by the concerned department and agencies.
- Monitoring system should be installed to ensure availability of sustained benefit to citizens.
- The concept of model office, based on computerized counter services in order to implement the citizen charter, be established.
- The minimum standard of public services reflecting the principles like social rights, fair treatment, entitlement, openness, participation, co-operation etc. should be adhered.

Decentralization and Empowering the Local Bodies

After the failure of 'community development programme' and 'national extension service' to channelize community efforts for granting a self-enduring base of development, it was realised that power and authority should be decentralized to the popular local bodies. However, in the absence of any popular movement demanding local democracy, the state took a long time to constitutionalize the local institutions through 73rd and 74th Amendments.[24] which provide that:

- A greater representation of various political, social, ethnic and tribal groups is anticipated in planning and its implementation.
- It calls for increasing the administrative capability of local institutions as well as to institutionalize the

participation of citizen in development policies and programmes by creating an alternative means of decision making.

- At the same time, it enhances the government responsibility to the needs and demands of various interest groups within the society.
- More importantly, it ascertains the appropriateness of the means by which policies and programmes are designed and carried out to achieve the goals of development.
- It is required that powers and responsibilities mentioned in 11th and 12th Schedules of our Constitution be actually transferred to the local bodies.
- Decentralized planning should be made functional through the institutions of 'District Planning Committee' (DPC) i.e. planning process should start from Gram Sabha, Gram Panchayat; Panchayat Samiti, Zila Parishad and must assimilate in the state plan and finally becomes a part of central plan on the lines of Kerala and Andhra Pradesh. Moreover, tehsil and block planning committees be constituted to provide meaningful inputs to the DPC.
- Funds on the pattern of M.P. local area development fund' may be created for elected representatives of local bodies.
- There is a need to weave and develop a new and responsible participation culture at grassroots level to sort out the problem of coordination.
- Development through evolution of effective policies with people's participation as suggested by Amartya Sen in Development as Freedom: A Framework, 1999.[25]
- Vigilance and monitoring committees for supervising the execution of development schemes may be constituted on the basis of Assam.

- Suitable structures and institutional arrangements may be made at the local level to integrate the people into governmental process as well as to take the administration at the doorsteps of the public.
- Autonomous district councils, village councils may be established on the pattern of Mizorum for the actual decentralization of powers.

Problems and Contradictions in 73rd and 74th Amendments

Even though we have been talking of decentralization for the last 58 years, actually a lot of centralization has happened. Moreover, the highhandedness of bureaucracy over the local autonomy still prevails and despite the constitutional amendments, it is not prepared to function in cooperation with the peoples' representatives. Moreover, we have certain problems like:

- Powers and responsibilities given in 11th and 12th Schedules of the Constitution have not been actually transferred to the people's representatives because the octopus like grip of the district bureaucracy is not prepared to shed any of its colonial legacy out of fear of being marginalized in the development process.
- There exists a dyarchical situation at the district level—DRDA and Zila Parishad. Due to this, the Central government recommended the merger of the DRDA with the Zila Parishad. But except for a few states (MP, Kerala, U.P.) the recommendations have not been implemented because of the collusion between the bureaucracy and state level political leadership.
- Ineffectiveness of the gram sabha is another constraint in the decentralized governance. This is a matter of great concern because grassroots democracy can't be

successful unless gram sabha is vigilant and sensitive to their own problems.

- It is quite ironical that we are creating another center of power at the local level in the name of area development funds of MPs and MLAs. It could be because the political leadership of the state is apprehensive of the fact that if PRIs are given a free hand, the dominance of state leadership will gradually recede.
- Another weakness is the problems of co-ordination among the three levels of PRIs, which has created ambiguities related to the distribution of their powers and functions, lack of clarity on the role of PRIs as planning and implementing agencies, absence of understanding with regard to the relationship between the PRIs and local level bureaucracy.
- Financial resources of PRIs of local bodies are really inadequate.
- Despite the provision of a district planning committee under Article 243ZD, the experience is quite discouraging.

Restructuring Police Department

The documents of civil liberties organization of 1990s contain details about the arbitrary and naked exercise of power by the police without any regard to the legal restrictions imposed on their authority.[26]

Manu recommended that the police jobs should be entrusted to only persons with local knowledge of people and regions and the main duty was to maintain law and order. Even now also, this basic duty has not changed.

The philosophy and procedure of the Indian Police Act, 1861 needs a drastic and rigorous changes to address the public needs and problems. In this regard the Supreme Court has outlined certain police reforms in the Prakash Singh (a retired CRPF-DGP), Public suit, on September 22, 2006 which are :

- In order to make it more accountable and protect it from political interference a State Security Commission may be set-up in every state comprising the Chief Minister or Home Minister as Chairman, the DGP as ex-officio Secretary, a member of Opposition, a Judge and eminent non-political member of civil society. The Commission would select DGP from a panel of three recommended by the UPSC.
- The tenure of top police officers from the rank of Superintendent of Police upwards would be for a minimum period of two years in order to minimize the political interference.
- A Police Establishment Board under the DGP is to be created in every state to appoint and transfer officers below the level of S.P.
- Scientific research is to be introduced to enhance crime detection.
- A Police Complaint Authority under a retired Supreme Court or High Court judge is to be created in every district to hear public complaints against cops upto the rank of DSP and its recommendations would be binding.
- Separation of crime investigation and prosecution from the maintenance of general law and order. The verdict of the Court is based on recommendations of NHRC, the Julio Ribeiro Committee and Soli Sorabjee Committee to revamp the Indian Police Act, 1861.[27]

The Court has taken 10 years to give its verdict and directed the government to implement it within a period of three months.

K.P.S. Gill supplements some more areas of reforms like :

- The status of Security Commission should be like that Election Commission.
- The appointment of prosecutors should be made by the Commission.[28]
- The ratio of police to the population should be based on global standards.
- The salary and emoluments of police must be hiked to level enough to carry out investigation in a fair manner.
- A tremendous increase in the police personnel, police station buildings, jails and houses is the need of the hour.
- A massive investments in forensic facilities and high-quality training is required.
- Need to establish a police training center including the legal segment and the contents of training may be over-hauled.
- Focus on field training not only be limited to urban based officers but also be extended in rural areas.
- More important is to provide counselling to police to change its mind-set that it is for serving the people and not to terrorize and exploit them.
- Police administration be decentralized and be given independent status under the police Chief instead of D.M.
- Need of rationalizing the pay structure, amenities, perks and allowance, working hours of police officials.
- Provision of waiting-cum-reception rooms, drinking water etc. in the police stations.

Making District Collectors, other Officers Accountable[29]

There is a need to sensitize collectors to track key social

indicators. A system of competition in achieving quality in key schemes can be introduced. Commendation certificates for good performers and extra grants for districts can be given as awards.

- Tenures of collectors be made fairly stable and non-productive and time wasting activities should be reduced.
- In order to ensure proper implementations of schemes and better coordination, a monthly video conference between the collectors and departmental heads should be held. Responsibility of district level officers needs to be spelt out clearly.
- Flat hierarchies instead of tall ones to ensure an employee focus functioning, a critical desidertum missing in the old-line bureaucracies.
- Segregation of law and order bureaucracy and development bureaucracy.
- Separate cadre of panchayati raj bureaucracy be created at all levels of administration.

Defining the Role of District Collector[30]

Collector is a jack of all trades and is held responsible for whatever happens in the district. Greater clarity is required about what a collector is responsible for and what he is not. He should be enabled to perform the coordinating role to the best of his ability. The role of collector is required to be redefined and repositioned in view of the increasing emphasis on PRIs and urban local bodies.

Effective monitoring of a variety of departments requires that he should be able to comment and evaluate the performance of the functionaries of these departments with regard to the schemes involved.

- The district collector should be assigned the

responsibility of regulatory functions whereas the development functions should be assigned to district panchayats.

- The district magistrate should have a supervisory control over district police but it must be under full control of the police chief in peaceful conditions.
- Collectors be given institutional support and be encouraged to innovate and initiate appropriate solutions to local problems. The existing programmes should have enough flexibility for local variations subject to achievement of objectives.
- An innovative fund should be created at the state level to support such initiatives.
- Each collector starts several worthwhile initiatives which are either dumped or forgotten when he is transferred. So each initiatives should be documented and their continuity ensured if they addresses problems of the people.
- Delivery of service by each department should be evaluated by an external agency in which beneficiaries have representation. If the quality of service delivery is unsatisfactory, the department should redesign the schemes.
- The training and capacity building of district level officers should be enhanced to effectively support the development initiation. Yearly refresher courses should be mandatory for all functionaries with carefully designed curricula and training of personnel.
- The staff of the DRDA should be professionalized. Experts should be accessed from outside government and better salaries be offered for the required skills.
- For transfer and posting an independent Civil Service Boards should be instituted for transparency in the process. Minimum/maximum tenure period for various categories of posts should be prescribed.

Punishment, Reward System

- Simplification of procedures for major penalty should be considered. There should be a provision for summary time-bound enquiries in case of minor penality.
- 'Employees of the Year' award for each category of employees should be instituted.
- Identification of best collector/best district every year may be started.
- Personal information system and pay module should be introduced at all levels with a data base of employees and career profile which should be regularly updated.

Moreover,

- There is a need to reduce duplication of schemes.
- Element of discretion in implementation of projects should be minimized and accountability be ensured.
- Mechanism of district plan should be revived and sufficient funds should be made available for this purpose.
- Regular feedback on the impact of schemes should be arranged through open fora, surveys, NGOs and score cards.
- A discretionary fund should be available at the district head quarter to take care of viability gap funding, contribution to village communities to build assets, assist destitutes, etc.
- There is a need to modernize work place with better designs and aesthetics to ensure clean, hygienic and motivating environment.
- Some flexibility should be allowed at district level to right size and reallocate staff to improve work ethos.
- Better communication system viz. satellites, video-conferences etc. should be available at district level to take care of situation like disaster management.

Following facets may be considered crucial for high quality functioning of district administration:

- *Morality:* It should observe certain basic norms like freedom, democracy, neutrality, human rights, values and ethical behaviour.
- *Knowledge Intensive:* It should strive for knowledge society with vigor.
- *Committed to future:* It should be founded on the consent of the people and really democratic in spirit. It also permits alternative forms of consent appropriate to different values, cultures, societal traditions and situations.
- *High energy but selective:* The administration must perform tasks leading to weaving the future for the better rather simply a night watch. High energy is an essential attribute of the administration, with its long-term responsibilities. This does not mean more but effective management.
- *Deep thinking:* The need for action-oriented thinking directed towards fundamental issues rather than focusing on symptoms.
- *Holistic :* The management thinking, choice and action must be holistic.
- *Learning* in context of rapid change and need of creativity and innovation.
- *Pluralism:* It refers to providing for mufti-level, mufti-skill and mufti-culture oriented administration.
- *Decisiveness:* It requires that the various elements of governance reinforce yet correct one another and result in a clear choice, rather than neutralizing each other. This requires workable rules for decision-making, controlled hierarchical authority and democratic power concentration.

Public Private Partnership (PPP) Initiatives:

- Each state government should enunciate a policy

framework for PPP clearly laying down, *inter alia*, the areas of participation, bidding/selection procedures, nature of viability gap funding support to be provided by public agencies, etc. These needs not be left to the District Administration to be worked out anew in each case.

- Model bidding documents and model contracts may be drawn up by specialized agencies having expertise in the domain of PPP. Adequate technical support should be made available to district administration to take up PPP projects as they have neither the time nor the capabilities.
- A number of PPP initiatives in district administration are already in operation (e.g. SETU Project in Maharashtra). It is necessary to document and disseminate these initiatives so as to evolve models of best practices.
- A list of selected areas of public services delivery at the district level, which are potentially amenable to PPP, may be prepared by a group of experts.
- A set of middle level officials of district administration may be identified and trained in PPP so as to build a core group in each district to take these initiatives forward.
- A National Fund for Innovations in Governance may be created with a corpus to support PPP initiatives in district level administration. The task of screening of eligibility of proposals for assistance from this Fund may be entrusted to reputed agencies.
- The services provided by various departments should be evaluated by beneficiaries periodically. The Score Card mechanism has been utilized with good effect in some states to estimate the quality of services rendered. This needs to be replicated.
- The skills available in civil society, especially that of retired civil servants, could be utilized for evaluating government services.

- Support should be given to establish citizen centers to provide all information relating to government programmes as well as critical evaluation of government's policies from the point of view of the citizen. Standardized software is now available to quickly set up consumer kiosks providing services online. These should be established in each district within a defined timeframe.

Thus, the success of governance depends on the reinvention of government, re-engineering of bureaucracy and re-invigoration of non government sector, with a social motive. There is also a need of political will, normative concerns and organizational flexibility. The state, the private sector and the community based organizations should co-operate and co-ordinate with each other to make good governance possible. The district administration should carefully observe that:

- Do people fully participate in governance?
- Are people fully informed?
- Do people make decisions?
- Are women equal partners with men in governance?
- Are the needs of the poor and disadvantaged met?
- Are people's human rights guaranteed?
- Are the needs of future generation taken into account in current programmes?
- Do people own their structures of governance?

Thus the client character of administration is to be adopted.

The key question is : whether the district administration is effectively guaranteeing the right of health, adequate housing, sufficient food, quality education, fair justice and personal security to the general public?

NOTES AND REFERENCES

1. S.S. Khera, *District Administration in India,* New Delhi, National, 1979, p. 79.
2. Ibid, pp. 99-127
3. Aftab Alam, (ed.) *Crisis of Governance,* Delhi : Raj Publications, 2003, p. 14.
4. Narmada Bachao Andolan, Mazdoor Kisan Shakti Sangthan in Rajasthan, etc. can be cited.
5. The New Public Management gained currency in 80s to make the public service efficient, economic and effective. Similarly, the Public Choice Theory suggested a new paradigm of administration laying more emphasis on competitive and efficient service delivery. Pradeep Sahini and Uma Medury, (ed.) *Governance for Development,* New Delhi : Prentice, 2003, pp.22-23.
6. Vjay Kumar, Re-engineering Indian Bureaucracy to Meet the 21st Century Challenges, in *Governance for Development: Issues and Strategies* (ed.) by Pradeep Sahni and Uma Medury, New Delhi : Prentice, 2003, pp. 147-48.
7. See the recommendations of National Conference of District Collectors, May 19-20, 2005.
8. The sanction required under this Section is not needed now as per judgement of the Supreme Court delivered on December 6, 2006. While taking this decision, the Court dismissed a batch of writ petitions filed by three former Chief Minister Lalu Prasad Yadav, K. Karuna Karan and Prakash Singh Badal and several other politicians facing charges of corruption. For details see the Judgement, *The Tribune,* Chandigarh, December 6, 2006.
9. Lecture of N. Vittal, C VC, at the IMA Seminar in Chennai on March 13, 2002.
10. See the recommendations of National Conference of District Collectors, May 19-20, 2005.
11. *Economic Times,* New Delhi, October 16, 2005.
12. E. Vayunandan and Dolly Mathew, (ed.) *Good Governance: Initiatives in India,* New Delhi, Prentice, 2003, pp. 1-2.
13. See the recommendations of National Conference of District Collectors, May 19-20, 2005.
14. Ibid.
15. Vijay Rattan, *E-governance by Information Technology : Limitations in India* edited by E. Vayunandan and Dolly Mathew, New Delhi : Prentice, 2003, pp. 92-93.
16. Sanjay Jaju, Information Technology and Governance in Good Grievance : Initiatives in India edited by E. Vayunandan and Dolly Mathew, Ibid, pp. 70-74.

17. Ibid, pp. 102-103
18. Ibid, pp. 120-135
19. *The Tribune*, Chandigarh, August 4, 2005.
20. S.P. Nanda, Governance for Development: New Initiative Gram Pilot Project Orissa, in *Good Governance: Initiatives in India*. Edited by E. Vayunandan and Dolly Mathew, New Delhi, Prentice, 2003, pp. 109-20.
21. See the recommendations of National Conference of District Collectors, May 19-20, 2005.
22. Ibid.
23. See the proceedings of the Training Course on Citizen Charter, Haryana Institute of Public Administration, Gurgaon, June - July 2004.
24. Alka Dhamija, *Contemporary Debates in Public Administration*, New Delhi : Prentice, 2003, pp. 179-80.
25. Dhruba Jyoti Bhaumik, *'Economic Reforms and Role of Bureaucracy in India : A Study in the Perspective of Administrature Reforms'* in R.K. Arora's (ed.) Public Administration : Fresh Perspective, pp. 112-13.
26. G. Hargopal, The Failure of Organisational Reforms : A Tragic Story of Indian Administration in Contemporary Debates in Public Administration edited by Alka Dhamija, New Delhi : Prentice, 2003, p. 287.
27. *The Economic Times*, New Delhi, September 28, 2006.
28. *The Tribune*, Chandigarh, September 29, 2006
29. See the recommendations of National Conference of District Collectors, May 19-20, 2005
30. Ibid.

2 District Administration in India in the Era of Globalization

*P.L. Sanjeev Reddy, IAS**

For a complex, plural and large country like India bottom-up-approach is the key rather than topdown-approach. The Prime Minister while addressing the collectors conference said that[1] India's great strategic resource is its people. It has a billion opportunities in its people and you must all see that those opportunities are converted into a permanent advantage for our country (demographic dividend). The challenges you face in your district, be it the education challenge, the water challenge, the health challenge or the employment challenge, the solution lie in enabling people to handle change and improving service delivery.

The cutting edge of a government's function is at the district and lower levels. India lives in states, I could amplify that to say that India lives in districts, and villages below. Vast changes are sweeping India and indeed the world over for the last two decades. We are living in an increasingly integrated and globalised world. Distances are shrinking and markets are merging. Competition is the name of the game and the role of the state is being redefined in many sectors.

Government is moving from being a provider of goods and services to being a regulator and facilitator ensuring fair play and adherence to higher integrity, efficiency and accountability. Government's attention and indeed expenditure pattern is shifting towards the provision of physical and human infrastructure to enable individual

* Director, Indian Institute of Public Administration, New Delhi.

players to compete in the evolving enlarged and global markets.

The government has also the obligation to ensure that the benefits of growth trickledown to all sections of the society, to ensure that they become equal participants in development processes. At the same time, the government has to ensure that those who are adversely affected by the winds of globalisation are able to adjust to new realities and techno-economic opportunities.

A major shift in our administration through the 73rd and 74th Constitutional Amendments, which seek to revitalize local bodies and empower the elected representatives down the line. Our development experience so far has been that decentralization is not merely a political imperative but as much a managerial necessity given the large size of the country, its huge population. Even a district in our country is similar to a province in other countries. It is a managerial imperative to strengthen the middle management level in our delivery system for effective distribution of public services and this has to be at the level of the District Collector.

Sensitive to the imperatives of democracy and majority rule, you must be alert to minority opinion. You must learn not merely to tolerate but respect dissent because your job requires forging a consensus among contentious claimants. We are on the threshold of an era of immense opportunities and immense challenges and all stakeholders of our social, economic and political system have to work together to realize our manifest destiny.

We are living in a world where human knowledge is increasing at an unprecedented pace. We all have to be willing to think new. Your job is precedent and procedure bound but working in the 21st century, you have to be sensitive to the fact that you are living in an innovation-driven world, in a demanding polity and a plural society. Old solutions may not work. You should be able to provide a leadership in tune with the demands of our time. Therefore :

- Be idealistic enough to take up this challenge of building a new India free from the fear of war, want and exploitation;
- Be innovative enough to look for new opportunities.
- Be sensitive enough to contribute to creating a just and humane society;
- Be modest and lead decent but simple lifestyles eschewing conspicuous consumption and extravagant living;
- Have concern for those who work for you and inspire them through example;
- Combine your commitment to idealism with a passion for excellence;
- Compassion must be combined with competence.

The Concepts of Government and Governance

Government

It includes :

- Superstructure
- Decisions
- Rules
- Roles
- Implementation
- Outputs

Governance

It pertains to :

- Functionality
- Processes
- Goals
- Performance
- Coordination
- Outcomes

E-Government

Its focus is on :

- Electronic service delivery
- Electronic workflow
- Electronic voting
- Electronic productivity

E-Governance

It is about :

- Electronic consultation
- Electronic controllership
- Electronic engagement
- Networked societal guidance

What is meant by Governance?

Governance implies set of traditions and institutions by which authority in a country is exercised. This includes :

- The process by which governments are selected, monitored and replaced;
- The capacity of the government to effectively formulate and implement sound policies;
- The respect of citizens and the state for the institutions that govern economic and social interactions among them.

The major dimensions of Good Governance are :

- Voice and accountability
- Political stability and absence of violence
- Government effectiveness
- Regulatory quality

- Rule of law
- Control of corruption

Effective governance is to meet the challenges of :

- Promoting a professional, merit-based and neutral civil service.
- Functional reviews in public administrative reform.
- Strengthening transparency and accountability within the civil service.
- Training of civil servants.
- Promoting the use of information and communication technology.
- Effective governance to meet the challenges of poverty and social justice.

Main Four Elements of Good Governance are given as under :

- Accountability
- Participation
- Predictability
- Transparency

Characteristics of Good Governance

Civil society contributes to three complementary domains of good governance :

- Developmental effects on individuals (Efficacy, information, political skills, civic virtues, critical skill);
- Public sphere effects (Public communication and deliberation, representation of difference, representation of commonality);
- Institutional effects (Representation, resistance, subsidiary, co-ordination and co-operation);

Good Governance : Mission

The follower-to-leader transformation also requires profound adjustments in the organisation, processes, recources and culture. These are summarised in the contrasting requirements.

Good Coverage : Strategy

Reforms approach for good governance :

(1) Reforms under G-G : Transforming government
(2) Reforms under G-B : Growth friendly government
(3) Reforms under G-C : Citizen centric government

Good Governance : Capacity Building

It includes :

- Managing policy, strategy and performance;
- Managing continuous quality service to citizens;
- Managing programmes, projects and finances;
- Leading people, innovation and change;
- Right-sizing governmental, organizational structure and functions;
- Strengthening of civil society organization;
- Human resource development;
- Setting up of a National Centre for Good Governance;
- Potential networking of existing institutions.

Vision of good governance was very close to the heart of Late Shri Rajiv Gandhi.

Major initiatives taken by the Union Government led by Manmohan Singh include the following :

Bharat Nirman (Rs. 1,74,000 crores)

- A business plan for developing rural infrastructure;

- 100 per cent connectivity to Indian villages through roads, electricity and telecommunication;
- To ensure 100 per cent coverage under safe water supply;
- To construct additional houses for the poor;
- To bring additional rural land under assured irrigation;
- National Committee on Rural Infrastructure to monitor all programmes under Bharat Nirman.

Ensuring Sustained Economic Growth

- Liberalisation of the economy through a sustained reforms process;
- Easing of limits on FDIs in infrastructure;
- Special Purpose Vehicle for infrastructure investment be created;
- New Investment Fund be created;

Setting up of—

- National Urban Renewal Mission;
- Announcement of National Electricity Policy;
- Enactment of Patents Act, 2005;
- Strengthening of autonomy of RBI and all national banks;
- All the ports/airports are being modernised.
- The Golden Quadrilateral providing highways, connecting the entire country, is fast progressing;

To ensure the transparent governance the following is undertaken :

- Right to information has been enacted;
- National Action Plan for e-Governance (NEGAP) is under implementation;
- Communal harmony has been strengthened;
- Innovation fund to promote innovation in governance at the grassroots level;

- Inplementation of Citizen's Charters;
- Effective grievance redressal system.

A New Deal for Rural India includes

- National Rural Employment Guarantee Programme;
- National Rural Health Mission;
- National Food for Work Programme;
- Rajiv Gandhi Grameen Vidyutikaran Yojana;
- National Horticultural Mission;
- Food Security through Antyodaya Anna Yojana;
- Increase in Agricultural Credit;
- Market Intervention Scheme/Market Support;
- Development of Market Infrastructure;
- Increased Plan Outlay for Agriculture;
- Increased outlay on drinking water supply and sanitation.

Late Jawaharlal Nehru, in his famous 'Tryst with Destiny' speech at midnight hour on 15th August, 1947, had pledged that "service of India" will be the mission of free India's administration; What the "service of India" means, he explained, it means the ending of poverty and ignorance and disease and inequality of opportunity. The ambition of the Father of the Nation—Gandhiji has been to wipe every tear from every eye. That may be beyond us but as long as there are tears and suffering, so long our work will not be over.

Grassroots Institutions

- Panchayati Raj Institutions (PRIs) and Urban Local Bodies (ULBs) have the backing of Constitution 73rd and 74th Amendments;
- Community Based Organizations (CBOs) like User Associations, Self Help Groups;
- Civil Society Organizations-NGOs.

All these institutions are at the grassroots, occupying the same geographical space, working mostly in the same or similar sectors. Therefore, there is a need for synergy and their linkages for greater output, better outcomes and larger harmony :

- PRIs and ULBs represent the democratic power of the people and thus, have legal sanction to provide governance.
- CBOs have specific purposes like water use, irrigation, livelihood support, etc.
- NGOs or the 'Third Sector' provide an alternative channel to the service providers.
- But the local bodies have greater reach and capacity to touch the lives of people. They are closest to people and can feel their pulse.

Why Emphasis on Grassroots Institutions?

They work closest to the people—touch their lives, represent their aspirations with greater credibility and legitimacy. With them at the helm of affairs matching of resources with needs is possible, more efficient governance and delivery of services can be ensured, greater representa-tion to vulnerable and marginalised groups can be given, women, poor, voiceless and disadvantaged, and space for more players depending on activity can be ensured.

They are friendly institutions, can match outlays with outputs, to generate new ideas and new plans in consonance with peoples' needs and aspirations, for channelising energies of the community, for better feeling of the community, fraternity and togetherness and they can hear the grass grow.

Moreover, implementation of pro-poor plans and programmes is ensured and that is why the institutions like the World Bank support such institutions for their effectiveness. They are helpful in better use and leveraging of local resources, more cohesive community, society and sustainable development through increased participation and involvement, give shape to Gandhiji's Idea of Gram Swaraj and village level planning, to resonate, peoples' power and voice and local development. They do better leveraging of technology, management, human resource and societal networking, extensive use of ICT for establishing linkages, trigger and radiate positive impulses in the community and ensures sustainable growth.

Important Features of Grassroots Institutions

The main features are :

- Pro-poor, gives representation to vulnerable sections and women,
- Stand for delivery mechanisms and systems transparent and accountable to the people -more vigilant
- Spread the fruits of development all over,
- Institutions like the individual players in an orchestra— harmony important,
- Decentralizes powers, functions and authority — more democratic and people friendly,
- Taps the community and collective wisdom and knowledge—the present century is the 'Knowledge Century',
- To be based on knowledge power.

The grassroot institutions enable the people, communities and institutions of self-governance, with Spatial Data Technologies, for informed participation in decision-making for integrated development of local areas. They perform as geo-informatics for finding solutions to locale specific problems related to natural resources and provide the necessary information to the planners to make objective decisions. They are helpful in developing methodologies for building and promoting the use of spatial data management and analysis technologies in local area planning as well as technological and institutional capacity building in a mufti-level framework, so that people can plan their own development, utilizing the local resources. They can provide tools and techniques for assessing local level natural resources endowment, their utilization, potential and generating alternative scenarios for development.

The ultimate goal is to develop a system of data sharing, data access and data use for solving locale specific problems.

Wired Village Warana - A model solution framework for EG at village level

It is an unique effort to bring IT at the doorstep of Warana (a cluster of 70 villages) with goals of providing agricultural, medical, educational information to villagers thru' networked facilitation booths and also providing greater transparency in village administration as well as potential for sustainable and participatory rural development 29 subject areas earmarked for PRIs (under 73rd Constitutional Amendment)

In the end it can said that the focus of good governance must be on SMAART i.e.

- Small/Simple—decentralized and empowering grassroots,
- Moral—equitable and honest,
- Accountable—easily tracked,
- Accessible—geography and community,
- Responsive—service orientation,
- Transparent—corruption-free.

REFERENCE

1. PM's Address—Collectors Conference (May 20, 2005, New Delhi)

3 Modernization and Re-structuring of District Administration

*N.C. Wadhwa, IAS**

The present day District Administration is a legacy of British system which has continued throughout the country with small changes here and there. In fact, the Britishers had not copied this administrative set up from England but adopted the native system with some modifications to suit to the changed circumstances. There were two main objectives before them. The first was collection of revenue and second was consolidation of its authority in an alien land. The Britishers, therefore, adopted broadly prevalent system but prepared a detailed programme for ruling a vast country.

The origin of present district administration may be traced to the times of Mauryan Kings. The Mauryan empire was a vast and unwieldy empire but the Mauryan Kings were very wise and to rule the country in an effective way, they had split up the vast empire into administrative units of manageable sizes. The imperial agent of that time was Rajuka who can be equated with the present day Deputy Commissioner or District Collector. The Rajuka would perform all essential functions on behalf of the empire in revenue administration and exercise judicial functions alongwith responsibility for proper condition of roads, carried out public works such as irrigation, construction of essential buildings and roads etc. He was responsible for promotion of trade and industry also. Similar arrangement continued during Gupta's period and empire was divided into

1. Divisional Commissioner, Rohtak, Haryana.

provinces known as 'Dedas' and the provinces were further divided into *'Bhuktis'* which were about the size of a Commissioner's Division and the Bhuktis were divided into *'Visayas'* which almost corresponded to a modern district. Visayapati, who was incharge of Visaya, was responsible for maintaining law and order and collection of taxes and revenue.

The Mohammadan rulers, when they arrived in the country, followed almost old system of district administration. Under the Delhi Sultanate, the empire was divided into provinces and tributary states. The provinces were further divided into Shiqs and with the weakening of Sultanate empire, the Shiqs later on became Sarkars. Sarkar was counterpart of a modern district. Later on, Shershah Suri divided his empire into Sarkars and Sarkars into Parganas. This system served as a model to Mughal empire during the period of Akbar, who with the help of his Revenue Minister, Raja Todarmal, completely overhauled the revenue administration which formed the basis of revenue administration of British system. During Mughals, the empire was divided into Subas, the Subas into Sarkars and Sarkars into Parganas which have continued till modern times though with changed names. However, during Mughals, the incharge of Sarkar was Faujdar, a Military Officer, whose duties were to maintain peace and order, to keep the army well equipped and ready for service and to assist the collection of revenue. He had of course different officials under him to assist him in various duties.

The Britishers after adopting the native system of administration, divided the country into districts by putting each district under a centrally appointed official called the District Collector who was having full confidence of the government. This system made it possible for small number of foreigners to rule a vast country. The District Collector was vested with both civil and judicial powers as per system introduced in 1772 and this system of centralized revenue administration, continued for some time. However, in 1786, a new system based on de-centralization was followed in which Collectors were made incharge of civil administration of the district exercising revenue, judicial as well as magisterial powers. The Collector was, therefore, also made judge and magistrate and he was very powerful. The scheme was altered in 1793 by Lord Cornwallis who separated the revenue and judicial functions and entrusted them to different officials. However, in contrast to Cornwallis system, Monro School of district administration was adopted in the first decades of 19th century in the provinces of Madras, Bombay and North-west frontier province. This system was in favour of ancient custom under which an officer responsible for collection of revenue, was also vested with extensive judicial authority. Under this system, the District Collector was responsible for welfare of the people and the general administration of the district and this system was gradually favoured by the British authorities in India. However, after the revolt of 1857, two offices of Collector and Magistrates were re-united and the Collector became head of the district in 1859. This concept of the office of District Collector remained basically unaltered until the country became Independent.

After independence, we have adopted our new Constitution from 26th January, 1950 and India has been declared a democratic sovereign republic. There has been a complete change in thinking and objectives of the state. The present state is a welfare state and the final authority in selecting a government, rests with the people who elect representatives of their choice and through them, the political executive runs the administration through permanent bureaucracy. There has been complete division of legislative, judicial and executive functions of the state and these three organs are enjoying independence in their respective functions through a working arrangement as per constitutional provisions and enactments passed by the Parliament as well as state legislatures. However, the framers of the Constitution looked into all relevant aspects in view of historical, social and political background of the country and decided to continue more or less with the administrative set-up which was prevalent during British system except that the revenue and judicial functions have been completely separated. Though, there has been complete change in the thinking of the district administration when it relates to running of day-to-day administration, maintaining of law and order and undertaking of developmental activities but the basic form of the district has been retained as such. It does not mean that the framers of the Constitution and the successive governments which have been functioning both at the Centre and the state level, did not think of making any changes in the set-up of the district administration but it was realized that the basic change was required in the objectives and psychology of the administrative set-up and there was no necessity of completely altering a system of administration which had been continuing through centuries in the country and was easily understood by the people and acceptable to them.

It is not that the Muslim rulers or Britishers who ruled over the country, imposed this type of administration on the basis of any background in the countries of their origin but in fact, they adopted the prevailing administrative set-up in the country with certain modifications which suited to their way of ruling and running the administration effectively. It is quite relevant and understable also that the basic structure of administration which has evolved through centuries of different regimes and kingdoms and which has been accepted and adopted by the people of this country, can not be suddenly given goodbye just for the sake of introducing a completely new set-up because we are now an independent country and, therefore, totally new district administration is must to give credence to the independent and democratic set-up. What is really needed is a good system of administration which is conducive to the aspirations of independent India and is capable enough to effectively discharge its duties for providing proper law and order and bringing about alround development in the country, which is need of the day. This debate has been continuing unabated since we attained freedom and it is due to this background that certain experiments have been made here and there for restructuring the district administration and making it competent enough to rise to the new situation and effectively perform its functions keeping in view aspirations of the people. It was in this background that late Prime Minister, Lal Bahadur Shastri, while addressing the National Development Council in 1964, emphasized the importance of good administration and advised the Chief Ministers of different states to restore to the district officer, whether he is known as Collector or the Deputy Commissioner, the status of a Co-ordinator of all government developmental activities in the district and confer upon him the responsibility for guiding all the efforts undertaken on behalf of Central and the state government concerned. He went to the extent of saying that for more compact administration, even larger districts can be split into more compact units so that there is no confusion amongst common man to deal separately with representatives of different government agencies.

Accordingly, in effective administration, which is the hallmark of a welfare state, it is essential that proper implementation of all the developmental programmes takes place and the main objective before the administration is welfare of the people and to ensure for them a better standard of living and a respectable life. It is, therefore, necessary that district administration is geared-up to the path of impartiality, honesty and independence while dealing with problems that face the people both in urban and rural areas of the district. The concept of development administration is not a new one these days. The district administration is no more an old styled organization which has continued for centuries and there are no signs of any new change. In fact, the approach and functions of district administration have suddenly changed from the traditional role of maintaining law and order and coordinating other activities into a proactive and vibrant set-up, whose role is not restricted to age old routine work like maintenance of law and order, issue of licences, registration of sale documents, maintenance of land record and collection of land revenue, etc. It is now a set-up which is pro-active and taking up important and challenging tasks like preparation of District Development Plans, framing of schemes for provisions of basic services to the people, upgrading of existing infrastructure and initiating lot of efforts to bring modern industrial ventures into the districts and generating economic activities for increased employment opportunities.

The present day scenario demands much more. People are not just satisfied with the routine development works. They are interested for replacement of manually operated regulatory mechanism through IT. enabled services. It is a day of E-governance and people want performance of day-to-day administrative functions and maintenance of services through E-governance. There is demand for total transparency and accessibility to all type of information which has so far remained in iron curtain. There is complete awareness and the public at large insist for accountability at all levels. In case of failure of the system or something going wrong suddenly, the society wants the responsibilities fixed for the lapse. Under such an atmosphere, the moot question is whether the present district administrative set-up is still relevant or is it capable enough to withstand the pressures and burden of fast changes which are taking place all around or has it became outdated and redundant? There have been deliberations and seminars on this topic and the consensus which has emerged is that the basic structure of the district set up may be quite different to be changed and it is the approach and the methodology for providing the services which need to be matched with the technological and ideological changes which have occurred with the passage of time. When every thing around has changed and IT boom in the country has replaced the centuries old manual system of working in almost all walks of life, the administrative set up has to give lead in such matters. It is in this background that basic information in all governmental organizations has become data based which is now being computerized and it has brought about revolutionary changes in the work culture and style of functioning of officials who were hitherto uninfluenced or unimpressed with the need of modernizing and restructuring the centuries old administrative system.

The institutional networking of administrative organizations has further done an excellent job in this connection. The feed back from the field agencies specially through young administrators has helped the pioneer administrative training institutions for probationers and middle and senior level administrators in evolving new administrative system befitting the need of the modern day society. The administrative set-up at district level may be having almost similar legal and administrative frame-work but there is sea change in approach of the modern administrators backed by technological inputs which have been utilized by them in revamping the district administration. The district administration has again risen to the occasion as per need of the modern times as it had earlier completely transformed itself into a new mould and role at the time of independence of the country.

It is no secret that when the Britishers left and the same lot of administrators who were running the administration as servants of the Crown suddenly found themselves in totally different atmosphere and as agents of an independent nation, they were expected to behave like public servants and lookafter the welfare of the people and to guide their destiny and help them in realizing the aspirations of a sovereign democratic republic. It appeared to be a difficult role and daunting task but the administrative set-up came out with flying colours inspite of very trying situations before the country. The nation at that time suddenly faced problems of division of the country into two divergent nations with huge population migration from both sides and scars of religious hatred communal riots, looting and burning of properties of migrating population and thereafter huge task of restoring communal harmony in the country and rehabilitation of huge population of refugees. Inspite of very trying situations, the administration restored order and peace in the country in no time and resettled the migrants through a very rational and balanced approach, helped them in rehabilitating themselves in agriculture, industries, trade and commerce and the nation pursued the course of rebuilding through Five Year Plans which by and by put India on a track towards peace and prosperity.

Today we are one of the front runner developing nations which commands respect in the world community and economic growth and development is our mainstay for respectable place but this has been possible not only through visionary policies of our national leaders and programmes of alround development but the credit goes to the field agencies also which include administrators, engineers, doctors, educationists and of course people at large who have together joined hands to transform this country into a progressive nation. Inspite of many bottlenecks like red tapism, favourtism, corruption and inefficiency at various levels, still the set-up has kept the country moving towards path of peace and progress. We can feel the real difference when we compare ourselves with our neighbour Pakistan, which was part of our country just before independence. It is again a matter of debate whether the administrative set up there has delivered the services or not as compared to its counterpart in India. Of course, there has been basic difference in the policies of both the countries but still the district level administration in both countries shared many traditions in common. Presently, the district level set up in Pakistan is quite different as we are told and they have experimented with lot of basic changes but the scenario in that country has not been quite encouraging. We cannot blame the new experiments undertaken there but the primary reasons there may be basic ideology of that country. In a non-democratic set-up, the objectives of the field level set up can not be expected to be pro people.

The present day society is quite different from the initial period of our independence when the goal of nation building was undertaken. The administrative set-up of that time was faced with basic problems like rehabilitation, illiteracy, poverty, untouchability, social evils like child marriages, sati and backwardness. The present day administration is faced with problems which an awakened and enlightened society faces. In addition to universal problems like unemployment, achieving goal of total literacy, widening gap between rich and poor, the immediate tasks before the set up are removal of corruption and inefficiency, empowerment of women, safeguarding human rights, advancement of higher and technical education and mainstreaming of disadvantageous sections of society. In the background of these tasks, the society needs a set up to which it has easy access, the same is more transparent, accountable, free from favouritism, nepotism and corruption and it is pro people and friendly. The society wants the credibility of the administration restored back which has been eroded to a great extent due to excessive political interference and succumbing of the bureaucracy to political bosses who had been always looking for a committed bureaucracy.

It is in this background that there is talk of modernizing and restructuring the District Administration so that it is relevant to the present day needs and requirements of the society and it does not become redundant in the ever changing circumstances. We are a much more matured and enlightened society and can not allow the bureaucracy to keep on treating the people at large in a casual or arrogant manner. The out-dated rules and regulations and regulatory measures which need replacement and updating naturally have to be attended to immediately. Due to fast moving life styles, the slow and lengthy procedures in day to day functioning have become obsolete and the same need replacement by quick, innovative and technologically assisted systems. People do not feel satisfied with small changes here and there and they do not feel hesitant to criticize the erring officials and want the government to provide quick relief or face the consequence of throwing them out of power during the next elections. The political parties are consequently more prone to acceding to lot of reasonable and unreasonable demands of the society through their manifestos at the time of elections. When the society is more demanding, it is but natural that the political parties will succumb to pressures from different opinion groups. The task of bureaucrats becomes more difficult in such situations. However, the same has to be balanced with objectivity, neutrality, transparency and consistency. All sections of the society should feel that justice has to be done to them and then only the bureaucracy can claim that they are running the administration as per provisions of the constitution and as per aspirations of a true democratic set-up.

The state governments realizing the daunting task of keeping the administration alert, active and easily accessible to the people, have introduced necessary changes to suit local requirements but there is no denying the fact that all those changes have not upset the basic framework of the district administration. It is a fact that lot of inputs have been introduced which have modernized the district administration and restructured it to suit to the social, economical and technological changes but it is again an admitted fact that the basic frame work of the administration set up has remained more or less common throughout the country. We have a federal set up which is called Union of states with integration of All India Services and, therefore, it is natural and good also that basic features of the district administration remain common which are easily understood by people throughout the country and it is easy both for the

Centre and the states to run the administration in an efficient, smooth and effective manner. Since All Indian Services are being recruited and controlled by Centre and such officers are on deputation to states, there remains uniformity and cohesion in the administration. In modernizing efforts, the outdated manually operated public dealing branches which cater to large number of people who visit the offices of Deputy Commissioners or Sub Divisional Magistrates for various jobs like issuing of domicile, caste and Income certificates, registration of their vehicles, procuring of driving licences and applying for arms licences, etc. are no more delayed for days together and some of the documents which are data based are processed then and there and are issued through single window system. Similarly, other important branches which have direct interface with people like Complaints and Enquiries Branch, Peshi Branch and Revenue Record Branch are also being handled through computerized softwares and necessary details are supplied to the public through electronic processing. Not only delay and corruption have been eliminated to a great extent, people feel more attuned and comfortable with the technological inputs in the administration which have streamlined the working of this organization. Same exercise has been repeated in the offices of Sub Divisional Magistrates who are dealing with registration of vehicles, renewal of arms licences, issuing of NOCs and other standardized certificates and permission for holding of rallies processions, various functions and use of loud-speakers, etc. At level below Sub Division/Sub District, which is known as Tehsil, the registration of various documents including sale and conveyance deeds has again mostly been computerized and as and when some changes take place, the some are automatically reflected in the revenue record which are being totally computerized and put on line. The record of rights popularly known as *Jąmabandis*, has been mostly computerized in states and bi-annual entries of cultivation of crops and change of ownership in record on the basis of sale deeds, inheritance, gift deeds, wills, etc. are automatically incorporated when the same are reported to the tehsil offices. The modernization of the official working through technological inputs popularly known as *E-governance,* has revolutionized the working of district administrative set up and people feel more satisfied and comfortable due to lot of transparency and elimination of corrupt practices. This has happened not only in Haryana and some southern states but most of the states have adopted it under guidance from Government of India through standardized software and financial help to set-up IT enabled services. More and more innovative efforts are continuing at local levels to further streamline the various jobs being handled manually so far.

Therefore, the most important aspect about the working of district administration is restructuring the same in line with the present day requirements of the society. There have been efforts to recast the supporting officers available to the D.C./Collector who further looks after the various jobs of the district administration. The pattern varies from state to state and the designations also vary. The officers who are immediately below the D.C./Collector, are IAS and State Civil Service Officers or Officers from Revenue Department and Rural Development Department who are equal in rank to State Civil Service Officers. Though there is almost uniformity in posting IAS or State Civil Service Officers as Incharge of Sub Divisions but at the HQ, the Civil Officers who assist the Deputy Commissioner vary from one state to another. The rural development work has been mostly assigned to District Rural Development Agencies (DRDA) which through poverty alleviation programmes, take up not only works of rural infrastructure development but create economic assets for individual as well as community as a whole. This agency is usually looked after by a senior administrative officer in the district who is next to D.C./ Collector and his designation is Additional Deputy

Commissioner or Additional District Magistrate. He is not only responsible for taking up development schemes and poverty alleviation programmes both in rural and urban areas (through DRDA and DUDA) but he also officiates as D.C./Collector in his absence. Some of the senior level jobs are therefore, automatically assigned by the D.C. to this officer. This post has almost become uniform throughout different states due to the fact that lot of Government of India schemes of rural and urban development are being handled by these agencies under direct supervision of Deputy Commissioner. Then there is one more State Civil Officer attached to the Deputy Commissioner and known as General Assistant or City Magistrate or Assistant District Magistrate who is looking after most of the work of the Deputy Commissioner relating to law and order and other regulatory functions like issuing of licences, issuing of various certificates, redressal of public grievances and lot of other miscellaneous jobs.

The other two important officers attached with the Deputy Commissioner are - one looking after PRIs and the second looking after revenue administration. They are either from State Civil Services or promotee officers from their respective departments. The Deputy Commissioner usually looks after these two important areas through these officers. In the PRIs, all the states have two or three-tier system of elected representatives from PRIs. Zila Parishad/District Panchayat at the top, followed by Block Samiti at middle level and the grass root level PRI is Gram Panchayat. Though these institutions enjoy lot of powers and their functions have been clearly defined through 73rd Constitutional Amendment, yet the co-ordination role in respect of PRIs has to be done by the Deputy Commissioner assisted by the officer who is called District Development and Panchayat Officer. Similarly, on the revenue side, District Revenue Officer assists the Collector in collection of land revenue and running of land administration. Ours being an agricultural country, the importance of maintenance and updating of land record on an efficient basis is the key to administrative efficiency. There have been extensive land reforms in almost all the states and accordingly there has been complete change in the work culture relating to maintaining of land records. The lower revenue functionaries (*Patwaris / Kanungos*) known for their lopsided approach are a great obstacle in bringing about transparency and corruption free atmosphere in land management but the introduction of computerization followed by on-line entries relating to cultivation, change of ownership and other details etc. has completely revolutionalized this important area of district administration.

The revenue hierarchy in court matters is as per stipulations in the relevant Acts and Codes and the court proceedings are conducted as per established practices within the parameters of laws of the land. The aggrieved parties after availing opportunities before trial courts get ample opportunities through appeals and revisions before the appellate courts of Collector and Commissioner. In case of still any desire for further relief, the cases are pursued through writ petitions before the High Court and Special Leave Petitions before the Supreme Court. The officers of the district level, sub-district level and tehsil level enjoy jurisdiction and powers under the state and the Central Acts as per the hierarchical principles.

There are other miscellaneous functions also which the district administration looks after but which vary from state to state depending upon the policies and approach of the respective state government. It is generally the district administra-tion set up which comes handy to state government as and when any new scheme/ programme is introduced for which there is no specific department to look. after or the concerned department is not capable enough to handle the same. This has resulted into multifarious facets of district administration and all odd jobs starting from flood, famine, disaster, epidemic, etc. are passed on to district administration and they are expected to deliver the goods in the shape of relief operations, crisis management and restoring back normal atmosphere through sundry jobs. The charitable and welfare organizations like Red Cross, Child Welfare Council, St. John Ambulance Association, Sports Bodies, Sports Councils and Olympic organizations are also put into the basket of the district administration. If we look at the list of ex-officio and honorary posts held by the Deputy Commissioner and his officers, the list is very large and really unmanageable. In nut shell district administration instead of squeezing itself, has been expanding out of proportions due to multifarious jobs.

The role of the district administration as co-ordinator of all activities in the district has in fact become the most important function of the modern Collector. The functions at the district level can be classified into regulatory and development related functions. D.C./Collector is in fact overburdened with number of activities which can be delegated and decentralized. He should in fact be relieved of certain responsibilities and should confine himself to law and order and regulatory functions. Developmental functions may be performed through some institutional mechanism. The Collector as a result will play effective co-ordinating role. The PRIs in hand with non-governmental agencies should monitor developmental schemes as in the case of Karnataka. At the level of second-in-command in the Collector's office, there has to be a very clear delegation of powers. It further needs to be institutionalized so that there is no conflict of tasks in case of developmental functions. This would imply that the main executive office will have no interference into the extension agencies. This would avoid unnecessary duplication of efforts and expenditure and wind up unnecessary branches and sections in the organization.

In the background of the economic restructuring in the country, the government has to think accordingly in terms of restructuring the administrative set up also. The government has to improve organizational culture and performance in the public sector. The changes in the structure have to be introduced by pruning size of the bureaucracy and by winding up departments and organizations which are redundant or duplicating work. The improvements have to be further effected through professionalism through development of managerial orientation which can be brought about by measures like training, zero based budgeting, jobs and positions as per activities, change in the organizational culture, etc. In this background, the improvement which can be brought about at the level of district administra-tion, is to ensure people's participation and reducing the workload of the District Collector.

The emphasis should be on transparency, accountability, responsibility and redressal of public grievances and preparation of citizens charters. The ultimate responsibility of civil servants is to solve the genuine problems of the citizens along with having a sense of commitment for advancement of the state and nation as a whole. There should be no place for indecision and confusion. A civil servant has to consider all aspects of a situation and take decision promptly though not hastily and then take action accordingly. The policies and programmes of government should be well publicized and known to the common man. Right to Information Act has already been introduced in the country in May, 2005 and now anybody can have any information unless the same is a privileged one exempted from disclosure. The district administration is further expected to enforce punctuality and promptness. Since there is direct interface with the people, therefore, behaviour and conduct of officials will have direct bearing on the image of the government. The officials are supposed to extend due courtesies. Though the present system of redressal of public grievances is effective, but it still needs lot of improvement. Complaints against officers/officials should also have to be dealt with promptly. Regular inspections of offices and regular review meetings are extremely important. The heads of offices need to have a mechanism for weekly review of pending references. Basic data has to be maintained and officials have to be trained and the departments should be armed with proper skills for proper decision-making. There has to be adequate delegation of powers to streamline the system. All these important aspects are necessary to revamp the district administration.

In the end, the District Collector who is leader of the team in the district and upon whom the state government banks upon for day to day affairs and again when anything special or untoward happens, has to discharge his duties in such an excellent way that the people of the district should start feeling that they are being administered very well and the governance by the state is minimal. In the present day environment, in fact the least governance is the best governance. Though all important infrastructure development works are being performed by concerned Line departments and District Collector has only a co-ordinating and unifying role with selective intervention, yet it is the office of Collector around which the whole administration revolves. He is symbol and authority of government. He is the single authority who provides direct and immediate link between the people and the state government departments may be set-up and disbanded or re-organized, yet the office of District Collector would remain forever in one form or the other. With the passage of time, his role as regulatory authority has become diminished but his role as symbol of development administration, has increased manifold. He has now quite a different set of officers as compared to his counterparts at the time of independence but the restructuring has not changed the basic frame-work of his organization. Whatever changes have occurred, have taken place to dove tail the role of his office with the requirements of the modern society in the changed circumstances when technological changes have revolutionized all the sectors but the authority and responsibilities of District Collector have not been diluted even after introduction of new techniques and technologies.

The need of the day is therefore, that let the district administration not resist the structural changes or modernization efforts which at times are taking place automatically and the approach should be to try to synchronize the same with the traditional and well defined role of district administration. The bureaucrats manning the district administrative set up may go in for new managerial skills and orientation so that the public at large do not feel that this office has lost its past glory and touch and it has become redundant with the advancement of new techniques and technologies. Its new and modern outlook will be welcomed by the people and this will further enhance the image, prestige and effectiveness of the district administration, which it had been enjoying from time immemorial in the hearts of the people. Let the district administration serve the people and not rule them, as the framers of the Constitution had desired and aspired.

4 District Health Care Administration
A Reformative Look in Karnataka

*S.L. Goel** and *Shalini Rajneesh***

The district is the most peripheral fully organized unit of local government. It is geographically compact and every part of it can normally be reached within a day. The district is often the natural meeting point for "bottom-up" planning and organization and "topdown" planning support. It is a place where community needs and national priorities can be reconciled. We can develop good plans for a small area and ensure their implementation.

District level health structure is a middle level management organization and has been set up to provide an organic link between state level health infrastructure as well as regional level infrastructure on the one side and district level and lower level health institutions on the other. District health administration is the nerve center of health infrastructure as upon its efficiency depends the efficiency of primary health care to a substantial extent.

A district health system based on primary health care is more or less self-contained segment of the national health system. It comprises first and foremost "a well-defined population living within a clearly delineated administrative and geographical area. It includes all the relevant health care

* Vice-President, Indian Institute of Public Administration, New Delhi. Emeritus Professor U.G.C, Panjab University, Chandigarh, Director SBI, Local Board, Chandigarh, Former Member of U.G.C., All India Board of Management, MOTE, Distance Education Council.

** IAS, Deputy Commissioner, Belgaon (Karnataka).

activities in the area, whether governmental or otherwise. It therefore consists of a large variety of interrelated elements that contribute to health in homes, schools, workplaces, communities, the health sector and related social and economic sectors. It includes self-health care personnel and facilities, whether governmental or non-governmental efforts including the hospital at the first referral level, and the appropriate support services, such as laboratory, diagnostic and logistic support. It can be most effective if coordinated by an appropriately trained health officer working to ensure as comprehensive a range as possible of promotive, preventive, curative and rehabilitative health activities.[1]

The actual organization of district health systems depends on the specific situation in each country and each district, including the administrative structure and personalities involved. Nevertheless, the general principles for developing such systems are based on the Declaration of Alma-Ata and the global strategies for health for all. They incorporate the elements of equity, accessibility, emphasis on promotion and prevention, intersectoral action, community involvement, decentralization, integration of health programmes, and coordination of separate health actitivies.[2]

The head of the district organization is designated differently in different states of India, e.g. Chief Medical Officer or District Health Officer, or District Health and Family Planning Officer. He has under him a lot of staff to supervise, co-ordinate and control the field activities as well as report to the headquarters. In some of the states of the Indian Union, district health system has been entrusted to the control of Panchayati Raj Institutions while in others, it is still under the total control of the state government.

In order to lightens the works of the upper echelons in administration as well as to promote quick disposal of work, decentralization in health care assumes greater importance. It generates participation which increases the motivation of employees as they get the opportunity to express themselves and not simply act as ordered.[3] It has a more important justification than mere administrative efficiency and bears directly upon the development of a sense of personal adequacy in the individual citizen; it has spiritual connotations.[4]

Larger (and fewer) decentralized units will find it harder to ensure the required adaptability, flexibility and efficiency and to promote devolution of power and accountability towards the grassroots, where the services operate. There is growing evidence that an important cause of the limited efficiency of the health care system is often found at the "district" level i.e., the level from which the basic Primary Health Care (PHC) services are organized and managed, and where the primary backup services are situated. The weakness of district level organization often leads to the breakdown of support and supervision, to shortage in essential supplies, and to lack of facilities for training (and retaining) grassroots health workers.[5]

Conversely, strong and well-organized district health teams with access to relevant information sources appear to be an essential ingredient of the PHC approach. It may even be argued that district PHC teams are the key units of the entire organizational structure, and that their leaders are placed in the most critical positions of the health sector. Such teams can be responsible for all basic health care activities, and for the operational link-up between PHC and hospital activities. The district, therefore, needs resources and authority under its own control to be able to fulfil its tasks properly.

The World Health Organization[6] urged countries to strengthen further the health system infrastructure based on primary health care, laying particular emphasis on district health systems and defining targets for the integrated delivery of essential elements of primary health care until all districts and all elements are covered.

With regard to development, the objective of the WHO Programme on Strengthening District Systems is to improve the quality of life and reduce mortality and morbidity by strengthening the effective implementation of primary health care in participating countries, with due consideration to equity, effectiveness, efficiency, and flexibility within the context of national, regional and global strategies for reaching the goal of Health for All.[7]

Organizational Structure of District Health System in Karnataka

In Karnataka, the management of district hospitals and dispensaries is under the direct control of Zila Parishad. Moreover, the implementation of maternity and child health programmes; family welfare programmes; immunization and vaccination programmes, etc. are also administered by the Zila Parishad. The taluka panchayats deal with the promotion of health and family welfare programmes; promotion of immunization and vaccination programmes and health and sanitation fairs and festivals, etc. At the village level, the gram panchayats deal with implementation of family welfare programmes, preventive measures against epidemics, regulation of sale of food articles, participation in immunization programmes, licensing of eating establishments and regulation of offensive and dangerous trades.

Apart from operating the district sector budget, the Zila Panchayats also implement such state sector schemes as are entrusted to them by government.

The state plan and centrally sponsored or assisted schemes and the normal schemes of the district are budgeted accordingly. Only innovative district specific schemes have to be funded under decentralized district planning for which either DPB provides 100 per cent discretionary funds or funds flow under incentive outlay where local community has to contribute on 50 : 50 or 25 : 75 basis of its proportion of the funds or from special outlays for backward areas. Otherwise, the district budget is proportional to the number of institutions functioning in the district and the norms set for central and state programmes being operated in the district under various approved budgetary heads of expenditure. Each programme officer at district level is drawing and disbursing officer and there is no integrated budget for the district. The delay in release of budget is generally the normal constraint affecting the utilization.

Administrative Machinery

Below this political set-up, there is administrative health machinery to implement the plans made by zila parishad (ZP). This machinery helps PRIs in the formulation of health plans as well. The district administrative machinery under ZP consists of the Chief Executive Officer (CEO), an IAS, as head of the administrative organization.

Besides CEO, the ZP secretariat comprises two deputy secretaries incharge of administration and development respectively, a council to assist in planning exercise and a Chief Accounts Officer to supervise the money transactions in the ZP. There are field officers, i.e. Executive Officer, Block Development Officer and gram panchayat secretary. Besides, there are departments headed by specialists. Let us explain with the examples of one of the District, i.e. Dakshina Kannada, where there are 17 departments.

District Health Department

It may be interesting to note that the Health Department in the district is the second biggest department. For example, in Dakshin Kannada, out of total employees of 14184, 3130 belong to health, more than 20 per cent of the total. In Group A, out of 216 employees 137 belong to Health Department, more than 50 per cent. Thus, CEO has to devote a lot of time to the Health Department in the district.

Functions of District Health and Family Welfare Officer

The district officer with the overall responsibility for health is designated as the District Health and Family Welfare Officer (DHO).

In a district, the overall responsibility of implementation of health care delivery system, lies with the DHO, who is assisted by a number of other district officers (Family Planning, Health, Malaria, T.B., U.LP., etc.) These district officers are declared as "Head of Office". The head of office declared as the head of department under certain rules framed by the state government/central government. The head of office has overall responsibility of carrying out all office functions. In this task, he is assisted by Administrative Officer/Office Superintendent/Office Assistant, etc. The office work is allocated amongst the employees of the office by dividing them into different sections, i.e. Establishment, Accounts, Store, Statistics, Transport, General, etc. The number of employees in a section depends upon the workload in that section and the number as well as the nature of sections may vary from office to office depending upon the type and the quantum of work.

In line with the government of India guidelines in the implementation of minimum needs programme, the state has revised its health policy, and decided to establish a 3-tier health infrastructure, viz. sub-centres, primary health centres and community health centres to provide Health for All under the overall supervision and control of district health system (see Chart 1.1.)

Role of DHO

DHO is responsible for the personnel, money and resources allocated to health department. Authority in the managerial context of a DHO is usually identified with the legitimate base of power. It may be defined as the legal right to command action by others and to enforce compliance. A DHO, however, might gain compliance in a number of ways

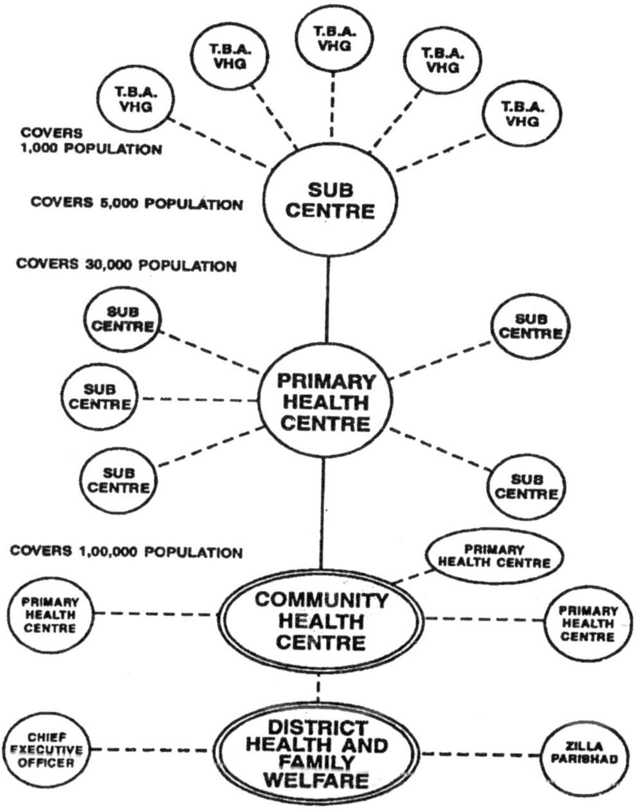

Chart 1.1 : Primary Health Care Infrastructure of District Level

through persuasion, sanctions, requests, coercion, cooperation or force. The responsibilities of a DHO are made clear by the State Health Administration through the statement "Function, Duties, and Responsibilities of DHO." In the absence of such role description, it may lead to role ambiguity and ultimately to role conflict, where role boundaries have an overlap. The working relationship with other district health offices, district hospital and other programme officers has to be clarified and clearly understood. In fulfilling his responsibilities, the DHO often delegates authority and responsibility to other district health officials. By delegation, we mean conferring authority from

DHO to another in order to accomplish particular activity/ programme. Of course, such delegation has, in most districts, been very limited. When a DHO delegates authority and responsibility, it can never be abdicated. That means, the DHO cannot throw the blame on others to whom he has delegated. Ultimately, it is the DHO who is accountable for everything in the district health services delivery.

For every recognized position in any organization, there is an expectation widely shared by members of the organization as to what would be the behaviour of persons who occupy that position. What a typical occupant of a given position such as DHO is expected to do, constitutes the role associated with that position. A role can be seen as encompassing, among other things, the duties or obligations of the position. DHO being the supreme authority of the district health care services structure is expected to translate into action, the broad health policies and programmes. In doing so, DHO is expected to provide direction and guidance to the peripheral health care structure in the district.

The roles of DHO are several and they are interlinked; he is the district health-action planner : he is director and supervisor of peripheral health structure in his district. He is the manager of entire district including lower levels of health care structure. In addition, the DHO might also have other roles in the district development administration and activities. DHO should create "prideful tradition of integrity, excellence and fellowship. Human beings breathe an ethos around them almost unconsciously and these traditions make for that ethos."[8]

The administrative functions of DHO include-health planning, implementation of health plans, intersectoral action, leadership, supervision, communication, co-ordination, control, finances, delegation and monitoring.

Functioning of District Health System

The functioning of district health system can be traced in (i)

Headquarter Field Relationship (ii) Field Reports : (See Chart 1.2)

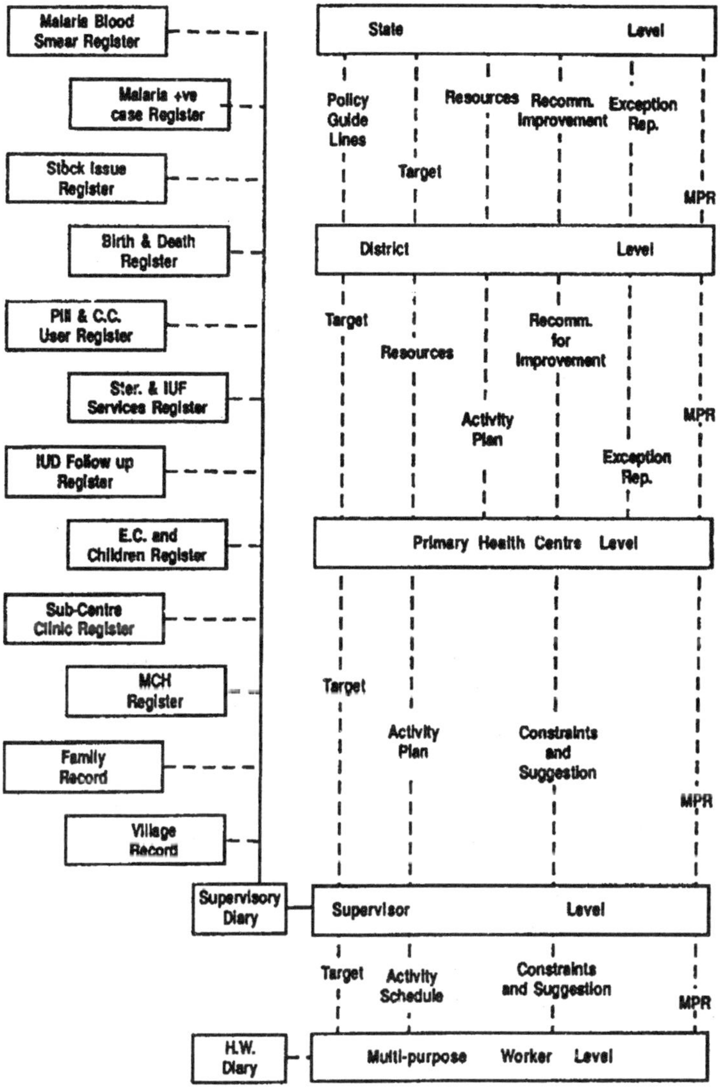

Chart 1.2 : Headquarter-Field Ralationships Through Health Management Information System

A large number of reports[9] and returns are procured from the field by District Health Office, like : household and family register, village register, target couple register, sterilization and IUD register, oral pill and nirodh distribution register, sterilization and IUD follow-up register, MCH register, malaria blood slide proforma, malaria positive case register, stock and distribution register, birth and death register, subcentre clinic register, health worker male diary, health worker female diary, health worker monthly report proforma, supervisor compiled report proforma and monthly report on health and family welfare programme.

All the reports after compilation at the district level are sent to the division level and from there to the state level.

The purpose of such reports is to:[10]

- Measure the progress in the field.
- Locate problems in the field.
- Confirm that the arrangements for implementation of policies are adequate.
- Prepare statistical data for comparison, assessment and future policy-making and planning.
- Guide the field staff in future on the basis of past developments.

A brief analysis of reporting done by CHCs and PHCs to District Health office shows that it lacks in quality. Most of the staff responsible for this task has a very lukewarm attitude towards the collection of data, leave aside their concern about its quality. In their own words, some of the field staff remarked during our field visits that 'data are collected to check the work and thus figures are mostly inflated.' At the district or the State level where it is used for the decision-making purpose, data are mostly found inconsistent and incomplete. The obvious answer submitted by the concerned staff is 'proforma needed to be simplified' or 'less information should be collected'. As a matter of fact, whether the concerned staff is worker, a supervisor or an official, the feeling is that the information collected has no relevance with their assigned jobs. Thus, attention paid to its quality has been minimal. The reports are usually prepared by a person with statistical backgrounds who is quite junior in status and has very little exposure of happenings in the field. It is also observed that whatever is prepared by him/her is forwarded blindly by the responsible officer to the next higher authorities. This has led to the gap between the real achievements and the reported figures. Further, since district authorities do not consider the utility and relevance of the records maintained and the reports received with the service delivery component, quality of the information has been rather poor.

Besides, the health staff feels that there is not much utility of such reporting. Our observation has been that most of the data does not get processed, analyzed or utilized at any level. Majority of the reports submitted to higher level after nothing the achievements remain within the files and thus there has been very little utility of the information collected. In other words, no efforts are made to compare the resources utilized with that of the results obtained (cost-effectiveness or cost-benefit). Further, the data is so fragmented and objectives of data collection are so vague and limited that excepting matching of achievements with the set targets (family planning and health programmes), nothing more is done. Same holds true for follow-up data. For example, the follow-up cards are kept at the PHC level whereas field workers are supposed to do follow-up in the field. As a result, the followup cards are either not prepared or incomplete or not updated.

One of the reasons for the indifferent attitude of the workers towards information system is that very little administrative monitoring at the level is done by the district authorities. The only monitoring which has been made as a regular feature of the family welfare programme is whether targets have been met and respective feedback is given. Again, feedback is mostly to warn the staff, if achievements not commensurate with the targets or to congratulate those who have completed the targets. This is not adequate. To make the system effective and increase its use, adequate processing and appropriate analysis is needed.

Reporting and its analysis cost time and money. Therefore, only standardized, authenticated and useful reporting may be used to have genuine field control and field development. For this purpose, there is a need of designing and installing Management Information System (MIS) to suit the needs of the organization. This would hasten the exchange of information between headquarters and field. Besides, it would help in improving efficiency in operational functions, controlling organizational performance, and supporting intelligent planning by providing such information to the decision-makers which is most relevant, accurate, complete, concise, timely, economical, reliable and efficient. In addition, the use of electronic gadgets can speed up the flow of information. In this context, district information centers set-up by the Government of India can serve as an effective link between headquarters and the field agencies.

Supervision and Inspection of Field Organizations

The effectiveness of workers depends largely on the supervision they receive from district staff. In other words, quality of work is directly related to the degree of supervision. High/degree of supervision improves the quality of work; poor supervision leads to poor work. So good supervision is very important for health workers, health guides and dais. Even well trained, highly motivated health workers eventually become discouraged and ineffective when supervision is lacking. The objectives of supervision are to help subordinates to do their job skilfully/efficiently, develop subordinates capacity to the fullest extent, to guide/ assist in meeting pre-determined work objectives (targets), to promote effectiveness of subordinates, to motivate subordinates and maintain high morale and promote teamwork.

In addition to formal reporting, observation and inspection are indispensable if field operations are to be kept under effective control and the mistakes made in one field are not to be repeated in another. The inspection should not be conducted for isolated activities as is the practice in most of the organizations, but should combine together all the issues needing attention at the field level. This combination of aims is necessary partly because travel costs have to kept within the limited budgetary allocations and also to economize the use of staff time.[11]

However, in practice, inspections are not planned and no use is made of reports prepared and are done hurriedly.

In spite of all these handicaps, the cumulative insight gained by the headquarters over field offices through observation and inspection helps in developing good relationships between headquarters and field agencies, as well as in effective evaluation.[12]

Meetings between the District and Field Staff

One of the most common and useful techniques of improving workers' performance is staff meeting. It is held by supervisors at various levels of an organization, who are responsible for getting the work done through a group of individuals placed under them. Staff meetings are productive if staff members participate freely, feel responsible, and contribute to the achievement of the organizationals goals. Staff conference may be held for different purposes. A staff conference may be called for (a) giving staff members certain information or to explain certain decisions taken at higher levels and to clarify certain points or doubts; (b) solving problems arising out of day-do-day work situations for which the supervisor may have to draw upon the skills and talents of staff; (c) giving instructions about a new skill which may need detailed explanation and demonstration. Thus, a staff conference is not always a single-purpose meeting, and the supervisor who calls and conducts it must be aware of the variety of objectives, each of which may require different patterns of leadership and participation. If staff meetings are planned and held regularly, they can certainly contribute to the development of teamwork.

The purposes of meeting are to discuss and solve a problem, communicate information, plan and organize, evaluate staff performance, evaluate the health services, coordinate the work of a health team, give training, motivate health workers and seek intersectoral meetings.

Every staff members should be well prepared for participation in a meeting. They should study the agenda and note carefully the topics to be covered. They should think about the items in terms of their own information and experience, and plan to share their ideas with others. They should feel free to make suggestions regarding the topics discussed during the meeting. Staff members should remain open-minded to listen to others reactions and accommodate the ideas of others. They should follow the discussions carefully and make notes of important decisions.

Findings and Suggestions

While district health systems have been developed and strengthened in varying degrees, a number of critical issues and problems remain like :

(i) the main emphasis has been on coverage, and quality of performance has been neglected;
(ii) policy guidelines are inadequate to support planning and implementation at district level;
(iii) decentralization is rare;

(iv) the roles, responsibilities and procedures of district health staff are poorly defined and their leadership and manage-ment expertise is usually weak;

(v) the integration of vertical programmes is still facing difficulties, and unipurpose workers, who have been trained as multipurpose workers, continue to give preference to their earlier programmes;

(vi) there are deficiencies in collaboration within the health sector, and between the vertical programmes and the general health services;

(vii) much of the information generated at district level is neither for the district health managers, nor required for decision-making, monitoring, and evaluation but only for transmission to the upper echelons, from which feedback is rarely provided;

(viii) community involvement in health is weak and attempts to foster leadership capability in the community are inadequate;

(ix) in district development committees, insufficient attention is paid to identifying health problems that require intersectoral action and individual sectoral priorities and different administrative structures often prevent the pooling and sharing of resources between sectors;

(x) Finally, there are not enough financial or skilled human resources, at the district level and those that are available are usually neither equitably distributed nor efficiently used.[13]

Based on the discussions in the preceding paras, we seek to highlight various issues affecting district health system and also propose suitable suggestions to make this system effective.

Poor Quality of Health Care

In the new millennium, quality is becoming an essential part of the health system in both developed and developing countries. There is a great pressure from patients and general public for quality health care which is based on certain standards, accreditation, certification and bench marking. The quality of health care needs continuous improvement in services. Quality of health care should be effective, efficient, technically sound, safe and accessible. A WHO report of a meeting held in Indonesia recommended the following to improve quality health care[14]:—

- Ensure that quality of health care is an integral part of health services delivery at all levels covering public and private sectors;
- Organize advocacy/awareness workshops on quality assurance for policy-makers, administrators and the leadership of health care to get their commitment for quality assurance;
- Establish a coordinating mechanism for quality assurance activities at national level and constitute a multi-disciplinary task force of national experts to provide advice on technical aspects of quality assurance;
- Initiate quality assurance of health care in selected hospitals and in primary health care through the district health system approach, document the experiences and expand gradually to more health care facilities;
- Organize national strategic planning workshops with technical assistance from WHO;
- Formulate guidelines to set standards and select national key indicators on quality assurance to monitor compliance and measure performance;
- Invest on building local capacity in health care quality through the creation of a critical mass of expertise within the country;

- Mobilize potential resources form within the country including support from international agencies; and
- Ensure that orientation on quality assurance be integrated in both basic and in-service training programmes of all health care professionals.

Lack of Equity in Health Care

In the new millennium, we have to change our priorities to benefit the most deprived from the health services. We must plan and implement our health system to ensure quality health care to the poorest section of the society. For this purpose, it is suggested that :

- An attitudinal change among the health service staff has to be brought in so that they can make the patients feel important, wanted, cared and well looked after;
- This change in affective domain must start early as part of the teaching objectives for all medical and paramedical students. They should be made to realize that the hospitals of medical colleges need the patients for clinical teaching; thus the academia is dependent on patients and not vice versa;
- Empowerment of patients will lead to medical uprising of the society by creating a class educated and aware, informed and health conscious, striving to improve their quality of life with justified use of their rights. They can curb exploitation in the name of medicine and ensure a decline in quackery;
- The empowered can be easily motivated and channelised to enlist support for health programmes and achievement of health goals. Thus, health programmes will be a truly people's programme since indifference will cease to exist in health matters. Voluntary participation in health activities will increase;
- We have to empower the poor people so that they

can take their due from health care system. As long as the services do not reach the needy people, there cannot be any perceptible change in the health status of the people. Services are not to be merely accessible but must reach those most in need;

- Today, there is great alienation between the goals of district health system and the personnel working in them resulting in inefficiency, tensions, conflicts, and low morale. Personnel system needs overhauling and reform to suit the health needs of the people in the next century. We may not get the result from the existing health personnel in the district without bringing about changes in them to usher in an era of hard work, ethics, responsiveness and transparency.

Bureaucracy Resistance to work in a Democratic Decentralised System

The greatest contribution of PRIs is breaking the hegemony of a few and empowering the masses. The concepts of transparency in administration and accountability to the people have a potential for being translated into reality through PRIs[15] :

- It is for the government to take certain tough decisions in overhauling the work culture and infusing ethics in administration;
- It is argued that appropriate action be initiated by policy-makers, administrators, political and social scientists to overcome the obstacles undermining the potential of these local institutions;
- The motto to Health for All can't be achieved by mere investment of further resources for buildings, residence, training centers, etc., but a call for both professional and local accountability to the community is required. Unless the health care work force in a district remains accountable to the

community and takes a large hand in health education and public information, primary health care system can never do justice to its challenges.[16]

Ineffective Primary Health Care Delivery Programmes

Implementation of national health programmes at the district level is weak. Therefore it is suggested that :

- The routine operations should be managed well, campaigns should be properly organized and integrated properly with other health activities;
- Promotive health programmes such as health education, school health, nutritions, food adulteration and environmental sanitation are usually neglected. Therefore, the district officials should be able to plan, implement and monitor such programme on priority basis.
- Epidemic control activities need to be streamlined.
- The district health system has to perform several functions in order to be supportive in the functioning of PHCs which at present suffer because of resources and lack of guidance. Therefore, the following may be taken care of :—

(i) Proper guidance/supervision to PHCs.
(ii) Adequate financial and administrative power,
(iii) Maintenance of equipments,
(iv) Supplies,
(v) Allocation of staff,
(vi) Appraise performance of PHCs systematically, scientifically and objectively,
(vii) Assess training needs of Mos, and
(viii) Create favourable community environment for health workers and PHCs to function.

Inadequate and Non-functional Infrastructure

In order to deal with such problem, it is suggested that :

- Committed and reputed NGO's may be involved in the development of primary health care system by handling over certain proportion of infrastructure facilities, namely, sub-centre or primary health center along with building, funds and staff with relatively more management freedom to VOs/NGOs depending upon their capability of funds, staff, etc. after ascertaining their credibility.[17]
- NGO supported and organized health care services must be an integral part of the total health system of a country, including the referral system.[18]

Lack of Community Participation and Involvement

In order to make the health care system more effective people's participation is necessary.[19] Therefore, it is suggested that :—

- The community members be given a say in decision-making about health and health care issues that affect them, and a measure of control over the persons that are supposed to serve their needs;[20]
- Community participation also has political implications when community members are involved in monitoring the services from which they are supposed to benefit. They can demand that the necessary attention be paid to the needs of the people at the grassroots, and of those expected to serve them;
- The community involvement is also important to give the authorities responsible and adequate information about the grassroots functioning of the health care system: without direct inputs from the communities,

those authorities may only receive information from the very system they are supposed to control;[21]

- The elected bodies should be given the real power to monitor the health care system;
- For this purpose, adequate resources and functionaries should be provided to them.[22]

Lack of Inter-sectoral and Intrasectoral Coordination

The concept of primary health care encompasses the overall socio-economic development of communities concurrent to the improvement of the health status :—

- It is admitted that the health sector cannot function in isolation while implementing primary health care programmes.
- More important and relevant in the socio-economic development—agriculture, housing, public works and communications, education, mass media—that they cannot work in isolation to the exclusion of the health sector.
- The broader aim of increasing well-being and resistance to disease as a whole while promoting and maintaining good health will require the combined efforts of many sectors not immediately related to health.[23]

Non-Involvement of Universities in Promoting Health Care

- Therefore, the universities must act as bridges between the community and the government. We have various universities and medical colleges who can help in the promotion of Primary Health Care.
- Now universities are seeking new relationships with

health policy-makers, extending the concept of health care beyond that of the individual to that of whole communities, and adapting their undergraduate curriculum to ensure that education equips students to undertake those supervisory and managerial roles which have not hitherto been seen as appropriate for health professionals.[24]

- Now at last, the universities seem prepared to lend whole-hearted backing to three of the main imperatives of Health for All, political commitment to social equity, community participation and the use of appropriate and affordable technology.[25]

Stereotyped Health Management System

- However, the challenge of 'Health for All' calls for a permanent and systematic managerial process, ranging from planning and policy-making, in collaboration with other sectors, to implementation, monitoring and evaluation, for the development of an effective health system.
- The managerial process entails the formulation of a health policy with defined priorities, and the preparation of programmes and budgets to put the policy into effect. It also calls for the assessment of manpower requirements and the formulation of plans to train the requisite manpower, together with the integration of well-formulated programmes into the general health system.
- A dynamic civil society and a professionally trained and dedicated civil service (Insulated from political interference) are the twin pillars of a constructive relationship between State and Society.[26]

Lack of Reliable and Scientific Referral System

At present, the referral system does not function effectively to overloading of hospitals with self-referrals, lack of confidence in lower level facilities because of perceived low quality of care and lack of organizational and management links between hospitals at various levels.

- Therefore an effective referral system has to be designed by focusing on three important areas: (i) the structure of the referral system, (ii) management coordination and (iii) quality improvement.

Thus, the new millennium, district health system has to introduce new technology of Telematics, and ensure equity and quality in health care.

Health Telematics is defined as a composite term for health-related activities, services and systems carried out over a distance by means of information and communication technologies for the purpose of global health promotion, disease control and health care, as well as education, management and research for health.

The process of its planning includes the formulation of policy and strategies is followed by the choice of technology, which is implemented in three phases.

The first phase of implementation includes the development and adoption of standards and laying down of specifications to meet the health telematics strategies. Standardization is required at different levels varying from Data Standards; Technical Standards; Work Standards and Equipment Standards to Training Standards and Professional Standards.

The second phase deals with the selection of computing hardware, peripherals telecommunication infrastructure, operating and utility software.

The third phase concentrates on procurement, implementation, training and support.

Health Telematics raises certain ethical issues, such as the acceptability of transmitting personal information across cultural boundaries; young doctors getting professionally affected, and the confidentiality of the relationship between the patient and the treating doctor. Full cooperation of the medical and paramedical staff involved, as well as patients is essential. Even in the most advanced form, Health Telematics might not provide a blanket solution for each situation. There would be cases where human intervention is needed. It also raises concern on widening the gap between the poor and the privileged.

Based on the presentations by various resource persons, and the experiences shared between SEAR (South-east Asia Region) countries during the workshop, the participants appreciated the potential of Telemedicine. However, the group proposed to change the term "Telemedicine" to the broader term of "Health Telematics" in order to avoid a narrow interpretation of the scope of technology.

The participants made the following recommendations:

- Conduct advocacy and awareness of Health Telematics so as to gain the commitment of policy-makers, administrators and professional groups at state and district levels.
- Incorporate Health Telematics into the renewed HFA policies/strategies of a state.
- Conduct situation analyses, and define priorities for initiating plans of action, through pilot projects on Health Telematics.
- Develop the local level capacity, through training of human resources required to set up and manage Health Telematics activities.
- Constitute state and district coordination committees for the development of Telematics as an internal component of social development, thus ensuring the participation of relevant sectors right from the beginning.
- Build Health Telematics on the available infrastructure, and choose appropriate technology

based on local resources and the health needs of the people.

- Develop the monitoring and evaluation criteria as integral parts of the project.
- Develop partnerships with various stake holders: the industry, academic institutions and research centers, and public and private sectors in support of Health Telematics.

NOTES AND REFERENCES

1. Eighth General Programme of Work Covering the Period 1990-93, Geneva, WHO, 1987 (Health for All Series No. I 0).
2. WHO, SEAR : Health Situation in the South East Asia Region, 1994-97, New Delhi; 1999, p. 185.
3. James C. Charlesworth, *Government Administration*, Harpur, New York, 1951, p. 207.
4. Ibid.
5. WHO : Strengthening Ministries of Health For Primary Health Care, Geneva, 1984, pp. 31-32.
6. WHO, 39.7, May 1986.
7. WHO, District Health Systems, Geneva, 1995, p. 8.
8. WHO, Technical Report Series, 215, 1961, p. 4.
9. Walter R. Sharp, *Field Administration in the United Nations System*, The Carnegie Endowment, London, Stevens, 1961, p. 266.
10. S.L.Goel, *Advanced Public Administration*, New Delhi, Sterling,1994, p.290
11. Ibid.
12. Ibid., p. 291.
13. WHO, District Health Systems, Geneva, 1995, p. 28.
14. WHO, SEARO, Report of a WHO Inter-country Meeting, Sarabayo, Indonesia, 16-20, December, 1996, New Delhi, p. 8.
15. Shalini Rajneesh, *Democratic Decentralisation in Karnataka*, a Ph.D. thesis, unpublished, p. 293.
16. A.P. Banabas, Good Governance at Local Level, in *IJPA*, July-Sept, 1998, p. 453 (Special Number on Towards Good Governance).
17. Mechai Vira Vaidya, Untapped Potential, in *World Health*, March 1985, p. 4
18. S.K. Vettivel, *People's Participation in Social Development*, Role of NGO's, New Delhi, Vetri Publishers, 1992, p. 5.
19. P.K. Bajpai, *People's Participation in Development*—A Critical Analysis, in IJPA, Oct.-Dec., 1998, p. 817.

20. WHO, Strengthening Ministries of Health for Primary Health Care, Geneva, p. 42.
21. Ibid., p. 42.
22. Documents, Action Plan for an Effective and Responsive Government Prepared by Department of Administrative Reforms and Public Grivances, Ministry of Personnel Public Grivances, New Delhi, Quoted in *IJPA*, Vol. XLIV, No. 3 (July-Sept. 1998), p. 637.
23. WHO, *World Health*, April, 1984, p. 3.
24. George C. Salmot, *New Problems, New Strategies in World Health*, January, 1980, p. 15.
25. WHO, *World Health*, April, 1984, p. 3.
26. R.K. Sapru, Development Administration : Crisis and Continuities, in *IJPA*, Oct.-Dec., 1998, p. 779.

5 MPLADS and District Administration

Problems and Prospects

*Mohinder Singh** and *Vijay Kumar***

On the demand of MPs, the then Prime Minister P.V. Narasimha Rao introduced MPLADS on 23rd December 1993 with a view to develop local area falling in the constituency of concerned MP. Under the MPLADS each Member of Parliament from either house has been given an authority to recommend various developmental works for his or her constituency to the concerned Deputy Commissioner. Elected member of Rajya Sabha representing the whole of the state may select works for implementation in one or more districts anywhere in the state. Nominated member of Lok Sabha and Rajya Sabha may also select works for implementation in one or more district, anywhere in the country. MPs can also recommend works outside their constituencies/state for construction of assets that are permissible in the guidelines for rehabilitation measures in the event of natural calamity of rare severity in any part of the country. Expenditure on each work may not exceed Rs. 25 lakhs out of a total expenditure of Rs. 2 crore every year. At the initial stage a total sum of Rs. 5 lakhs per MP was released, which became Rs. one crore from 1994 and was further stepped upto Rs. 2 crore per annum per MP from 1998-99. Since, the inception of the scheme, 8,77,571 works were recommended throughout the country by the MPs and out of that 7,76,675

* Chairman, Department of Public Administration, Kurukshetra University, Kurukshetra.

** Research Scholar, Department of Public Administration, Kurukshetra University, Kurukshetra.

(88.43%) have been completed at the cost of Rs. 12732.16 crores (88.98%) out of the total sanctioned amount of Rs. 14308.80 crores.[1]

Administration

In the beginning this scheme was implemented by Rural Development Ministry but since October 1994 the implementation of this scheme was transferred to the Ministry of Statistic and Programme implementation. At the state level, each state and union territory designate one nodal department for effective implementation of works taken up under this scheme and co-ordination with the Ministry at the centre. The head of the district, where the MP recommends works, is directly responsible for implementation of the scheme at ground level. The authority and power to receive the MPLADS funds from the centre; to sanction the works recommended by MP after scrutinizing its conformity to the guidelines; to sanction the expenditure involved; to get the work executed; and to ensure maintenance of the assets created under this scheme vested in Deputy Commissioner.

Reality

We see that MP is confined only to recommend the works. The funds are not directly disbursed by him/her the MPs. In the implementation of the work under MPLADS, vital role is played by the Deputy Commissioner but the review of various studies shows that district administration has failed in effective implementation of MPLADS. Serious irregularities are found on the part of Deputy Commissioners while implementing this scheme. For instance, the C&AG Report 1998 reviewed the scheme from 1993-94 to 1996-97 in 24 states and 6 Union Territories through sample check in 165 of 488 districts. The relevant records maintained by DCs and in the department of programme implementation were examined and it was found that the scheme had not been implemented economically, efficiently and in an effective manner and had failed to achieve its objective. The C&AG of India in its another report submitted in 2001 revealed that the implementation of the scheme had become worse during the period 1997-2000 as evidenced by the low utilization, i.e., 64.2 per cent of the released fund and a very poor record of completion of works. Even 64.2 per cent utilized expenditure did not yield commensurate assets. Overall failure in operational ising the MPLADS in meeting its stated objective both by MPs at the recommendation stage and by Deputy Commissioners at the execution stage, was found.[2]

Evaluation report of the Planning Commission (2001) also highlighted various irregularities in the implementation of MPLADS such as poor position of monitoring and supervision and meagre allocation of funds to most of the works in the selected districts.[3] The above mentioned studies also revealed that the Deputy Commissioners have failed to check corruption in MPLADS. There are so many cases of fraud in implementation of MPLADS. Test check of Audit Report 1998 disclosed 11 cases of suspected fraud involving Rs. 50 lakh. For example, in Nagaland DC of Kohima paid Rs. 1.50 lakh in February 1995 for construction of a bridge over a seven feet *nullah* across a footpath in Khuzama village after approving the work recommended by the MP without preparing any estimate. The DC made payment on the basis of a certificate from the Block Development Officer, Kohima about completion of work. But actually the bridge consisted of only six local bamboo laid horizontally across the *nullah* alongwith side railing supported by Wooden poles which could not be expected to cost more than Rs. four to five thousand. The DC released the total payment without examining the correctness of the cost.[4]

In another case BDO, Nirsa in Dhanbad district of Bihar paid Rs. 1.05 lakh during June 1995 to July 1996 for carriage charges of morrum for construction of two roads. But records in the local transport office revealed that truck number shown in the voucher for carrying of morrum were that of motor cycles and public bus. So it is clear that the actual carriage of morrum was fictitious which cannot be happen without the involvement of the DC. In Faridabad district of Haryana, against the actual expenditure of Rs. 1.41 crore during 1993-96, ADC submitted utilization certificates to the Ministry for Rs. 1.81 crore. In Himachal Pradesh, Rs. 0.70 lakh transferred in March 1995 by DRDA Shimla to BDO Mashobra, were not traceable in the books of the latter. In Bidar district of Karnataka, out of Rs. 102.30 lakh released to the executive engineer of Zilla Panchyat Rs. 99.80 lakh only was accounted for and deposited into the bank account. There was no account of the remaining Rs. 2.50 lakh. The Deputy Commissioner of Khurda district of Orissa, sanctioned works worth Rs. one crore forwarded by the Resident Commissioner without the recommendation of MP. This is a clear violation of guidelines on the part of Deputy Commissioner.[5]

The corrupt practices were highlighted recently in a T.V. sting operation where some MPs were shown accepting bribes for sanctioning of the works under the scheme. The MPs only recommend/sanction the works. The implementation, i.e., scrutiny of works, technical estimation, administrative and financial sanction, supervision and monitoring is taken care of by the district authority. So it is clear that if a corrupt practice is followed by any MP all this happens with the involvement of district administration.

We also conducted a study in Kaithal, Kurukshetra and Yamunanagar districts of Haryana state to examine the implementation of MPLADS and observed certain weaknesses on the implementation part of MPLADS which is the responsibility of district administration. When it was asked to the development functionaries as to whether state government provided them any training for effective implementation of MPLADS, the views of the respondents clearly indicate that no training was given to them for the said purpose. During 2002-03, an amount of Rs. 1.20 crore was released for 121 developmental works in the 92 selected villages of six blocks. But out of 121 works. 5 (4.1 %) works were not found on the ground, though they were shown completed in the official record of ADCs. It seems that once the work is recommended, sanctioned and fund released, nobody keeps track of progress. It was also observed that money was released for C.C. streets whereas on the ground, there were brick made streets in place of C.C. streets. This indicates that there was manipulations of funds in implementation of MPLADS. According to the MPLADS guidelines, the MPs are authorized to recommend works only and not allot funds for them. But in practice, funds are allocated by MPs themselves and the district officers succumb to their pressures. Estimation of the cost is done after the allocation of fund by the MPs. What is the use of such type of estimation ? As a result out of total 121 works. 40 (33.1 %) works were found incomplete. Para 2.2 of the guidelines clearly shows that the works under the scheme should be of developmental nature based on the locally felt needs. Majority of selected Panchyat representatives (78.7%) and villagers (76.8%) stated that MPs did not keep in mind the felt needs of people while recommending works. The district authorities admitted that while sanctioning works they gave first priority to MPs' purposal instead of local felt needs and demands of the people. Thus, local felt needs and demands of the people are ignored at the time of making recommendations by the MPs and sanctions of funds by the DCs.

Involvement of Panchyati Raj Institutions in the effective implementation of MPLADS is must at the stages of recommendations, sanctions, monitoring, supervision and maintenance of the assets created. But 40.9 per cent of the development functionaries mentioned the non-involvement of PRIs. This demands that the representatives of PRIs should be involved at different stages of MPLADS. The task of monitoring and supervision become easier if the elected representatives are actually involved. Villagers can act as a watchdog to ensure the quality of the assets created. So non-involvement of Panchyati Raj Institutions by the district administration is a biggest drawback in the effective implementation of MPLADS. The guidelines issued by the ministry do not permit deducting of any contingency expenditure out of the funds released for works but 20 to 27 per cent development functionaries admitted that contingency charges were deducted which resulted in reduction in the net amount for the works taken up under MPLADS.

It was also found that assets are not used for the intended purposes. For example, many old age homes are constructed under MPLADS but our aged people do not like to go there as they think it is against the Indian social norms. As a result only stray dogs and animals take shelter in these homes. Thus, district administration has failed in ensuring the intended use of the created assets.

In order to make local people aware about the MPLADS signboards bearing the inscription. 'CONSTRUCTED UNDER MPLADS' ought to be erected at the work-sites by the implementing agencies but during field visit, the MPLADS signboards were found absent in majority of cases. Regarding signboards one interesting thing which has been observed is that in a village named Kheri Lakha Singh of Radaur Block, an old age home was constructed under MPLADS with an amount of Rs. 2.50 lakhs. It was shown completed in the official record of ADC Yamunanagar, but the signboard on the old-age home bears the words 'CONSTRUCTED UNDER SARKAR AAPKE DWAR PROGRAMME'. How can there be awareness about MPLADS among the people when the assets created under MPLADS bear the signboards of other programmes?

During the field visit, it was also observed that inferior quality of material was used for creation of these assets. Efforts should be made for ensuring the good quality of assets and this may be possible if sincerely attempts are made on the part of district officials and non-officials directly or indirectly responsible for creation of assets under MPLADS.

Information relating to quality of maintenance was also collected. It was rated poor by 45 per cent of development functionaries, 5I per cent of Panchyat representatives and 48 per cent of the villagers. If the good quality of maintenance is ensured by the district administration more benefits may accrue to the recipients.

Para 5.4 of the guidelines provides that the Deputy Commissioner should send monthly progress report about the status of works to the MPs. All the selected 5 Deputy Commissioners told that they were sending progress reports to the MPs about status of works every month but out of 6 MPs, 4(66.7%) pointed out that they did not receive any report about the status of works from the concerned Deputy Commissioner.

As per the guidelines of MPLADS, the Deputy Commissioners should invariably get the concurrence of MPs in identification and selection of implementing agencies but on enquiry, 5 (83.3%) out of 6 MPs, said that the Deputy Commissioners did not take their advice in selection and identification of implementing agencies.

The desired result from the MPLADS can be expected only through a proper and effective co-ordination mechanism among the MP, Deputy Commissioners and the development functionaries executing the work. Lack of co-ordination may lead to delay in preparation of cost estimate, sanction of works, release of fund for a particular work. Inappropriate co-ordination may also lead to the released amount for works lying unutilized with implementing agencies. Only appropriate co-ordination can ensure elimination of above mentioned drawbacks. While rating co-ordination among the concerned MPs, DCs and development functionaries for implementing the scheme, all the DCs rated it as satisfactory but 72.7 per cent of the development functionaries rated it as partly satisfactory and out of 6 MPs, 2 MPs were of the opinion that the position of coordination is less than satisfactory. This reflects that the co-ordination has remained unsatisfactory.

For effective implementation of works under MPLADS proper monitoring and supervision is required but it was found that position of monitoring and supervision for effective implementation of MPLADS is not so satisfactory. An overwhelming majority of the respondents reported the shortage of staff to look after the MPLADS works. This had resulted in poor monitoring and supervision.

From the above findings and observations, it is clear that there are several weaknesses in the implementation of MPLADS which require appropriate solutions.

Suggestions

For effective implementation of MPLADS by District Administration the following suggestions are given:

- The Panchayati Raj Institutions should be fully involved right from the stage of recommendations and sanction through monitoring supervision and maintenance of the assets created. If we do so villagers as a watchdog can ensure the quality of assets created. If inferior quality of material is being used by the implementing agency, villagers can object and stop such type of construction.
- To check the practice of manipulation of funds, village level Vigilance Committees may be constituted with the involvement of NGOs and viral youth clubs. These committees should keep themselves aloof from the petty politics and narrow considerations. If some flaw is noticed it should bring it to the notice of the concerned authority and the Gram Panchayat. The corrupt persons should be punished to bring them to the book. If the required information is not made available and inordinate delay takes place the notice

may be given under the Right to Information Act, 2005 to seek information.

- Sufficient funds out of the funds available with the MPs may be earmarked for ensuring proper and timely maintenance of the assets. At least 2 per cent of the estimated cost of the project completed under MPLADS in the previous year should be released for the maintenance of the assets created under MPLADS. Even local contribution by the user can also be utilized for this purpose.
- To overcome the problem of co-ordination, it is necessary to set-up a co-ordination committee at the district level which should consist of MP, MLAs, DCs, development functionaries including office holders of rural and urban local bodies. It is expected that such committee will not only ensure proper co-ordination among various functionaries but also check the problem of overlapping or duplication of works under MPLADS and MLALADS.
- As it was observed that some of 'the assets were not used for the intended purposes, so it is suggested that District Administration and Village Panchyats should be made responsible to ensure that assets created under MPLADS are used for intended purposes. Such persons as are found misutilising the assets must be brought to book. MPs should recommend employment oriented development works to enable the rural youth for getting employment.
- The assets under the MPLADS bore signboards of other programme such as constructed under Sarkar Aapke Dwar Programme instead of constructed under MPLADS. Signboards bearing the words constructed under MPLADS should only be engraved on each asset constructed under the MPLADS. Besides, we can also use electronic and print media for making the people aware of the scheme.

- As guidelines issued by the Ministry do not permit deducting of any contingency charges out of the funds released for works. But contingency charges were deducted which resulted in reduction in the net amount earmarked for the works taken up under MPLADS. Only strict adherence to prescribed guidelines can stop this practice. If necessary the guidelines may be amended.
- It should be made mandatory for the Deputy Commissioners to send monthly status reports of works to apprise the MPs of on-going works under the MPLADS.
- Deputy Commissioners should take MP's advise in identification and selection of implementing agencies. This will create good working relations between the MP and the Deputy Commissioners. This would also strengthen democratic functioning.
- For effective monitoring and supervision of MPLADS work, one post each of Research Officer, Assistant Research Officer, S.D.O. (Civil Engineering), a clerk and a peon should be sanctioned for regular monitoring and supervision of works undertaken under MPLADS. The monitoring team should be provided with a vehicle to take appropriate steps to required feedback.
- The Union and state governments should organize workshops, seminars and refresher courses from time to time for providing training to the officials to update their knowledge and skills for proper and effective implementation of MPLADS.
- As many as 40 (33.1%) assets were found incomplete due to low allocation made by the MPs. To overcome the problem, it is suggested that first the estimate should be prepared by the experts and thereafter requisite funds should be allocated and new projects should not be sanctioned by the Deputy Commis-

sioners unless the project already recommended are fully completed.

- Last but not least, funds should be channelized through the District Planning Committees constituted under 74th Constitutional Amendment.

NOTES AND REFERENCES

1. See, *The Tribune*, Febuary. 5, p. 10.
2. See, C. & AG Report No. 3 of 1998 and Report No. 3A of 2001.
3. See, Evaluation Report of Planning Commission on MPLADS 2001.
4. See C&AG Report No. 3 of 1998.
5. Ibid.

6 Modernization and Restructuring of District Administration

*Vikas Gupta**

The country has seen a systematic and sustainable development after the independence. Specially in the last decade of the 20th century the pace of development has picked up with the opening of economy to the global trade and commerce. The liberalisation and globalisation has seen a faster pace in the beginning of the new century. This change at a faster acceleration has created many gaps. This is being felt in various fields including the individual and social behaviour. Inspite of rapid changes in the field of science and technology, trade, commerce and industry, the human resource in the country has not been able to keep pace with the fast changing scenario. Notwithstanding our growing hold on the international human resource market, we have not been able to change the response quotient of the individuals in the society. We are struggling between the contraries. We move in the global society with nostalgic feelings of the past which has become very difficult to be shed off for us. This internal conflict has spared no field of life. We have a hidden but strong-tendency to live simultaneously both in the past and the present.

The modernisation and restructuring of administration at the district level has to be seen and appreciated, apart from other things, under the above background also. The present period of the Indian society, from this point of view,

* I.A.S, Additional Deputy Commissionar, Jhajjar, Haryana.

may comfortably be termed as a transit period of Indian psyche. During the first half century, of the independence we remained stagnant as far as our mindset towards the public administration is concerned. We adopted and accepted not only the British enactments, but also completely gave ourselves to the centuries old administrative set-up without much of the resistance. The old statutory enactments, were allowed not only to continue but were completely obeyed and exercised. Although the Constitution of India was the principal post independence enactment, but even the mode of enforcement of this Constitution flowed from the old English codes and statutes. We adopted the old system as ultimate without even an effort for an alternative. The sense of reverence and respect for governance was assimilated in our blood and that is why the relations of the governors and the governed remained almost static. Of course, the British rule was replaced by self-rule but the system of governance remained uncharged to a great extent.

This continuation of the British rule under the self-rule had its impact. This could be discerned both in the governors and the governed. The common masses had the faith in the government almost from the same sense of reverence which they had under the British regime. This could be seen as a positive development as far as it saw the continuity of respect for the rule of law among the common masses. That is why the law and order situation in the country as a whole remained much better than what it is today, in the third quarter of the 20th century. In addition to it the past impact of the freedom movement had ensured a sense of commitment and dedication among the Indian masses towards the glory and respect of our motherland. As a matter of fact the euphoria of patriotism continued in the same spirit and with the same intensity many years after the independence. Its impact was clearly visible in various fields of life. In the political hierarchy it could be recollected that the moral standards set up by the first generation of our political leadership are still remembered and cherishes with nostalgic reverence. The pace and direction given to the future of the country during the first decade in the form of futuristic infrastructure were remarkable. The blotless public life of this leadership was enviable. It was further reflected in the public life in the field of administration. The faith of the people in the rule of law was correspondingly fortified by the clean administration. All the three organs of the government—Legislature, Judiciary and Executive had a blotless track record. The modern evils of corruption, nepotism. and crisis of moral values had not touched the public life at large. The instances of these evils were exceptions only.

However, inspite of its glory and glamour the public life lacked openness and it resulted in the creation of a new class within the society. The number of people having direct access to the administrative authorities was very-very, limited. The old division of society between the rulers and the ruled still continued as such. One of the causes and effects of this division was the continuity of a selected section of the society in the higher echelons of administration. The isolation of the lower section of the society from the public administration was further aggravated even after the country became free. This resulted in the absence of responsive administration. The public life of administrative authorities remained eclipsed from the public scrutiny. That is why the first generation of the administration in free India enjoyed the air and aura of rulers rather than the public servants as envisioned in the Constitution of the free India. The public at large was isolated from the close scrutiny of functioning of these public servants.

But with the advancement of education among the common masses the old order gave way to change. The growing awareness among the people regarding their rights removed the iron-curtain and the people had a chance to come close to the administration. It was also due to the fact that the advancement of education enabled the lower middle class people to join the main stream of administration. The entry of this class in the administration acted as a tonic to ameliorate the situation. They allowed the isolated sections of the society to see the administration in action closely. It reduced the sense of awe and fear towards the authorities. The constitutional reservation for the downtrodden sections of the society in higher services proved epoch-making in this regard. The poor Harijans were able to see the interior of the administrative set-up when their offsprings adorned these high offices.

But it had an adverse impact also. The reduction of distance between the public and the administrators resulted in many evils of today. Corruption and break down of law and order was the problem which took a stride in the free India. The proximity of the authorities with the public became one of the reasons of corruption. It became a common temptation both to the authorities and the public. The public had a direct access to identify the blacksheeps among the authorities to axe their grind and reciprocally such blacksheeps saw an opportunity to deal directly with such elements in the society. Thus it facilitated both. However, notwithstanding this fall out, the public at large was highly benefited with easy access to the administration.

Against this background the present malaise of the administration came into existence. The main maladies are corruption, procrastination, inefficiency lack of credibility and lack of timely response to the public problems. The roots of corruption have gone deep to the extent that the people have more or less accepted it as essential part of the system. This has further deteriorated the credibility of the administration. The people have lost faith in the system. Delay in disposal has also become an essential ingredient of administration. As a matter of fact there is crisis of credibility which has been generated by lack of commitment and conviction among the administrative machinery. All pervading apathy among the administrative machinery has gulped up both efficiency, credibility and vitality of the system.

While making an attempt to modernise and restructure the District Administration in the country the main thrust areas could be identified on the following lines :

1. Eradication of : (a) Corruption
   (b) Procrastination
   (c) Inefficiency
   (d) Indifference
   (e) Demoralisation
   (f) Interference
2. Establishment of : (a) Credibility
   (b) Quickness
   (c) Efficiency
   (d) Commitment
   (e) Transparency
   (f) Confidence
   (g) Independence

The remedial measures to achieve the desired goal would have to be result oriented. The exercise to modernise and restructure the administration could be done as an evolution of the system rather than an abrupt change leaving all concerned confused and confounded. Before introducing the latest technology in communication and the tools of E-Governance, it has to be ensured that the people have first developed adaptability for the concept. It has to be continuously remembered and recollected that the real beneficiaries are not IT trained professionals but majority of them are almost illiterate in the new concept. The computerization process in the government departments has also proved that keeping apart beneficiaries, the govt machinery executing such process themselves needed to be educated and that is why the modernization process has remained restricted to the purchase of computers only. Practically the large purchase of computer hardware in government offices is sans result. Computers have just been able to replace the type-writing machines and nothing more than that. This is basically due to the fact that the actual writing on the wall has just been not taken care of. In an attempt to change everything quickly, we have put the cart before the horse.Therefore, the first phase of modernization of district administration should start with the process of education of both the beneficiaries and the government machinery. The meaningful and practical training of the concerned staff in the latest technology of their concern should be the first step. They must know what is to be delivered by them and how. They should be made well versed in their new responsibility. Once they are fit to deliver, their services may be utilized to address the same problem among the beneficiaries. Once both of the sections are aware of their respective roles, the system may take a start. We may discuss here the practical aspect with a specific instance. The project of the computerization of revenue record is under process in various districts of Haryana for the last many years. In some districts it has been claimed to have been accomplished also. However, the desired impact is not coming forth. It is primarily due to the lack of the required know how at various levels. Inspite of the revenue record being made available on the computer network, the farmer who is the real beneficiary, has not been able to make use of it. It is due to the same reason that firstly the revenue officials are not well acquainted with the process of updating the data nor they have been facilitated for the same. Thus, the revenue record without the latest update is of little use. Similarly, the real beneficiaries don't understand the process. They have still to depend upon the govt officials to get the documents. Thus the net impact has not been felt.

Then this modernisation at the level of district administration should first identify the real problem areas in each and every department e.g the district level. Each department has selected areas of operation which are directly connected to the people. After identifying such areas a cause and remedy study be got conducted through well equipped professionals. The process of modernization should address such problems on priority. For instance essential services like health and education are badly failing in public sector and private sector is fastly flourishing in both these fields. Briefly the reason for this could be the lack of credibility of govt sector. Inspite of heavy investment of public money these hospitals and schools have remained the forced resort of the poor and under privileged. The modern technology, if effectively enforced in such services can do wonders. The computerised display of availability of medicines and testing facilities to the patients in the govt hospital and the availability of consultancy could help the patients a lot. Corruption cases of selling of free medicines in the market could easily be checked once the daily stock is made public. Similarly, in other services like the supply of electricity, drinking water etc. can easily be made transparent.

Apart from it, the modernization process may take care of the effective monitoring system. The present administrative set-up depends entirely on the lowest field functionary of the department. The collector of the district has to depend upon the information given by the *patwari*. Similarly, the superintending engineer just has to endorse what the J.E. reports. This practically results in the non-application of mind at the senior level and the public has to suffer on account of carelessness and malafides of these lower- functionaries. But if the information technology provides the latest data at every level in the district it could easily take care of the problem. However, again it is reiterated that to ensure the real benefit of modernisation to those who require it, all concerned would have to be duly educated and enlightened regarding the system. If it is not done crores may go down the drain.

Another aspect which has to be simultaneously

addressed is the updation of law and rules/regulations to make them commensurate with the technology. The legalty and acceptability of E-documents for various purposes would have to be ensured. Here, the problem of attestation of the documents by the competent authorities would have to be taken care of. In each department of the district the alternate remedies would have to be identified. The same has to be endowed with the legal sanctity also, failing which the credibility would be jeopardised. It may be taken note of that each department has typical problems in this regard and the same have to be addressed separately. In the same sequence, to sustain the new system, duties and responsibilities to maintain and update the, data should be clearly defined and the same may be made the part of the departmental/service rules.

The restructuring of the district administration has to be commensurate with the modernization process. The same has to be done inter-departmental as well as interadepartmental. It has also to take care of the growing participation of elected bodies in the administration. Practically speaking, the majority of the problems at the district level take place due to the lack of coordination among various departments of the govt. During the British Regime as well as many years after the independence, the district administration remained closely knit headed by the District Magistrate. The institution of District Magistrate provided an umbrella of protection as well as the coordination to the administrative machinery in the district. It used to provide an ultimate source to the public as well as a single responsibility centre of district administration through which things could be controlled and coordinated by the govt. A strong institution of District Magistrate provided a hub around which all the activities could revolve. However, with the passage of time the administrative machinery of almost every department began to grow both vertically and horizontally. It was required also to some extent because with the increase in volume of work the system was bound to expand. However, this departmental growth had a tendency to grow like islands without linking-up properly with other coordinates of the district administration. Resultantly, the centre of gravity weakened. Some of the departments like police started almost a parallel centre of power while ignoring the authority of the Civil Magistracy. Similarly, others created their own hierarchy of vertical control. This decentralisation of district administration has created a very peculiar situation where the interdepartment coordination is badly lacking. The public has to run to the state capital for very small jobs because they fail to get remedy at the district level. The political powers are over burdened with such complaints and people get harassed. Therefore, while restructuring the district administration, it could be handled keeping in view the problem of coordination and to ensure an effective and responsive administration at district level itself. Firstly, the inter-relation of various departments has to be clearly defined. The hierarchy of district administration should have no confusion and who has to monitor and supervise has to be clearly identified. Let every department should work independent of each other as far as the professional expertise is concerned. But every department should be bound to respond to an institution who would lead the district administration. There should be no scope for this authority to be diluted. Correspondingly, the head of the district administration should be made completely responsible to the govt. for the entire administration of the district. Once every department is made responsible to such an office, he/she has to be responsible for the perfect coordination.

Apart from it the already existing concept of single-roof administration should be enforced in every district. The concept of mini-secretariats in the district should be further enhanced and enforced so that the entire district administration is available to the public at one place. It would save time, energy and money. It would ensure greater service and satisfaction to the public. This has already been done to a considerable extent and, it has to be further strengthened.

Then, while restructuring the district administration realistic assessment of workload is essentially required. Both the manpower and the machinery like computers, etc. should be realistically assessed, keeping in view the volume of work to be performed and accordingly it may to arranged, it is to be noted that inefficiency and delay both breed many other evils like corruption. Once proper resources are identified and arranged a considerable improvement could be expected. It would help in using the surplus and under utilized resources of some other departments of the district. For example the Junior Engineers with Civil Engineering qualifications are employed in more than one wing of different departments. There have been cases when the JE's were surplus in irrigation department but there was shortage of JE's in Public Health and PWD (B&R) wings. On the one hand it is shortage but on the other hand it is unutilized. Therefore, a scope should be left in the system itself to take care of it at the district level itself. It may also be remembered that these problems are not new but the same are continuing for years. However, these problems have just been ignored at the senior level, leaving it at the competency and discretion of individuals to handle. As a matter of fact, rather than giving a solution for these problems the same has-been exploited. The denudation of powers and control of the District Magistrate over the police in the district has given birth to new means of getting the things done. Rather than asking the senior officers to take care of the problem the communication has gone down to the junior functionaries. There have been cases when the Chief Minister or his office directly giving directions to the SHO in the police station. Thus the senior district authorities in the police are also being by passed. It has the tendency to jeopardize the discipline in the force as well as the break down of rule of law as well as law and order. It may also be appreciated that for individual gain or loss the institutions should not be allowed to be denuded and destroyed. Moreover, ignoring a problem is no solution. While restructuring the administration the reality has to be read and aberrations have to be removed. such aberrations are not to be misused at the cost of public malaise.

It could be restructured at two levels. The inter-departmental level should be clearly defined and notified and the responsibility to respond should be clearly defined and declared. No scope should be left for individual ego and whims while responding to the public responsibilities. The institution of head of the district should be allowed to play a dominant role in the district. The course of action and the mode of administration once defined and declared after consulting all the concerned quarters, it should be allowed to function strictly in public interest. Apart from it, the infra-departmental complexities within the departments should be clearly identified and the same may be rationalized keeping in view the actual requirement. Almost every department has created a complex hierarchy of levels with a very heavy top. If to go to the root cause of the problem, the genesis could be seen in an attempt to create more and more posts at higher levels to accommodate more and more officials in promotion. There have been offices in the district of some departments who had continued for years without relevance. Such redundant offices without work are normally used to punish the officers who annoy the powers that be on some account. This trend is available in almost every department and still it is prevalent without much of the noise regarding the misuse of public money. Not only at district level, it is equally available at the state level. However, this has to be done away with at all levels. Such an exercise would save the state money and the misuse of forced jobs without work would be checked.

The next and perhaps the most important problem to be taken care of is the quality of man power to be deployed at all levels in the district administration. Any exercise to revamp the system would be simply futile, if merit does not prevail in the postings of the officers in the district. It is really unfortunate that this aspect is being ignored recklessly which defeats the very purpose of the public service. The government will have to realize that the real cutting edge of administration are the officers working in the district administration. If such officers are posted and transferred on considerations other than the merit how is it possible to expect real public service from them? For this purpose a self-searching exercise is required at the level of those who has to decide it. While modernising and restructuring the administration this aspect should not be ignored and some modalities must be worked out to ensure the posting of only of meritorious officers with an excellent past record, at least on key assignments in the district administration.

In this process another exercise to be essentially conducted is the review of the service rules of each and every department in the district. It is unfortunate that the District Administrative manual prepared by the Britishers in India is still prevalent without any amendment or modification. Resultantly, it has become redundant and the officers in the districts including most of the District Magistrates, do not know even its bare contents. We have crossed half century mark after independence and have failed to respond to even the basic needs of governance, which ultimately has resulted in a situation of confusion. Let the service rules and other manuals be studied and examined by those who are really aware of the practical working and functioning of the respective departments. Let the basic needs and requirements be identified along with the redundancies. The ground realities may be kept in view throughout this exercise and the rules should be allowed to operate strictly in public interest. The district administration manual should be accordingly revised and replenished with the latest update.

Another very important aspect which requires to be kept in view during this exercise is the relations of the district administrations with the local self-government. These institutions have gained a constitutional status. The constitutional provisions have given a boost to these institutions and these institution at various levels have come into existence. It is a very happy development for the growth of democracy in the country. Every effort should be made to impart a real power to these institutions. However, this process has to be achieved cautiously. The practical experience at district and field level indicates that the members of these institutions are after more and more powers without owning the responsibility attached to such powers. As a result of it, clash is bound to appear between the PRI's (Panchayati Raj Institutions) and the functionaries of the district administration dealing with them. This is a natural outcome also in the sense that they are not aware of or they don't want to know the responsibility. One of the reasons is the fact that no academic qualification is prescribed in the Act for the members of these institutions. Many of them are illiterates or semi-illiterates and they are not even bothered to learn as members. In addition to it the all pervading corruption in the system adds fuel to the fire. Resultantly, these members of the PRI's spend heavy amount on elections and they try to recoup the same with multiplications when they are elected and get responsible positions. Therefore, at the time of restructuring of the district administration this aspect has to be appreciated alongwith the ground realities. Firstly, the relations of the official machinery with the PRIs has to be reviewed and redefined keeping in view the practical part. It is not meant here that the PRIs should be kept under the complete check of the official machinery, because doing so would mean throttling of democracy at the grassroot level. What is required is to transfer the responsibility also alongwith the powers. Let them be empowered to every extent possible but with the provisions ensuring that nobody can escape after floundering the state exchequer. A frame of rules should make these institutions powerful but equally responsible. These rules may envisage a situation where they may work for the welfare of the people as much as they like, but once they try to use such powers for personal gains, they are not allowed to escape. Thus a detailed exercise in this regard is essentially required while restructuring the district administration.

Last but, the most important point to be ensured is the proper mindset of the powers at the state level. It goes without saying that the district administration can't be visualized isolated from the state authorities. It is a fact that district administration is the reflection of the will and intention of the state government. The district administrative machinery draws its strength from the state headquarters. Therefore, it is the thought process at the highest level which actually matters. While conducting the exercise in this regard the state authorities both political as well as bureaucratic should be convinced to impart some independence and security of tenure to the district administration. As a matter of verbal consent no state government would decline to grant it but actually, so far none has been able to grant it upto the desired level. Therefore, the security of tenure and independence of working should take a statutory form subject to the effective control of the state government. But such control measures may be made applicable only on account of substantial reasons on record. The point here to be made is neither the authorities be allowed to go berserk and belligerent nor they are allowed to be used for the personal interests and gains of the powers that be.

Therefore, it is submitted that the modernisation and restructuring of district administration is a very noble cause but simultaneously it is very complex and ticklish also. There are many facts which require an intense and indepth study alongwith what is actually happening on day-to-day basis in the district administration. The past experience and strength of those who could deliver the goods at district level and the weaknesses of those who badly failed in public welfare, could be used also as a study material in this regard. Otherwise, if modernisation mean addition of a few computers in the office and restructuring mean abolition of a few posts and creation of another few, it is meaningless and such exercises have been done in the past also by some departments which went unnoticed without any tangible results.

7 Revamping District Rural Development Agency

*Mohinder Singh**

Rural development is one of the priorities of our development policy. For developing the rural areas, well-planned efforts are going on. Appropriate administrative arrangements have been made from time to time to achieve the goals and objectives of rural development. The then existing agencies popularly known as SFDAs were renamed as District Rural Development Agencies (DRDAs) with effect from 2nd October, 1980 to implement IRDP and allied activities in all the districts. The DRDAs were registered under the Registration of Societies Act XXI of, 1860 to provide benefits to the target group consisting of small farmers, marginal farmers, agriculture labourers, rural artisans and other weaker sections while focusing on the poorest among the poor. The DRDA administration was changed w.e.f. from 1st April, 1999 to strengthen and professionalise it. The staff costs of DRDA establishment are met by the Central and State Government in the ratio of 75:25 respectively. Under the DRDA administrative scheme, DRDA is visualized as specialized agency capable of managing anti-poverty programmes of the Ministry of Rural Development on one hand and to effectively relate these to the overall efforts of poverty eradication in the district on the other. During the year 2002-03, Rs.19,918.64 1akh were released under DRDA

* Chairman, Department of Public Administration, Kurukshetra University, Kurukshetra, Haryana.

administrative scheme. This amount reached to Rs.22,000 1akh in 2003-04, and to Rs. 1,8464.16 1akh up to 24th January, 2005 during 2004-05.

Organizational Structure

There is a Governing Body of each DRDA which has to be headed by the chairman of the Zila Parishad and it should have other members as follows :

(i) All MPs, MLAs, MLCs of the District;
(ii) One third Panchayat Samiti Chairpersons to be nominated by rotation in alphabetical order for a tenure of one year, one of whom must belong to SC/ST and another a woman;
(iii) CEO of Zila Parishad/District Collector-Chief Executive Officer/Executive Director;
(iv) Head of the Central Cooperative Bank of the district;
(v) Chairman, Regional Rural Bank;
(vi) District Lead Bank Officer;
(vii) Representative of the Reserve Bank of India at district level;
(viii) NABARD representative at district level;
(ix) General Manager, DIC;
(x) Representative of KVIB;
(xi) District officer in charge of Scheduled Caste/Scheduled Tribe welfare;
(xii) District Women and Child Welfare Officer;
(xiii) District officer dealing with welfare of disabled;
(xiv) One representative from technical institutions;
(xv) Two representatives of NGOs;
(xvi) Two representatives of the weaker sections, one of whom may be from SCs and STs; and
(xvii) One representative of rural women.

Project Director, DRDA-Member Secretary

The administration of DRDA works under the governing body, which provides the policy directions; approves the annual plan; and reviews and monitors the implementation of the plan, including the different programmes. The governing body gives such directions to the DRDA, as it deems necessary from time to time. This body has to meet once in a quarter. Before the 73rd Constitutional Amendment, the District Collector or the Deputy Commissioner used to act as the chairman of the DRDA.

It has been observed that in some of the states, the DRDAs have not been placed under the control of the Zila Parishad despite the clear instructions, the chairman of the Zila Parishad has not been made the chairman of the governing body of the DRDA. The Conference of the Chief Ministers held on 2nd August, 1997 recommended that the DRDAs be restructured so as to function under the overall control and supervision of the District Panchayats. Accordingly, the State Governments and Union Territories were advised to merge DRDAs with District Panchayats and make the Chairpersons of the District Panchayats as Chairpersons of the DRDAs, which have not taken place in all the cases. Moreover, the meetings of the governing body are not being convened every quarter and the representatives of the weaker sections also do not get opportunities to actively participate in the deliberations of the governing body.

As per the guidelines issued by the Union Ministry of Rural Development, the DRDAs are to be equipped with appropriate manpower and functionaries. The state governments are allowed to make modification in the structure and staffing pattern of DRDAs depending on circumstances. The staffing pattern of the DRDAs is given below—

A Project Director usually of the rank of an Additional Deputy Commissioner heads the DRDA. In Haryana, he is designated as Chief Executive Officer who is the overall in-charge of all the activities of the DRDA and is responsible for interaction with the district/state administration as well as with the Government of India. In those states where Zila Parishad is fully functional, the CEO is appointed to the Zila Parishad. In such cases the so appointed CEO also acts as the project director of DRDA.

Wings

Each DRDA is expected to have the following wings :—

- Self-employment wing;
- Women's wing;
- Wage employment wing;
- Engineering wing;
- Accounts wing;
- Monitoring and evaluation wing; and
- General Administration wing.

Self-employment Wing: This wing is also under the administrative control of the CEO and is staffed by assistant project officers in the area of planning, credit, social mobilization and technology. This wing also has women wing, which is responsible for women development programmes and gender issues. Assistant project officer who works under the overall supervision and control of the CEO also heads this wing.

Wage-employment Wing: The DRDA has the responsibility of overall planning, monitoring and technical evaluation of the works completed under the wage employment programmes these days, SGRY is the major centrally sponsored wage employment programme which is implemented by the Gram Panchayats and the line departments at the block and the district level. The DRDA provides guidelines and ensures effective implementation of the programme.

Engineering Wing: This wing is also under the overall control of the CEO and it should have one Executive Engineer to be supported by Assistant Engineer and one Junior Engineer.

Accounts Wing: The CEO with the help an accounts officer who is further assisted by two-three accounting personnel looks after all accounts matters.

General Administration Wing: As it is clear from its name, it deals with all administrative matters of the DRDA. It works under the control of the CEO.

Monitoring and Evaluation Wing: This wing is no doubt under the CEO but it works through the APO (monitoring) who also ensures evaluation relating to schemes and programmes of the DRDA. The staffing pattern according to the guidelines is expected to reflect a clear departure from that of a purely administrative organization. Thus, the staffing structure of the DRDA includes positions for planning for poverty alleviation, project formulation, social organization and capacity building, gender concerns, engineering supervision and quality control, project monitoring, accountancy and audit function as well as evaluations and impact studies. The following principles have been laid DRDAs for the personnel system :

- The DRDA is not to have any permanent staff and no longer any direct recruitment is allowed.
- It is better to have employees on deputation for a specific period.
- It is necessary that at least the project director, project officers, APOs and all technical posts should be manned by officers with proven capability and motivation to be selected in an objective manner by specific selection committees.
- The project directors and APOs selection should be from amongst officials not more than 40-45 years of age and in any case not more than 50 years of age.

For the effective administration of the DRDAs administrative cost per district is fixed as follows:

Category A District	having less than 6 blocks	Rs.461akhs
Category B District	having 6-10 blocks	Rs. 57 lakhs
Category C District	having 1-15 blocks	Rs .65 lakhs
Category D District	having more than 15 blocks	Rs. 67 lakhs

The above amount limits were applicable from the year 1999-2000. The limits are raised every year on compounding bases, up-to 5 per cent to set off increases due to inflation, etc.

Functions

The functions of the DRDA are:

(a) to keep all the concerned district and block level agencies well informed with regard to the basic parameters, the requirements of the anti-poverty programmes and the tasks to be performed by them;
(b) to co-ordinate and oversee the surveys, preparation of perspective plans, annual plans and action plans of the development of the district;
(c) to give publicity to the achievements made under different programmes and disseminate knowledge and build up awareness about the programmes;
(d) to secure inter-sectoral and interdepartmental coordination and cooperation;
(e) to conduct monitoring and evaluation of the programmes to ensure their effectiveness; and
(f) to send periodical returns/reports from time to time to the state government in the prescribed formats.

Observations and Suggestions for Revamping DRDAs

A close examination of the structure, functions and role of DRDA clearly indicates that some of the posts of APOs and other supporting staff are lying vacant and there is general reluctance on the part of deputationists to take up the assignments in the DRDAs because of lack of special benefits. The Protect Directors/CEOs are frequently transferred, which greatly impairs the efficiency and effectiveness of the DRDAs. The officials are also not imparted training on regular bases as a result of which the effectiveness of the programmes suffers. In some of the cases it has been observed that the DRDAs could not check the wrong flow of funds. In most of the cases, the requisite training for starting new trades is not arranged for the self-help groups and the main funding is confined to the dairy programme. It has also been noticed that there is lack of proper nurturing of the self-help groups. No doubt, there is a provision of Rs.10,000 for NGOs for the success each SHG but in practice, the amount is not being spent on the NGOs. A meagre amount of Rs.1,500 is being given to the Anganwari workers for guiding the SHGs. The monitoring pact is also weak. The activities are also not being jointly identified by the representatives of the DRDA, Bankers and the BDO.

Suggestions

For revamping the DRDAs following suggestions are given :

(i) The DRDA should be placed under the control of the Zila Parishad and the chairman of the Zila Parishad should be made the chairman of the DRDA.

(ii) It should be ensured that the meetings of the governing body of the DRDA take place as per the guidelines.

(iii) There is a tendency of creating parallel bodies/ committees such as vigilance committee, etc. which should be discouraged and the governing body of the DRDA should be activated by involving the weaker sections as are generally ignored.

(iv) The CEOs should not be frequently transferred and

there should be specific rule under which no such officer be transferred before completion of three years tenure.

(v) Well-trained staff should be recruited and training at regular interval should be arranged/imparted to the staff engaged in planning, implementation and monitoring of anti-poverty programmes.

(vi) The existing staff of the DRDA having a longer stay should be merged with the staff of the development and panchayat department.

(vii) To attract better personnel to be taken on deputation, handsome deputation allowance is required.

(viii) As there is lack of effective coordination among DRDA, bankers and development staff, therefore, all available means should be applied to establish effective coordination.

(ix) All the vacant posts should be immediately filled to ensure better services to the beneficiaries.

(x) All those officials who are hard workers, sincere and honest should be publicly honoured.

(xi) Strong and positive steps are required to ensure genuine selection of beneficiaries being covered under anti-poverty programmes.

(xii) As there is a provision of involvement of NGOs, therefore, it is suggested that reputed NGOs should be involved in the formation and survival of the SHGs.

(xiii) Last but not least, regular monitoring and supervision are also required to provide quality services to the beneficiaries.

8 District and E-Governance
Restructuring Service Delivery Mechanism

*Suresh Misra** and *Devendra Singh***

Introduction

The issue of governance has in the recent times emerged at the forefront of the development debate. To promote good governance India has recognized the urgent need for administrative reforms to enhance the capacity and capability of the administrative systems in carrying out goals for economic and social development. The deficiencies in the administrative machinery constitute a major obstacle to the effective implementation of development plans and priorities. The growing complexity of modern life in an age of rapid technological, social and economic changes has increased the role of the government, particularly in the provision of service delivery. Inspite of liberalization and privatization the government still continues to be the largest service provider with the largest resource base and catering to the largest section of the population. Improving the quality of administration and providing a responsive interface between the citizens and the public services requires a number of new initiatives.

The district in India is in many ways the most important unit of field administration. It remains the basic territorial

* Professor, Faculty of Public Administration, IIPA, New Delhi.
** Programmer, Faculty of Computer Sciences, HIPA, Gurgaon.

unit of administration in the states and continues to be the face of governance. It is a convenient geographical unit where the apparatus of public administration are concentrated. During 1991 census India had 466 districts and at present the number has increased to nearly 600. Within the districts are units called tehsils or talukas for departments such as revenue, education, health, etc. and blocks which are basic units for agrarian development. Local governments include panchayats and various municipalities.

With the passage of the 73rd and 74th Constitutional Amendment Acts the local governments have been saddled with major responsibilities, resources and political power within the district. The district administration includes all agencies of government and comprehends all institutions for the management of public affairs. As a unit of the administrative system it has been a pivotal point of contact between the citizen and the administration and truly the cutting edge of the administration or government and this is what constitutes its vital significance.

Genesis of District Administration

District administration has been one of the important institutional legacies passed on by the British. The genesis of district administration dates back to the East India Company and the principal representative in the district became the collector of land revenue. Trading was replaced by levy and collection of land revenue. As law and order had to be maintained and the army could not be present everywhere, the collector of the district also became the official responsible for maintaining law and order. Later on the district came under full governance and administration of the imperial power. Gradually with need the district administration grew into a complex apparatus with addition of a number of other staff to man various functions/services at the district level. As the functions and responsibilities of the district expanded the structure also grew with a large work force to man the various sub systems. Even though the local institutions particularly the District Boards were given charge of some areas of operation but by and large the local institutions of self-government tended to form administrative isolation within the district administration as a whole.

With independence the growing emphasis was on development planning and the implementation of welfare and development programmes. As a result the role and structure of the district administration changed. The district administration evolved from the basic purpose of maintenance of law and order, revenue administration to the implementation of developmental activities for the economic and social advancement of the people of the country. Today the district administration is burdened with multiple goals, objectives and functions ranging from maintenance of law and order to implementation of development and welfare schemes to delivering a range of public services.

The district administration faces many difficulties and conflicting challenges due to increasing demand for various governmental services, diminishing resources and general public distrust to name a few. Moreover due to a variety of factors the traditional homogeneity of the district administrator and the authority of the district collector are being challenged. Therefore, building capacity of the district administration requires a new thrust and aim to make the district administration more transparent, accountable and responsive to citizen's needs and concerns. The focus should be on improving the service delivery mechanism.

Excellence in Public Services

Citizens of today are more aware, more demanding, more informed and more knowledgeable. Service has become very critical. If governance at the districts level adopts the concept of service excellence it can become more productive and competitive. Excellence can simply be defined as the quality or state of being outstanding or superior. Excellence provides happiness and comfort to the citizens and also provides a memorable experience. Good organizational culture and developing a relationship of trust with the citizens will enable the districts to move closer to the concept of excellence. We need to have the employees and the citizens at the same wavelength. The cutting edge officials should be more motivated and competitive and need to improve their attitude. A positive environment is to be created where every citizen feels needed and important.

The new economy is customer economy and the customer/citizen is full of emotions and we need to understand their emotional needs. In the realm of service delivery at the district level we are still aiming for a 'satisfied customer' where as worldwide organizations are moving towards a 'delighted customer'. Total organizational excellence involves comprehensibly improving competitiveness, effectiveness and flexibility through planning, organizing and understanding each activity, and involving each individual at each level. No doubt there are many ways of achieving organizational excellence and enhancing the capacity of the delivery mechanism at the district level. Today technology can be used to create excellence in services. The points of contact have to be identified, where the cutting edge administration is in contact with the citizens. Adopting e-governance in service delivery is perhaps the best bet.

Promoting E-Governance

E- governance opens up a realm of possibilities for provision of cost effective transparent services. E-governance is fast emerging as an important tool for achieving good governance especially with regard to improving efficiency, transparency and making interface with government user friendly. E-governance denotes the application of IT to the processes of government functioning in order to bring about better governance, which has been termed as SMART. Use of ICT in government facilitates efficient, speedy and transparent process for dissemination of information to the citizens. In an attempt to promote convenience and facilitate e- governance the district administration needs to understand the citizens needs and expectations at all points of interface. i.e. at all stages in the service delivery process so as to determine key components of service quality and procedures that are citizens and employee focused, responsive, flexible and reliable. The irony is that the personnel at the district level have not realized the rewards that a good service can bring.

The strategy could be to make best use of technology in service delivery, systems improvement and improvement in the work environment so as to ensure speed, accuracy and efficiency. Attention has to be focused on potential failure points and service recovery procedures, which amounts to empowering employees to exercise responsibility, judgment and creativity in responding to citizen's problems. By the use of ICT the major benefits the district administration would gain are :

- Better delivery of services to the citizens,
- Improved programme management,
- Better resource management, and
- Facilitate planning process.

E-governance would help to improve the universal availability of quality services and universal access to these services. The information revolution empowers the citizens to access, transmit and transform information in ways that governments are powerless to block, and in the process it undermines authoritative controls. It also constraints the government to withhold information from citizens and there by help in bring about :

- Transparency in the working of the sub-systems at the district level,
- Ensure greater efficiency, objectivity, accountability and speed in providing services and information to the public,
- Provide cost effective services and ensure quality of the same,
- Provide single window for all government services at the district level,
- Make the administration more transparent and responsive,
- Eliminate middle men.

Apart from these it will also provide a friendly, speedier and efficient interface as citizens evaluate public services not only on the result but also on the behaviour and even the appearance of the individual delivering the service. The historical lack of interest in services at the district level can partly be attributed to the fact that the district administration was more designed to maintain law and order and to collect revenue. With democratization of the nation and also the society the role of district administration has changed substantially and it requires a different emphasis and approach. Increasingly with globalisation, liberalisation and privatisation quality is becoming a key variable in strategic planning at the district level. It is equally important to clearly lay down the range and standards of delivery to be achieved within well-defined time frames at the district level.

Citizen Centric Initiatives

During the last few years there have been a number of major initiatives taken by various states and local governments in India towards ushering in information technology in the functioning of government. Haryana has also been a part and parcel of this process. The emphasis has been on providing better services to citizens and improving the internal productivity of the departments and the line departments at the district level. It has been widely accepted that implementation of e-governance has been a difficult process due to a number of factors and hence requires careful planning and formulation of strategies for effective implementation. The experience of individual states in this regard needs to be understood and shared to evolve meaningful strategies. To enable us to understand and appreciate the transformation and changes that e-governance intends to bring about in service delivery in Haryana, select a governance projects from the state have been discussed. These "Quick Wins" will enhance the faith and confidence of the citizens in public bodies as they are much more citizen centered and cater to their requirements and at the same time improve the service delivery mechanism at the district level.

Critical Services for E-Governance

There are large number of government departments/ agencies at the district level, which have maximum interface with the public. It would be immensely beneficial to adopt e-governance to improve these critical services, to provide quality services to the citizens. The services could include specific departments like police, revenue, food and civil supplies, rural development, social welfare, education, public health and various offices of the district administration. Apart from these the specific public utility services that can be targeted are; vehicle registration, land registration, driving license, arms license, issue of certificates including ration cards, birth, death, domicile and caste certificate, registration in voters list and issue of voters identity card, grievance redressal, passport forms collection counters, public grievances relating to electricity, water, ration card, sanitation, public transport, revenue administration, disaster management and police. Rural services like land records, below poverty line cards (BPL), social services including old age pension, widows pension, ex-gratia payment and various services being delivered by the municipalities and panchayats can be improved with the help of e-governance. In the agriculture sector information regarding pesticides, fertilizers, crop disease, weather forecast-short-range/district wise, market pricing can be made available to the citizens to help increase productivity.

E-Governance, Haryana Initiatives and Case Studies

Haryana has emerged as an IT hub with some of the best multinational companies being located in the state. Though the process of e-governance is slow but it is gradually picking up. It would not be out of place to mention that in the recently held National e-Conference at Cochin on Feb. 2, 2006. Haryana has received two National a Governance Awards. The first award is for HALRIS software which Dynamically Integrates Property Registration and Land Records Administration. HALRIS software facilitates availability of Records-of-Right (RoR) anytime and any where with transparency. The second award is for the project "Result Through Binocular (RTB) Empowering Public with Knowledge". The RTB is a compendium of thousands of queries, in depth analysis and information bonanza. The online system has been developed to monitor the results of various exams , viz, middle, matric and senior secondary, open school (secondary, senior secondary) conducted by Haryana board of School Education. It facilitates students and teachers, guardians and school management, government and board alike in detailed anatomy of results. It empowers public with knowledge. The new initiatives taken by Haryana have been recognised and the state is moving towards a governance in a large number of areas to improve the delivery mechanism. The State IT Policy, 2000 is the first step towards creating an enabling IT environment in the state. It states that Information Technology (IT) would have a prominent and progressive role in the new millennium as the single most important enabler for improving efficiency and effectiveness in organisations. The State Government recognises the role of IT as an effective tool in catalysing economic activity, in efficient governance and in developing human resource. This policy seeks a deep impact initiative by the State Government in encouraging replacement of traditional delivery system of public services by IT driven system of governance that works better, costs less and is capable of serving the citizens' needs with ease. A high degree of public satisfaction through transparent and efficient functioning of public domain activities would be at the focus of IT initiative. Application of sunrise technologies in transition to a knowledge based society, providing equal opportunity to all in reaping the benefits of development, harnessing vast potential of human endeavour and enriching quality of life shall provide the long term underpinning of socio-economic transformation of the state. This policy further seeks to facilitate private domain initiative in e-transition of Haryana by providing critical infrastructure, systems framework and enabling environment.

Enabling E-Governance Environment

In order to create an enabling IT environment and operationalise e-governance projects in the state there is a need to integrate and network the state administrative structures both vertically and horizontally. Haryana was part of Punjab before 1966. Since then the state has travelled a long way as far as development indicators are concerned. The state is divided into four administrative divisions with 20 districts. The size of the districts is small in comparison to its bordering states, which makes it easier to be governed and also easy to adopt and implement administrative reforms. The trickle down of e-governance at the district level cannot be seen in isolation from the overall policy and initiatives being taken in the state. The organic link between the civil secretariat and the district administration and the link between the district headquarters with all sub-divisions, tehsils, sub-tehsils, blocks, municipal committees and district offices is very important in day-to-day administrative affairs and processes. To give a philip and guide the process of e-governance in the state important initiatives have been taken and the following four high powered committees have been constituted :

State Level Steering Committee (IT-PRISM)

(Planning, Re-engineering, Implementation, Steering, Monitoring) has been constituted by the government to set the priorities of sectors to be taken for computerization and review the progress of IT action plan of various departments, boards and corporations. It also intends to approve the budget and sanction posts and expenditure for IT Department and promote IT education in the state. The Chief secretary of the state heads the committee.

State Technical Committee

The committee is headed by Secretary Information technology for standardization of hardware, software and database packages, and to frame course curricula for all type of computer course and help the IT-PRISM.

Facilitation Committee

Principal Secretary to Chief Minister (PSCM) is the head of this committee. Under the PSCM society for IT initiative a fund of Rs. 10 crore has been established for e-Governance.

High Power Committee

Headed by Chief Minister of Haryana to consider special packages or incentives/concession for prestigious projects with an investment of Rs. 30 crore and above. Apart from this a number of initiatives have been taken to network the administrative agencies and systems. A few of these relate to :

(i) An E-Governance center has been established at the Haryana Civil Secretariat for Information Technology (SIT). The center has following facilities:

   (a) Server Rooms and LAN at SIT
   (b) Application/Data Center
   (c) Web Studio-cum-GIS Lab
   (d) Two Number of IT Training Labs
   (e) Executive Briefing Center and Lecture-cum-Conference Hall
   (f) Technology Showcase, Multimedia Presentations
   (g) Digital Library
   (h) Video Conferencing Room: Two VC cabins

(ii) Providing computer to officers and officials working in secretariat branches.

(iii) Local Area Network (LAN) is established in Haryana Civil and New secretariat. It has been decided to provide LAN cabling in each room in both the secretariats. NIC is responsible for the coordination and management of this internet and related activities.

(iv) Various application packages for e.g. Payroll, PIS have been developed by NIC for State Government departments. These packages are in use by government department for salary Pay Bill and Personnel Information System.

(v) Under Web site policy of the Government , web sites of 16 districts of Haryana and around 15 departments, boards and corporations have been developed and hosted on NIC's official web server.

(vi) The Geographical Information System of Haryana

(GISH) is a on line web enabled application which provides on line queries/information to the users on various aspects like state, district, block and village boundaries, road network, rail network and distance between two cities apart from other information. A database on tourism also provides details about various tourist facilities. A click on a particular tourist site displays details about the distance, accommodation facilities, expenditure and other details about the place.

(vii) Video conferencing facilities for interacting with Deputy Commissioners of Kurukshetra, Gurgaon, Hisar and Rohtak districts has been established in the first instance and is to be extended to all the districts of the state. This facility of video conferencing is also available at Haryana Bhawan.

E-Governance Projects and Case Studies

A large number of e-governance projects are already in operation in the state and are being implemented in a number of districts to provide a range of services. We have analysed some of the important e-governance projects in the state in order to understand and evaluate the improvement in the process of service delivery using information and communication technology. Only those e-governance initiatives, which would have long term effect not only on the quality of public services but also on the service delivery mechanism at the district level have been analysed.

District Minimum Applications Programme (D-MAP) and District Networking (D-NET) Project

This is one of the important initiatives being taken to make the district administration more responsive and transparent. District Networking [D-NET] project intends to network all the main offices under the deputy commissioners. It will also facilitate automation of workflow and provide single window information access and e-mail communication to the general public. Panchkula district has been identified as a Model D-NET district. *The standard replicable software product under "NAI-DISHA" (New Agent for Information District Level Integrated Services of Haryana for All) has been developed covering twenty-two types of citizen services. At present NAI-DISHA has been implemented in Panchkula and is currently being replicated in five more districts of the state (Sirsa, Sonepat, Hisar, Rohtak, Gurgaon) in the first phase. The backend software of NAI-DISHA is being developed.* The application packages identified under D-MAP includes Public Grievances, "Public Information and Facilitation System, Payroll, Periodic Returns Transmission System, DAK Monitoring System, Patwari Information System [PATIS], Revenue Recovery Information System, Rainfall Information System, Decision Support System, Court Cases Monitoring System, Village Information System, Arms License Information System, Certificate Issuing System. *The work has already started on D-MAP applications and some of the applications have already been implemented at districts. With the integration and networking of various offices in the district the citizen will be able to access information at a single point, there bringing efficiency in the delivery of services by reducing delay and harassment.*

Haryana Registration Information System (HARIS)

The HARIS is similar to Bhoomi Project of Karnataka and provides registration of documents within the premises of the Tehsil/Sub-Tehsil offices. HARIS features include various security checks, on-line capturing and storing of photos of buyers, sellers and witnesses, information of registration fee, printing of registration certificate and various other statistical report. This has been developed in-house by NIC and provides maintenance database and on-line query facilities. The system is being implemented at 88 Tehsils/Sub-Tehsils of the state and efforts are being made to extend the implementation of HARIS in all tehsils and sub-tehsils. The existing registry staff at tehsils/sub-tehsils has been trained to operate this system. With the application of this system, encouraging results are visible in terms of revenue maximization, cost minimization and public convenience. The HARIS website is also being developed to provide rates, procedures and other information to the public.

Land Records Computerization Project (LRCP)

Land remains a prime asset and there is a need to have a systematic process of managing land records. Due to poor records management large chunks of government land has been encroached. Moreover, due to corruption in registration and transfer of land there is a revenue loss to the public exchequer. To over come these problems the land records are being computerized and the system involves different sub-systems like Jamabandi creation, Mutation, Khasra Girdavari, Generation of New Jamabandi, On-line query on Land Records Information, Nakal (Record-of-Right) generation and distribution services to the public. The project is being implemented in 19 districts of Haryana and some of the districts have completed 100 per cent entry and verification of Jamabandi. Above 95 per cent of data entry of Jamabandi has been completed in most of the districts. Creation of New Jamabandi using semi-utomatic Jamabandi generation system and Nakal services started at select districts. The Land Records Query System [LRQS] has been developed with the objective of providing a Query Service to Farmers, Revenue Officials, and Town Planners. It is a tool to access information about the Jamabandi data at various levels; i.e. village, tehsil and district level. LRQS has been designed and developed using user-friendly Window based Hindi technology keeping in view future trends and requirements. To have an Integrated Land Information System the linkages to various sub-systems has been initiated.

E-Finance - Net (OTIS)

This is another important system. The objective of e-Finance-Net is to ensure the effective use of information technology within Finance Department and various other departments. There are 21 district level and 80 sub-district treasuries, all located in different regions. Associated with each treasury, there is a lead bank branch, which co-ordinates all treasury related work. Managing and tracking the funds inflow and outflow was done in the traditional manual manner, leading to inefficiencies in the process. The biggest problem was the time lag between when the funds came into a bank, and when the state treasury actually found out about the transaction. The treasury was totally dependent on the internal processes of the banks-which were often marred by inefficiencies.

The workflow based Online Treasuries Information System (OTIS) ensures smooth data flow between treasuries and banks and treasuries and departments. The implementation of OTIS in all Treasuries, has made available the real time information of the funds to the state helping it to keep track of the cash in low and outflow, and facilitating better plannings. The OTIS provides for an efficient, transparent mode of payments clearances, and facilitates faster payment processes, saving time and reducing red tape involved in conducting transactions with banks and state authorities. The biggest benefit to citizens however, is the improvement in government and administrative services—a direct result of better fund planning that the government will now be able to do.

House Tax Assessment and Collection System

One of the important duties assigned to the municipalities in the state relates to house tax collection. This has not been an easy task due to various reasons including poor data base management. To overcome this problem and also increase the revenue of the municipalities a new software has been designed. Based on the new House Tax formula of Haryana Government, the software for generating of house tax notices, house tax bills for collection of tax and issue of receipts, various forms, registers, reports and analysis has been developed. The survey has been carried out and data entry has been completed in all the 53 municipalities, and detailed analysis on house tax assessment has also been carried out. The notices of house tax have been issued in all 53 municipalities and whereever applicable fire tax has also been added. The collection of tax using this software has started in various municipalities.

Replicable Suite of Packages

The suite of five packages (Payroll, PIS, Dak Monitoring, Court Cases and Meetings Management) has been developed. *Payroll Information System*, completely conforms to the various forms approved by A.G. Office . The database maintains department code, employee code, and various heads of accounts as per the directions of Finance Department. The software is expected to form the important component of proposed Central Data Repository in future. Personnel Information System maintains basic permanent information, ACR, awards, punishment and integrity details. The S/W can help in deployment of staff, planning transfers, planning for promotions, filling of vacancies, deciding extension beyond 50 and 55 years, etc. Security has been provided at server based system and no unauthorized person can tamper the Database. DAK (Diary/Dispatch) Monitoring System keeps track of the dak marked to different officers in the department and the status of action taken by them. The software helps in building a basic database on all type of references. The Court Case Monitoring System, systematically monitors the status of the various types of court cases of the department pending in various courts. Timely alarms are provided so that various branches of a department can take forehand action. On the other hand the Meetings Management System maintains Meeting Notice, Agenda Items, Attendance Sheet, Minutes of the Meeting, etc. This will essentially help tone up the administration at various levels and help keep track of processes and documents.

E-Food. Net

This is a unique concept. The core functioning of the Food and Supplies Department of procurement and storage were traditionally managed manually. In the manual system, huge staff, which took lot of time, compiled information and by the time information was available it lost its relevance. With the implementation of e-Food. Net (e-storage and e-procurement) data was captured from mandies during procurement into web enabled software. Various reports and queries generated from e-procurement gave instantaneous picture of procurement done at all the mandies by various agencies. In e-storage, which is also a web enabled solution stock information is capture godowns/ storage location wise under various categories of stock.

The statistical and GIS report generated from the system helped in taking judicious decisions relating to movement and dispatches. The system drastically reduced the manpower engaged and time taken in preparing various reports and plans manually. The e-Food. Net has brought efficiency and also helped in reducing the cost incurred by the department for these functions. The system has also made activities like transmitting procurement figures from mandies in districts to head office through telephone and telegram redundant and thereby saving huge costs. All state agencies involved in procurement of food, distribution of food grains, etc, including Agriculture Department, Haryana State Agriculture Marketing Board (HSAMB), Food Corporation of India, Haryana Cooperative Marketing Federation (HAFED), Haryana Warehousing Corporation, Haryana Agro-Industries Corporation, Confed, etc. are connected.

Below Poverty Line Survey (BPL] Query System

The survey of all households living Below Poverty Line has been conducted in rural areas of Haryana. A database for this census has been created at all DRDAs. The application has been developed keeping in view the utilization of BPL database at DRDA as well as Directorate level. The system is a Web-Enabled query system and quite easy to use. This database is being used for implementing various schemes for BPL population in the state. The capacity of the DRDA's is also being upgraded to enable them to make use of ICT. This will provide a data base to effectively implement various programmes/schemes to those below the poverty line.

Transport Department Applications

The manual process of making a driving license is not only cumbersome but breeds delay and corruption. The process is being simplified with the use of technology. The Driving Licence (DL) software captures on-line photo and signatures. The DL is printed and database is created for quarrying. Different kinds of reports are also generated. The vehicle Registration Certificate (RC) software allows for registration of vehicles and printing of RC. The software is operational at seven locations in various district. The implementation of the software has resulted in increase in revenue greater transparency and improvement of service delivery to public and ease of data analysis. The standardization of the software as per standards provided by Ministry of Surface Transport and to meet local requirements of state is being done by NIC. The standard software will be implemented throughout the state. The out-sourcing of Smart Card based Driving License and Vehicle Registration has been planned.

Excise and Taxation Department Computerization

The Excise and Taxation department is one of the most important revenue earning department in the state. The geographical spread of the department and the volume of transactions, makes it an ideal organization for the adoption of e-governance. The process of computerization of this department is very comprehensive and caters to around 20 applications in a phased manner including installation of requisite hardware, creation of IT infrastructure, system and application software, historical and current data entry, facilities management, staff training and manpower deployment.

On-line Billing System of UHBVN / DHBVN

The billing system of various public utility organizations including electricity is a source of harassment to the citizens. The bills are not only faulty but due to lack of proper and timely availability of records the consumers are put to severe hardships. Keeping in view the need to streamline this service the focus has been on computerization of the bills of various public utilities in the state. The on-line billing system of UHBVN/DHBVN has been planned through out-sourcing. Currently, the billing is being processed off-line. The project involves complete solution on BOOT basis. This includes software development, installation of hardware, training, facilities management, networking and web enabled information access, etc. The web enabled billing system developed by NIC-Bihar is being explored for implementation.

Property and Financial Accounting Management System of HUDA

The project involves software development for Properties Management and Financial Accounting and Management. The software requirement cover all micro-level details related to properties including land acquisition and legal matters. The Financial Accounting and Management System includes all micro-level details in respect of finances of HUDA.

Integrated Budget Information System

The automation of the Finance Department is very important not only to help keep track of finances at the department level but also to enable the district administration to keep track of its finances and other related matters. The complete workflow automation of Finance Department has been identified as flagship application. The state annual budget has been automated and running for the last eight years. The computerized budget in the form of documents and CDs is presented in Haryana Vidhan Sabha by the State Finance Minister and also released on the Web. Ways and Means, Loans and Advances, Pay Revision packages have been implemented. Twenty applications have been identified. The networking of all branches and officers of Finance Department in the Secretariat is in progress.

E-Health Net

Health sector has high potential for extensive use of ICT resulting in better productivity, effectiveness, efficiency and economics leading to better health care to all. Tele medicine is fast emerging to provide quality health care to patients in remote and inaccessible areas. The NIC and Directorate of Health Services, Haryana have jointly initiated a mission mode project of E-Health Net during 2003. The project mission was to set up an efficient, effective, transparent and TI-enabled integrated system to provide the health care services to the people.

The NIC-HRSC has developed and implemented e-governance solutions for important key areas of health administration. The implementation of Medicine Inventory, Monitoring and Control System and Doctors Attendance

Monitoring System has reduce absenteeism resulting in increase in availability of doctors. It has also helped in monitoring distribution availability and consumption details of medicines supplied for public in all health institutions of the state. The system has helped in efficiently managing inventory function, distribution of medicine from central store, OPD inflow, population covered and consumption pattern.

The implementation of the system in all the districts of the state has resulted in checking the pilferage of medicines, increase in availability of medicines at government health institutions, increase in attendance of patients/doctors in health institutions and optimal utilization of medicines. The other systems in operation are, Disability Certificate Issuance System, Clinical Laboratory Information System and Burden of Death based International Code of Disease (ICD-10) System. The E-Health Net System work on low end ICT resources and e-mail based data transfer from district HQ to state HQ. The implementation of this system has helped in planning better health care system for masses.

Fatehabad First Fully Wired District

Fatehabad has become the first-ever district in the country to have computer network enabling it to transfer a government data file from its remotest corner to its headquarters. The inauguration of the network happens two years after the district came into being. The technological advancement, a brainchild of Fatehabad Deputy Commissioner V. Raja Sekhar, comes soon after the district launched for the first time in the country a CD-ROM of revenue data. The system uses a dual server to link district headquarters with all sub-divisions, tehsils, sub-tehsils, block, municipal committees and district offices. The network has been established by installing a package of computer, printer, modem, UPS and a telephone at each of the 22 sites in the district. The connectivity for these computers comes through 33.6 KBPS modems. The staff has been trained in collaboration with the National Informatics Centre.

Summing Up

The application of e-governance in the state demonstrates that there is a great need and demand for quality services at the district level. In a democracy, ultimately the goal of any government is to engage, enable and empower the citizen by mitigating their hardship while ensuring that the systems and institutions of governance deliver services that are efficient, reliable and cost effective. The district administration is the face of governance and bulk of services to the citizens are provided at the district level and below. There is a need to focus on improving the delivery mechanism at the district level so that the citizens can get quality services and grievances be redressed.

A road map has to be prepared to further enhance and give boost to e-governance in various sectors with citizen interface. The benefits have proved that such projects have greater sustainability because it is the citizen who sets the standards of performance and measures the success. The e-governance experiments have altered the way the government transacts business in many sectors. It represents a departure from the traditional pattern of working. Such departures have their own problems; the challenge is formidable but not insurmountable. An important point to be taken care is that IT in itself, does not offer all the answers, automation frequently does not produce the expected gains. Many public sector organizations putting in major new computer systems have achieved only the automation of the existing processes. However, inspite of this there is no doubt that the pace of change has been enormous and IT systems in a short period have enabled sweeping changes in the working of the organizations. Technology can help improve the service delivery mechanism at the district and below and ensure that quality services are delivered to the citizens. The districts need to be viewed as service centers and aim to achieve excellence in the delivery of services.

REFERENCES

1. Anwar Shah, *Public Services Delivery,* The World Bank, Washington. D.C, 2005.
2. Chaturvedi, T.N. and Jain, R. B, *District Administration,* IIPA, New Delhi, 1980.
3. Gupta, M.P., Prabhat Kumar and J. Bhattacharya, *Government ONLINE, Opportunities and Challenges,* Tata McGraw Hill Publishing Company, New Delhi, 2004.
4. Haryana Government, *Information Technology Policy,* Chandigarh, 2000.
5. John. S. Oakland, *Total Organisational Excellence,* Butterworth-Heinemann, Oxford, 1999.
6. Khera, S.S, *District Administration in India,* National Publishing House, New Delhi, 1979
7. Misra Suresh, E-Governance: Responsive and Transparent Service Delivery Mechanism, Amita Singh (Ed) *Administrative Reforms, Towards Sustainable Practices,* Sage Publications, New Delhi, 2005.
8. Misra Suresh, Re-Engineering Public Service Organisations, International Conference on Services Management Proceedings, IIMT, Gurgaon, 2005.

9 District Administration in Independent India

Need for a Fresh Look

*U.B. Singh**

Inspite of the fact that the administrative environment in the country has been undergoing changes, the district continues to be the pivot of structure of administration and is recognized as a unit area, earlier for regulatory functions and after Independence also for development functions of the state government. The districts are well-knit units of the administrative structure of every state of the Indian Union. The district administration has always been the backbone of the Indian administrative structure and services as the connecting link between the state and local population. Before Independence district administration largely confined itself to maintenance of law and order, supervision of local bodies and some minimal development efforts. After Independence and specially with the introduction of the Five Year Development Plans, the emphasis has been more and more on development works, drawing up plans and schemes. It threw up new problems of coordination and cooperation between various government departments as also those of initiatives in development schemes. But even now as before, the District Officer (Collector) remains the kingpin of the variety charged district administrative structure.

* Joint Director, Regional Centre for Urban and Environmental Studies, University of Lucknow, Lucknow. Email:ubsingh 56@yahoo.com, ubrcues@rediff com

Historical Perspective

District has continued to be the basic unit of administration since times immemorial in India. The code of Manu mentions that about 1000 villages were placed in the charge of an officer. The origin of the modern district administration can be traced to the Mauryan era when due to difficult communications, the unwieldy empire split up into smaller and more manageable administrative imperial agent called 'Rajuka'. He exercised both revenue and judicial functions. Under Muslim rulers provinces were divided into 'Sarkars', which was based on the principle of delegation of authority to the man on the spot. The district in the present form came to be established as a formal administrative unit during the administration of Lord Cornwallis.

The administration at the district level has not been static. Its functions and composition have changed according to the political philosophy of the ruling class. The main plank of district administration throughout the country in British days was to bring within the purview of one responsible officer the sum total of state authority, the state activities and government responsibilities. Even semi-government organizations like District Boards, municipalities were dominated by the District Officer.

During the British regime the functions of the district administration were largely limited to maintenance of law and order, management of land and collection of land revenue and administration of justice. The advent of the freedom brought enormous changes in its wake. The political power was transferred to people's representatives. The administrative structure left by the British outwardly underwent changes. With accelerated socio-economic growth through planned development as the objective, the government embarked on an organized planning effort for accelerating the development. The formulation and implementation of Five Year Plans has been a major plank of national policy of social and economic development. The government was also committed to separation of executive from judiciary and involving the people in the process of preparation of the local plans and implementation thereof.

Emerging Challenges

The institution of the collector is very much there but the holder of the post has no longer the image of the sole authority or the only symbol of government authority. He may even now represent the administrative will of the state government but does not represent the political will of the government. He has many more functions to shoulder but he is now essentially to function as a manager, a coordinator, a team leader.

At the advent of the freedom from the British colonial rules, the independent India accepted the parliamentary form of government with democracy at its centre. The people of the country are the sole master and sovereignty lies therein. The largeness and diversity facilitated the adoption of representative democracy, where people's representative are empowered for decision-making and the executive wing comprising civil servants is responsible for implementing those policy decisions. In this changed scenario, the elected representatives—M.Ps and M.LAs., etc. represent the political power of the state and the District Officer cannot continue to have undisputed power in district administration. This is a qualitative change in the scenario of administrative set-up at the district level in post-independent India.

With separation of powers as between the executive and the judiciary culminating in the enactment of Cr.P.C. Amendment Act, 1973, the control of the District Magistrate over the police has weakened without in any way making the police more responsible to judiciary or increasing the effectiveness of the police. The powers of the Magistrate under the Police Act remain intact but their exercise has been greatly affected.

The establishment of the Community Development Organization in 1952 to undertake integrated rural development represented a watershed in taking administration nearer to the people and the process of a coordinated all-round development of the rural areas with emphasis on the community. It was for the first time that the government organizations dealing with various development activities at the district level were brought under a single roof with one coordinating officer under the overall leadership of the Collector.

When the National Development Council decided to tackle the socio-economic problems of the poorest of the poor in rural areas, the state governments created District Rural Development Agencies, a government body with the District Officer as Chairman. They are outside the ambit of the Panchayati Raj bodies even though the village panchayats have a role in the selection of beneficiaries and the block staff in the preparation and implementation of projects.

On the lines of District Rural Development Agency responsible for implementing programmes for rural development, a new organisation in the name of District Urban Development Agency has been created in every district for undertaking poverty alleviation programmes in urban areas. The District Collector is chairman of both these agencies, but there is no coordination or integration in their approach. This has added a new dimension to the complex district administration. The multiplicity of agencies and departments at the district level might have added many feathers to the district head, but with no avail. This has made the messy district administration messier.

Panchayati Raj Institutions viz. Zila Panchayat, at the district level, the Kshetra Panchayat at the block level and the village panchayats at the village level as a consequence of 73rd Amendment to the Constitution have been created with the firm objectives of decentralization of specified powers and functions of the state to these bodies and democratization of the administrative structure at the local level so that the people could have an effective role in the planned development of an area. The supreme law of the land now endows these grassroot level units of administration with the powers of self-governance. The democracy has been decentralized and the people from all walks of society especially woman, Scheduled Castes/ Tribes/Backward Classes have been granted definite representation unlike the other levels of legislatures in the country. The facets of rural district administration have totally changed with the presence of people's representatives belonging to all sections of the society.

Simultaneously, in pursuance of the 74th Amendment to the Constitution three types of municipalities — Municipal Corporations for larger urban areas, Municipal Councils for smaller urban areas and Nagar Panchayats for transitional areas have come up with the objectives of taking administration nearer to the people, ensuring participation of people in administration and making local administration accountable to the people. The presence of people's representatives in large number in these urban local government units is bound to affect the working pattern of district administration. These bodies too have certain working relationship with the District Officer, who is at the helm of district administration.

In addition, a large number of public corporations and development authorities have been established during the last five decades or so to achieve certain specific objectives. These bodies do not have uniform relationship with the district administration. Actually their relationship at the district level is also ill-defined although their area of functional jurisdiction is spread over the district.

The independent developing India has been committed to diversified activities covering welfare, development, regulatory, maintenance, etc. Thus a large number of administrative departments have come up at the district level. As the departmental activities enormously expanded, government organisations at the district level both expanded and proliferated. Some of these organisations have an in-built relationship with the Collectors, others have not.

Further, there are a large number of voluntary organisations and institutions providing certain services, facilities and infrastructural support to a particular area with the aid of the government. Their activities contribute to the development of their area of operation. These are not part of the government set-up but are a definite aid to government apparatus at the district level. They act as a new facet of district administration.

The supreme law of the land (through 74th Amendment) provides for constituting a District Planning Committee in every district for preparing a development plan for the whole district. It consists of officials and people's representatives from rural as well as urban local bodies. The Constitution further provides for constituting a Metropolitan Planning Committee in every metropolitan area to prepare a development plan for the whole area. The metropolitan area is defined as an area having a population of ten lakhs or more, comprised in one or more districts and consisting of two or more municipalities or panchayats. These planning committees created under the Constitution are conceived as a unit for integrated planning at the district level. These are the instruments for associating people's representatives with the planning process as the basic unit of administration. Now, planning in the name of decentralized one is not the exclusive domain of district officials.

In addition, the grassroot level administration has been endowed with the preparation and implementation of planning for economic development and social justice. This whole exercise of socio-economic planning is in the hands of the people's representatives. In this changed context, district officials are no more repository of local planning.

Furthermore, the essence and scope of administration has now changed from regulatory and maintenance of law and order to the development administration and further to good administration which is based on the principles of participation, decentralization, responsiveness and responsibility, morality accountability, transparency, openness, simplicity and shortness. This all can be achieved through participatory governance, the governance short of secrecy and officialdom at the district level.

The country has been experiencing a transform in its development strategy from welfare to improvement, development, and empowerment. The empowerment pre-requisites the participation of people in decision-making and in plan formulation and implementation. The pace of participation of people is inversely related to the extent of officialdom. Less the officialdom more the people's participation. The benefits of imposed development have failed to percolate to the lowest level, hence a change in development strategy, which calls for change in pattern and style at district level administration. The district administration is now responsible for maintaining a lawful regulated environment conducive for development activities.

Summing Up

To sum up, as the government functions have expanded and the administration has become multi faceted, the problem of intra-organization and inter-organization coordination has become acute requiring some effective coordinating agency at the local level. The new challenges and problems thrown up by the process of development, political and social awakening, economic upsurge, large scale industrialization and growing urbanization have necessitated a fresh look on district administration, a basic unit of administration, and in all its facets becomes of paramount interest to government as well as citizens. The District Officer (Collector) has to play the role of an intermediary between the people and the government; between local bodies and government organizations; between executives at district level and the people's representatives; between rural development and urban development; and between deliberative and executive wings of the government at the district level. He is responsible for facilitating a peaceful environment conducive for bottom-up development approach aiming people's empowerment. The district officer is now no more an "administrator" heading the district administration but has to work as 'manager' of the district management. This is pre-natal stage of district government which is need of the new Millennium.

REFERENCES

1. Seth, J.L., 1990, District Administration in Uttar Pradesh, in R.D. Sharma (ed) *District Administration in India: Problems and Prospects,* H.K. Publishers, Delhi.
2. Chaturvedi, A., 1988, *District Administration: The Dynamics of Discord,* Sage, New Delhi.
3. Misra, R.P.(ed), 1990, *District Planning: A Handbook,* Concept Publishers, New Delhi.
4. Sadasivan, S.N. (ed), 1988, *District Administration: A National Perspective,* IIPA, New Delhi.
5. Report of the Commission on District Level Administration, Government of U.P. 1986.
6. The Constitution of India, Government of India.
7. Report of the Commission on Centre-State Relations (Sarkaria Commission), Government of India, 1985.

10 District Administration and E–Governance
A Holistic Approach

*Chaitali Pal**

Introduction

District is the basic territorial unit of development administration in India. District administration involves in the management of public affairs in the grassroots level. It is the key unit of our administration as the District Magistrate is '*sarkar* 'and '*mai-baap*' in the eyes of people. The success of any state government depends on how its policies are implemented and things are delivered by the district administration. If we want to have a society based on equity and social justice the need of the hour is to have a 'responsible and responsive' district administration. 'Responsible' administration implies commitment and devotion to the various policies, plans and projects with a view to serve the society. It also means that it has to deliver 'good governance'. Responsiveness implies that administration should be sensitive to the needs of the people. The administration must feel that they are not the 'masters but the servants' of the people. Jawaharlal Lal Nehru outlined the parameters of a responsive administration in his lecture on April, 06, 1957, at Indian Institute of Public Administration. He said, "Every

* Research Associate in Institute of Applied Manpower Research, Plot 25, Sector- A7, Narela Institutional Area, Delhi.

administrator, whether he is high up or low down in the scale, must give the impression, even if that impression is not wholly correct, that he is working through the public will and carrying it out."

To effect these changes a strong political will is required. With the changes taking place, the development of Human Resources can't be neglected as Information Technology has emerged as an all pervasive force that impact on lives of people across the world.

Background

Since 1980s two concepts, i.e., *"Information Technology"* and *"Good Governance"* have transformed the entire outlook on approaches to and methodologies of development administration. As a matter of fact, efficiency, accountability, digitalization, responsiveness, transparency, flexible and people oriented government—all these idioms of good governance can be realized through application of information and communication technology in the sphere of development administration at all levels of government. Accordingly, the developing societies have redefined their governance mechanism and technologies. One innovation attempted in the process of "E-governance" is "Community Information Centers" for sustainable rural development.

In the Liberalized Era

In the wake of privatization, liberalization and globalization, it has been realized that benefits of rural development have not percolated to the needy. The downtrodden and destitutes still lag behind in getting a share in the benefits of development, while rich are becoming richer. E-governance has been perceived as the best tool for administrative effectiveness to deliver benefits to people. E-governance is the application of Information Technology (IT) to the process of government functioning in order to bring about "Simple, Moral, Accountable, Responsive and Transparent (SMART)" governance. E-governance also involves transformation of administration from being a passive information and service provider to active citizen involvement.

ICT is increasingly used in administration to empower citizens with information and speedy delivery of services. Democratic, decentralized institutions needs good governance to reflect people's voice. Civil society organizations including NGOs and corporate sector are already taking many initiatives to improve the quality of governance and service delivery. Efforts have been made in independent India to create and strengthen the institutions of local self-governance. ICT will make such self- governance effective.

The world is marching towards 'e-governance' age. The last decade of the twentieth century saw a very rapid development and spread of communication and Information Technology (ICT). These new technologies have placed a powerful tool in the hands of the society that could be used to make life easier and better for all in several dimensions of human activities. Almost all areas of social and commercial activity have been touched by the electronic revolution.

IT as a Technological Revolution

IT has introduced revolution in the administration in the same way as the Industrial Revolution had brought in the methods of production. IT is the key to re-engineering administration. It has not only revolutionized the administration in terms of delivery of goods and services but also in terms of accountability, transparency and fulfilling the aspirations of the citizens. IT is a product of Information Technology. It is a vehicle for future development, opportunities, challenges and competition that enables information to be collected and used. It is changing every aspect of human life- communications, trade, manufacturing, services, culture, entertainment, education, research, defense and global security. IT is breaking old barriers and building new interconnections in the emerging global village and becoming the chief determinant of the nations, communities and individuals. It is clear that IT has made a great impact on the various facets of administration. It facilitates the development of Human Resource which is the asset of nations.

IT development is creating a fundamental change in the value system, quality of life, thoughts and visions of people. Many activities of society are based on IT like electronic commerce (e-commerce), government operations online (e-governance), online education (e-education), mailing through computers (e-mail), development of human interpersonal relationships (e-communities), etc. The increasing use of ICT in operations of govt. has led to what is described as e-governance whose dimensions include e-commerce, e-democracy, and e-citizen. The electronic tools and networking has made it possible to involve the 'citizen' in decision-making.

Government Policies

The government has suggested a plan of action to make India an IT superpower in the world. There has been an emergence of IT revolution on the national agenda which has been followed by announcement of IT policies by several state governments. Measures taken by Andhra Pradesh, Delhi, Goa, Gujarat, Haryana, Karnataka, Kerala, Madhya Pradesh, Maharashtra, Tamil Nadu, Uttar Pradesh, West Bengal, Orissa, Punjab, Rajasthan, Sikkim, Meghalaya have strengthened India's position in the software-driven IT sector in the world.

- Introduction of e-governance is the key to making IT relevant to ordinary citizens in India where a large population is poor and lives in villages. E-governance will allow the people to constantly interface with the government at both local and central levels. Now, mobile telephone is being used in villages also to have a better communication and information. This can improve the rapport between the government and rural masses and reduce the gap between them which stands in the way of good governance. There is however need to initiate a mass campaign for creating awareness with regard to the benefits of IT in the villages. Awareness of new technologies is important because it explains how the common man can solve his problems by taking help of these technologies. There is a need to open multipurpose information technology centers at the district, block and village levels to provide information on carry out one or more of the following roles:

- Multipurpose training and service.
- Training and skill development on computer operation, internet, and office automation.
- Institutional training in schools and colleges.
- Training schemes for SCs/ STs and women.
- Training of Panchayat functionaries, health workers, anganwadi workers, agricultural extension workers, teachers and other field functionaries.
- Information window samadhan kendras—to provide information on government schemes, agriculture commodities, health, education and employment, legal issues, self-employment opportunities, technologies and resources.
- Computer-aided coaching.

Keeping all this in view, this paper explains to what extent the IT is enabling district level administration to develop transparency, accountability, responsibility and responsiveness towards people. Since, the objective of development is to create good governance, e-governance is the means for good governance. People have a right to have good governance. In view of Kofi A. Annan, Secretary General of the United Nations, "Good Governance is perhaps the single most important factor in eradicating poverty and promoting development".

Initiatives by States

Villages in Punjab now use their government's portal to get information about the prices of the grains in various mandis and to decide where to sell them. This helps them earn more money and save their valuable time. The farmer now doesn't have to wait in the long queues to satisfy his small queries.

In Rajasthan, Nyala became the first village of the state to have the Jan Nidhi Information, through which citizens are also able to access information related to health, family planning, employment, taxes, water and electricity.

West Bengal Government has also designed a web education which aims to facilitate the use of computers in rural and semi-rural areas for access to information, telephone bills etc.

The tele-medicine project of Tamil Nadu allows doctors in remote areas to consult experts on special cases through a direct ISDN link.

The Gyandoot Programmes in the Dhar District of Madhya Pradesh is networked to 31 village centers. The service covers wide-ranging information needs of the villagers like agricultural process, auction center rates, copies of land records, on-line registration of applications and many others.

The e-bail system in Bihar that functions through networking and video conferencing, helps the prisoners in rural courts where it is difficult for the judges to reach frequently. With the help of video conferencing, the latter can give bail orders to prisoners which otherwise take many days or even months.

In Pondicherry, Villianur village is the hub of information

revolution. People in this village, along with those from Embalam and Kizhoor villages, are connected through an on-line database, which helps them to access the required information. The villagers go to the information centers to read the newspapers and to obtain the latest local news. Women get information about the wholesale and market prices of vegetables while farmers log on to find the market prices of fertilizers and grain. The centers also provide weather forecasts and thermal wave maps on those parts of the sea, which can yield large catches of fish to the fisherman. Students get news about their examination schedule and the timing of their school buses. They can also watch the latest educational compact discs.

A Holistic Approach

A holistic approach would pay attention to all emerging IT technologies which can be strategically used in the government and governance at the district level. On line local government which had been introduced after the success of this technology in the developed countries offering to the citizen friendly e-governance. The main objective is to provide citizens a secure and easy access to the key services through the e-governance infrastructure, any time, from any place, using any device. The power of the ICT has permitted the governments to adopt a *'linked-up'* or *'holistic'* approach by connecting various departments and organs of the governments with the grassroots administration so that they became aware of the benefits of technology and make use of it. India has been a developing country for more than half a century. We have to make it a developed nation now. For that to happen, it is required to strengthen the use of our technology in various activities to keep pace with global trends.

The Indian IT sector is broadly divided into two segments, domestic and export market. The domestic market can be further divided into software and services, hardware, peripherals, networking and training. The export market consists of software services and exports and ITs. A holistic approach is required when it comes to IT. There has to be an emphasis on quality higher education to ensure steady supply of the most important raw material for this sector, trained manpower. There is a need to provide easier and better accessibility to student loans for higher education. There is an urgent need to accelerate the speed of rural infrastructure renewal and development. Government must facilitate for the same.

Conclusion

The global communication revolution is throwing up many challenges and opportunities. This will give a boost to penetration and diffusion of information technology down to villages. This means that the *'Global Village'* is going to emerge in reality in India also. Information technology helps in optimizing the use of scarce resources and makes it possible to improve the quality of life by streamlining a variety of services. IT has the greatest potential for growth and development. The success of any state government depends on how its policies are implemented and benefits delivered to people by the district administration. District administration becomes the focus of reform. Involvement of NGOs and the media needs to be facilitated in order to organize IT awareness camps. For spread and use of IT services, it is necessary to develop solutions based on regional languages in the country.

If we want to restructure the grassroots administration in a meaningful manner we have to strengthen its mode of technology by the use of technology to have the e-democracy. Civil servants should adjust to the changes brought in by liberalization and globalization became aware of the advances made in science and technology gain and for information revolution, computerization and mechanization to speed up all round development. This change would strengthen democracy as well as positive response of the community to development programmes which is the ultimate goal of good governance.

REFERENCES

1. Agarwal, Satish, "E-Governance for Administrative Effectiveness" (2005) *Prashasnika*, Jan-June, Vol. XXXII, No. 1.
2. Dudeja, V.D. (2003) *"Information Technology and Human Resource Development"* Published by Commonwealth, N.D.
3. IT and Indian Administration, (Special number) 2000, *The Indian Journal of Public Administration*, July-September, Vol. XLVI, No. 3.
4. Nair, Sudarshanan, *"Holistic Approach to IT is Required"*, Asian Age, Feb, 27, 2006.
5. Rana Vaishali, (2004) *Information Technology and the Common Man: Areas of Investigation*, Published by Institute of Applied Manpower Research.
6. Souvenir, National Seminar on *"Technical Manpower Planning in India : Issues and Concerns"* Organised by National Technical Manpower Information System, Institute of Applied Manpower Research and Jawaharlal Nehru Technological University, Hyderabad (September 5- 7, 2004).
7. Souvenir XIX *All India Conference, Indian Public Administration Association*, Organised by Department of Public Administration, Punjabi University, Patiala (July 29- 30, 2005).

11 Ploughmen, Wild Tribes and the Spectre of Raj

Reflections on the Notion of 'Good Governance' through the Ages in Indian Context

*Shri Krishan**

The notion of governance and good governance are being increasingly used in development literature.[1] Governance is the process of decision-making and the procedures by which decisions are implemented or certain decisions are not implemented. In any hierarchically arranged social order, the apparatus of state wields the power to conduct public affairs and manage or mismanage public resources. It is believed that good governance accomplishes these tasks in a fashion that is free of abuse and corruption and in keeping in view the rule of law. Sustainable human development is another key notion of contemporary political and social discourse. Again, it is argued that state institutions must work to achieve the ideal of good governance, or they should follow a set of normative procedures that ensures transparency and accountability. Recently international financial institutions like IMF and World Bank are also increasingly linking their assistance and loans to the condition that borrowers must ensure steps in their home countries encouraging good governance. It is, therefore, emphasized by the policy-makers that good governance is essential for achieving progress of

* Professor, Department of History, Post-Graduate Regional Centre, Rewari, (Haryana).

any society. The idea of good governance emerged in the corporate management especially after the financial crisis of 1997 in South East Asian economies in a big way. It was felt that crony capitalism and corruption linked to its financial structures ought to be rooted out. Hence, there was talk of moral-ethical framework, which alone, it was thought would ensure transparency in the operations of corporate world. It was seen as an essential step towards realization of accountability and effective productive use of resources without any waste in any sector. In other words, the business organizations were advised by the management *gurus* to take into account moral dimensions in taking and implementing decisions. Such corporate governance, it was advocated, could only give real value to the investors in terms of creation of wealth, reasonable returns and a good market capitalization.

Starting with the corporate world, the issue of good governance became central in the political discourse also even to the extent that it eclipsed the earlier favourite term of civil society. The notion of civil society had depicted a kind of homogenized, harmonious society free of class conflicts. The notion of good governance is also a ploy to justify and seek legitimacy for the ongoing restructuring of welfare schemes of modern state in the name of liberalization and as response to the globalizing environment. A set of strategies have been advocated by international lending agencies. It is claimed that reform of institutions of state could lift underdeveloped countries out of stagnation, backwardness and absolute poverty because these conditions of underdevelopment are product of bureaucratic delays, inefficiency, corruption, poor quality of public services, leakage of public funds and an archaic judicial and legal system. It is maintained that no country or nation can afford to be less efficient in the age of globalization and good governance is a pre-condition for attracting capital, which is considered to be the sole vending machine churning out development and economic growth.

The political leadership of all hues has started glibly talking about the need for state to 'steer, not row'. In this environment of liberalization and globalization, the new mantra often chanted is to slim down the state bureaucracies and encourage private capital initiatives in order to expand productivity, to build new capabilities rather than just redistribute wealth to help the marginalized social groups. In fact, economics and politics are not separate or compartmentalized entities. The package of reforms which is being presented as the prerequisite for good governance is part and parcel of a larger agenda of economic reform and 'structural adjustment'. The neo-reforms envisage withdrawal and retreat of state from undertaking social welfare programmes. So, instead of political management of economy from 'above', the state is supposed to provide adequate infrastructure to attract capital which would ensure economic growth. As corporate world has acquired an image of sleekness, efficiency and rationality; to streamline public administration 'reformers' advocate of similar set of values and techniques that corporate management utilizes the profitability criteria, cost-benefit analysis and economic rationality. This could mean changing the nature of social goods provided. Applying the principle of economic rationality to basic social services like health and education would mean re-defining targets in terms of providing a supply of skilled manpower in accordance with the needs of market forces.[2]

However, it needs to be understood that government is only one actor in the process of modern-day administration. Other actors involved in governance may depend on the level of administration we are discussing. In rural areas, for instance, these other actors might be influential powerful landed magnates, peasant associations, cooperatives, NGO's, religious and community leaders, caste-hierarchies, and financial institutions (both formal and informal), etc. The situation at national level and in urban areas is far more complex. Here, powerful corporate houses and other business interests, organized and well-articulated urban elites, transnational companies, media, well-entrenched crime, landed and drug mafia and syndicates may play important role in decision-making.

In order to realize the goal of good governance, what we need is social empowerment of marginalized social groups. In the contemporary social setting in India, caste and class based social inequalities[3] are so deeply entrenched that they are bound to affect the developmental process and participation of deprived sections of society in our democratic polity. The rise and growth of Indian social classes in modern times was organically linked to structure of colonialism and it still continues to bear imprints of that association. The dominant proprietary class in urban areas is marked by its plurality and heterogeneity in composition. A clear-cut demarcation along the lines of merchant, industrial and finance capital is not possible in case of India. The Indian business classes exhibit a complex intertwining of functions. Initially, under the colonial rule, the Indian businessmen were relegated to small private trade, money lending or acted as the agents of foreign British capital. The British capitalists and merchants controlled the upper layers of Indian economy represented by the big joint stock companies, capital markets, managing agency houses, banking, and insurance and major export-import firms. Inspite of various constraints and obstacles, the Indian capitalist class grew slowly but steadily and breached white men's 'collective monopoly'. Certain groups of indigenous merchants like the Parsis, the Marwaris, the Khojas, the Bhatias and Gujarati traders benefited from security of private property and sanctity of contract guaranteed by the colonial regime and grew in establishing collaboration with British firms. The indigenous capitalist class not only grew but diversified and acquired important position by 1940.[4] This class thrived in independent India under the government's policy of import-substitutions and quantitative controls.

The 'Public-Sector' units provided the infrastructure and the intermediate and capital goods to this protected class while public lending institutions provided it with chief source of finance. The assets of the biggest of 20 industrial houses increased from Rs. 500 crores in 1951 to Rs. 23,200 crores in 1986. The subsequent liberalization drive has increased the wealth of this class manifold since then. On the. other hand, almost 70 per cent of Indian people live on merely subsistence level and 76.6 million agricultural labourers earn only 1/10th of what an organized sector worker in the city earns. Besides very high unemployment levels, there is a vast army of pavement vendors, domestic servants, porters and street hawkers working in unorganized informal sectors and dwelling in sprawling slums in our mega-cities. Similarly a class of rich landlords and rich farmers also enjoy disproportionate access to rural assets. The other pole of rural social structure is the world of poor agricultural wage workers who have little or no control over productive resources.[5]

In the urban bureaucratic-managerial elite also constitutes significant class of India as the relatively weak capitalist class at the time of India independence was not in a position to completely subordinate the highly developed administrative apparatus. The growth of non-market mechanisms and planning in the allocation of resources and economic patronages also resulted in the expansion of this bureaucratic-cum-managerial elite. So despite the egalitarian ideal of post colonial Indian state, there are still disproportionate access to resources, power and entitlements between different social classes and caste. The establishments of formal democracy and adoption of nouns of good governance are no guarantee that all citizens will enjoy equal participation in the political processes. Political privileges have been retained and remain ingrained in many non-elective institutions, especially the bureaucracy and the police.[6] The marginalized social groups are not yet sufficiently empowered to shape and mould the state's social and economic policies. The powerful landed magnates of upper castes in the countryside and the industrial and business classes of urban rich and various kind of mafia make use of authoritarian streak inherent in the non-elective institutions to deny genuine democratization of polity.

The nature of post-colonial state in India partially reflected the legacy bequeathed by its colonial past. Many features of the administrative and institutional structure of the colonial state were retained after independence. The Constitution of India itself was a product of British constitutional arrangement for India. The elected legislative assemblies of the provinces, created on the basis of Government of India Act (1935), elected members for the Constituent Assembly. Even the colonial notion of communal electorates played an important role in the formation of Constituent Assembly. This became a sovereign constitution-drafting body after independence. Although, the Constituent Assembly adopted many of the democratic and normative forms that the nationalist leadership had been espousing during anti-imperialist struggle, the basic framework comprised of a strong unitary centre, with limited devolution power to the provinces. Thus, the centralizing polity of colonial period was retained with some modifications. In districts also, the elite district collectors and Indian Civil Service norms continued to exist with same type of powers and privileges.[7] Although bureaucracy's responsibility and control through the system of regular reporting to the elective, non-bureaucratic political leadership did introduce changes in its functioning and orientation, many other features of colonial period were retained. The separation from civil society, permanence of tenure, and control over public resources as well as its functional orientation were some of the elements that remind one of its colonial legacies. The notion of establishing social control and attaching of primacy to the law and order instead of focusing on developmental initiatives reflect values and ethos of colonial civil service.

There was a great degree of autonomy for bureaucracy and armed forces during the colonial regime, as they were used to suppress and subordinate the indigenous social groups. The process of partial transfer of power during 1920s and 1930s established procedures by which the bureaucracy could bypass the elected political leaders. These procedures created a space where bureaucrats could deal with 'public matter' out side elected institutions, thus, paving the way for mediation between public and officialdom through elected representatives.

This type of military-bureaucratic machinery retained its autonomy and its mediatory role between elective institutions and public. The power and status of post-colonial bureaucratic managerial also grew manifold with the proliferation of non-market mechanisms in the allocation of public resources through arbitrary distribution of patronage in the forms of licenses, permits and governmental sanctions. The unrepresentative administrative machinery was neither civil nor service-oriented but encouraged a new nexus between the business and the state, thereby, empowering itself by appropriating power and resources. The developmental ideology of welfare was an important feature of postcolonial state in India and the Fundamental Rights enshrined in Articles 12 to 35 of our Constitution accord a guarantee against encroachments by the state on the civil and human rights of individuals as well as religious minorities.

The Directive Principles also provides a set of guidelines or instructions to the state to introduce certain basic socio-economic reforms so as to make fundamental rights more effective. Although, there is no legal sanction behind the enforcement of these policy measures, yet they mirror the basic welfare-oriented norms of the Indian polity. These normative features, however, only represent the declared agenda of the Indian nation state. As already shown, the functional and implementation aspects are hindered by other dimensions such as the power of urban and rural rich and the resultant increasing marginalization of the poor (the ploughmen and the wild tribesmen and women being the main social groups that represent such poor strata). We hope that our discussion so far makes it clear that there is a hiatus between norms and ideals and actual existing social situations in every society. Even our contemporary democratic polity espousing the goal of 'good governance' is not an exception to this gap between political rhetoric and practical reality. We ought to strive for a participatory, consensus-oriented, accountable, transparent, responsive, efficient and equitable society where the voices of the most vulnerable and marginalized sections are not only heard but a society where they get an equality of opportunity and a dignified human existence.

The contemporary globalized world economy especially at the periphery is marked by paid as well as unpaid labour activity of poor and pauperized children. The increasing pace of globalization also displaces and dislocates millions of children worldwide and creates conditions that can account for displacement of children from schools to streets. Urbanization in many cases is usually linked to rapid socio-economic change but in many underdeveloped and developing societies overstrains the resources and capabilities of local and national governments to provide even the basic facilities like water, electricity and housing. There are regions in which urbanization has occurred independent of economic development and growth and where it has been largely residential rather than production based. The lack of adequate and affordable housing and the scale of urban homelessness in underdeveloped urban mega-cities and large urban agglomerations, when compared to the developed world, are enormous. The number of homeless around the world is estimated from 100 million to one billion. The lower bound 100 million counts only those who have no shelter at all while the upper bound one billion includes those who are dwelling in sub-standard, insecure or temporary structures without provisions for the most basic services such as safe water, sanitation and drainage. The homelessness is a global problem and for many urban poor, displaced from their rural homes by the processes of development and globalization of economy and resultant agrarian crisis superimposed on agriculture of small cultivators, sleeping in public buildings, parks or other public spaces has become a part of their daily existence. In India, for instance, the homeless can be seen everywhere on pavements, in parks and even in unused water pipes or under bridges. A large number of them also consist of women and children who have run away from domestic violence and abuse.

There are an estimated 18 million street children who live or work on the streets of urban India, earning their "livelihood" as porters at bus or railway terminus, as mechanics in informal auto-repair shops, as venders of food, tea or other home-made items or simply picking through garbage and selling usable articles to local buyers. Many a times, their proximity to place of crime make them easy target of law-enforcing agencies. In the perception of society and police they are often seen as vagrant and criminals. This sort of exclusion and invisibility of the urban poor and street children is not unique to any one less developed country. Whether it is Sao Paulo in Brazil or Mumbai in India, despite economic growth, the underdeveloped mega-cities have been able to absorb only a tiny fraction of labour so that unemployment and underemployment remain persistent problems. A sizable chunk of labour including those of street children find employed in informal sector. In many parts of the world urbanization is being accelerated by the growing global economy. Globalization, however, has had a very uneven impact on the various regions and social groups around the world. It is associated with growing economic inequality and social polarization. It is associated with growing economic inequality and social polarization. In many places income inequality has multiplied dramatically, thus, increasing economic and spatial segmentation. The signs of economic absolute poverty and deprivations are quite pronounced in cities of South Asia. For instance, despite many slum improvements schemes over years in Mumbai, almost half of its population lives either in slums or on streets.[8]

Moving back on a temporal scale, we find that the British colonial state used various means and ideological strategies to justify their rule in the eyes of Indian people. The British Empire, even though armed with an efficient bureaucracy and a huge amount of information about Indian society and people at its disposal, lacked the financial resources and sufficient military capacity to rule our vast and turbulent country by force alone. The British ideologues, therefore, projected their state as an engine of better governance and modernization in India. They stressed on the positive virtues of colonial rule such as establishment of rule of law, a modern and scientific educational system and above all, an impersonal 'rational' bureaucracy that improved and professionalized the task of maintaining law and order. The conception of 'oriental despotism', the idea that India was governed by unchecked and absolute power of a despotic emperor and an administrative elite dependent on the ruler, was used by the Orientalists to analyze the precolonial political arrangements of India. Alexander Dow ('*The History of Hindustan*, 1770) and Robert Orme (*Government and People of Indostan*, 1753) used such notions to understand pre-colonial Indian polities. Subsequently other British administrators cited the tropical climate, Islamic religion and other racial factors as reasons that fostered the growth of despotism in India. The British rulers found, strangely enough, implicit rationalization for their own authoritarian rule in the subcontinent through use of such analytical categories. According to Thomas R. Metcalf, as the British endeavoured to define themselves as 'British', they had to make of the Indians whatever they chose not to make of themselves. Thus, they thought themselves as honest, laborious, masculine and rational and enlightened ones and as a natural corollary, Indians were depicted as deceitful, lazy, feminine, irrational, and superstitious.[9]

Under the intellectual sway of people like Adam Smith and Jermy Bentham, liberalism remoulded the British society and its institutions in the 19th century. The basic objective of liberal project was to secure liberties for the individuals and rights to property and life. This could be achieved only if citizens got freedom from bondage to the clergy, despotic rule and feudal aristocracy. This social transformation was to be introduced slowly through the agency of free trade, rule of law, reform of pedagogical practices and administrative organs of state and implementation of idea of representation and elective principle. The liberals wanted to change the ascriptive society which conferred patronage and status on the basis of birth into an achievement-oriented society where personal achievement of individual became the sole criterion of a person's competence and status in society. This liberal project expressed itself in Britain through the Parliamentary Reform Acts of 1832, 1867, repeal of Corn Laws, welfare-oriented labour legislation, establishment of new local administrative bodies like municipal corporations in urban areas and elected county councils in the countryside, reform of civil laws and introduction of modern 'secular' education. In the colonial setting, the liberal views were reflected in James Mill's *History of British India* (1818). In this work, Mill envisaged a programme to free India from age-old 'stagnation' and 'decay' and set it on the road to 'progress'. He advocated "light taxes and good laws" to achieve this goal. The aim of liberals was to 'civilize' India through replication of institutions and culture of Britain on Indian soil. The principal among these were private property, the rule of law, education in western scientific manner.

The principle of security of private property was made sacrosanct in India. The spirit of 'rule of law' became visible in the Codes of Civil and Criminal Procedure proposed by Macaulay's Law Commission and enacted in 1860's. This was supposed to introduce elements of transparency and predictability in the sphere of law that had remained arbitrary and ill-defined in pre-colonial times. The legal system of colonial India, however, was an adjustment of assimilative ideal of liberalism (Codes and Procedures of Laws) and the British assertion of the difference of Indian personal laws (defined in terms of being a Hindu or Muslim). But despite the liberal attempts to re-create India in the image and likeness of England, the Empire itself was a negation and reversal of liberal ideals. 'the inconsistencies and contradictions in liberal designs for India resurfaced over and over again. James Mill denied the representative government to India on the ground that happiness and not liberty was the goal of government. The well-known utilitarian and son of James Mill, John Stuart Mill, while recognizing the intrinsic value of liberty *per se,* was also of the view that representative government was not appropriative for all cases. In actuality, most colonial administrators had the conviction that a tough and decisive executive action was a necessity in colonial situations to secure order and social-control. Although, the colonial state relied on securing the consent of Indian people in various ways and attempted to legitimize its rule, in practice the colonial state maintained its domination by the use and demonstration of force and coercive display of power. The brutal suppression of Kuka Uprising in Punjab (1872) was a sort of precursor to the infamous Amritsar massacre (1919). The colonial armed forces were the basic sinews of colonial apparatus. The colonial government had also used the indigenous institutions in its early phase to control crimes.

Warren Hastings, for example, had retained the post of *fauzdars* and also utilized the policing functions of Zamindars in Bengal during early Company raj. However, this arrangement proved adequate and he subsequently appointed district magistrates and the districts were further subdivided into smaller sub-units, each unit being placed under a *darogah* who led a group of 20-30 armed policemen to maintain law and order in the countryside. The *darogahs* worked under the supervision of the district magistrates. The policing functions of Zamindars were abolished by Regulation XXII of 1793. The administrative machinery that evolved under Lord Cornwallis was based on the amalgamation of duties of revenue-collection and policing duties as magistrates in the person of district collector.

The districts were also modelled on the pre-colonial revenue-units called *sarkars*. These functions were briefly separated at the recommendation of Bird Committee (1808-12) but were recombined again in 1844. The police organization emerged as an autonomous organ of the state in 1840's. Sir Charles Napier modelled his police organization in Sind Province on the quasimilitary pattern of Irish Police (1836). In his scheme, the posts of lieutenant and an adjutant in the district were to be manned by the British army officers and *thanedars* or commissioned officers of mounted police were in charge of each sub-division of a district. Easy mobility, a clear and firm hierarchy, direct and official relation with army organization and a highly centralized command were the main features of this apparatus. This reinforced the frail political authority in the countryside. This style of police organization was later suggested by the Police Commission (1860) and enshrined in Police Act of 1861. The Act was applied to all provinces except Bombay and Madras for which separate Acts were passed. The colonial state not only modelled police on military structure in its administrative and organizational form but also frequently used army to deal with the 'disturbances' caused by peasant (ploughmen) and tribal masses (often depicted as 'wild and criminal'). The military character of the law enforcing agency also influenced the perception of dealing with crimes, which were seen primarily in terms of 'rebellion and disorder' or as aspects of public safety and political stability rather than as matters allied to lawlessness and security of property and persons. Lack of adequate financial resources and political will constrained to police to rely on method of selective controls, i.e., classification of particular social groups as their targets.

The organization of legal and judiciary machinery was further inhibited by the weight of racial ideology and its alignment with the powerful dominant propertied classes. The result was that in most part of the countryside it was the *daroga* and the local landlord who mattered as government for the peasants and labourers in the rural locality. In the field of justice, the Ilbert Bill Controversy (1882-83) reflected the racial prejudices of European administrators in India. The bill was based on liberal principle of equality before law and sought to authorize Indian magistrate in the rural areas to try British subject. The British opponents of the bill argued that Indian social and legal institutions were different from Britain and, therefore, such a conception of legal equality could not be applied. The colonial state, neglecting the traditional indigenous local governance, institutionalized the liberal ideology in 1860s and 1870s through the creation of municipality and district boards on the basis of elective principle. Seats in these local bodies, however, were prearranged to specific social groups and religious communities. They initiated the process of establishment of communal electorates. The government wanted to increase its revenue by raising local taxes and to incorporate powerful indigenous social groups in the process of governance. The British also established a new system of civil and criminals court to administer justice. Warren Hastings, for example, established *diwani* and *nizamat adalats* at the district level.

These were presided over by the European judges assisted by Indian *pandits* and *maulvies*. The British legal system was formally based on rule of law and the idea of equality before law. However, the racial distinctions were maintained and justice became costly and beyond the rich of illiterate peasants as a new class of professional lawyers, who were well versed in the knowledge of legal intricacies, had to be engaged and paid. The new notion of 'sanctity of contract' also favored the indigenous propertied social groups like landlord and moneylenders. The early nationalist leadership disputed the claims of British rulers that they were improving the conditions of Indian people. They held the colonial state responsible for unilateral transfer of resources from India to England to meet an array of Home Charges. Dada Bhai Naruroji claimed that India received no equivalent value of goods and services in return for a rising export surplus. This invisible resource transfer was held accountable for India's backwardness, poverty and lack of development.[10] The environmental historians have also shown how the legal and institutional framework of imperial forests acts of 1865 and 1878 completely marginalized the villagers and tribal communities except for narrow and meagre claims on the produce on the forest. The prohibition of grudging and shifting cultivation in forests destroyed the way of life of many pastoralists and tribal social groups. The indigenous knowledge of traditional conservation and management of forests was devalued and colonial commercial interests and priorities became the guiding principles of the new regime.[11]

Some scholars depict colonialism simply as the 'documentation project of the colonial state'. However, it was more of a combined project of colonial rulers and its powerful supporting allies to control and subjugate the 'dangerous and volatile nomadic and pastoral tribal communities' the colonial state paid special attention to the mechanisms of social control and process of pacification of internal frontiers the colonial social arrangements also due upon the preexisting institutional framework and methods of earlier polities to achieve its objectives. Forests were seen as the abode of robbers and criminal elements the tribal social groups were represented as unstable construction of power on the fringes of settled agriculture. The British government discontinued with the pre-colonial practice of not assessing forest and cultivable waste lands and tries to settle and discipline nomadic tribal groups. From the very beginning, the colonial state used surveillance and legal tools of social control to define certain groups as beyond the bound the civility. The colonial brand of anthropology and anthropometry created categories of the civilized and the barbaric. A number of community and tribes were stigmatized as 'the criminal tribes'. The legal language of the colonial rulers was used against a wide variety of marginal groups who did not confirm to the pattern of settled agriculture and wages labour, especially nomadic, pastoral community and the forest dwelling tribes.

Apart from British tradition of associating forest with crimes and out laws, the fear of nomadic and wondering groups among their Brahmin subordinates, the cultivators fear of hunting gathering people and high caste apprehension of people outside caste converged in the making of 'criminal tribes' ideology.[12] The belief in the professional and hereditary character of the crime was widespread among 19th century colonial administrators. The Criminal Tribes Act (1871) provided the institutional basis for registration of any or all members of such tribes who were notified as such. The registered members had to report themselves to the local police authority at fixed intervals and notify their residence or any intended change of place of residence. Any contravention of these legal provisions invited severe punitive measures. More than 150 tribes were listed under the Act and most of these belonged to marginalized social groups outside settled domesticity. The colonial state defined these groups as criminals by simple reference to their caste or tribal identity and this legal characterization rendered them defenseless to any claims to protection or impartiality of law. Their criminality was represented as an in-born trait or as a profession that they inherited from their ancestors. Such assumptions and legal enactments were also in congruence with the values of indigenous landed magnates and their notion of an appropriate social order. The authorities at district level administration especially Magistrates in Punjab and North West Province maintained that Provisions of Indian Penal Code and Codes of Criminal Procedure were inadequate to suppress their criminal activities. Therefore, they stressed the use of special surveillance measures to deal with the criminality of such groups. They were to be treated like wild animals—to be watched, tamed and hunted up.[13]

Recently, some scholars have maintained that the Kautilya's *Arthshastra*, a treatise on statecraft in ancient India can be taken as a model of good governance.[14] Before we proceed further, it needs to mention here that this textual source contain at best the views of Chanakya, the famous minister of the Mauryan king Chandragupta. The norms prescribed in the text of *Arthshastra* may be simply a theoretical construct or might not depict the existing realities of the times. In the words of Amartya Sen, "India's past has become an ideological battleground".[15] For him, it is important to recognize that the significance of past for us today involves selection and choice in which our contemporary concerns can have a reasonable role. But he cautions that it is also important to see that this connection between the present and our involvement with the past neither undermines the need to look for veracity and ascertained evidence nor removes the case for deliberately concentrating on those cases in which the lessons involved have particular relevance to our concerns today.[16] *Arthshastra* was one of the greatest political books of the ancient world. Max Weber said that this, "truly radical 'Machiavellianism' in the popular sense of the word, is classically expressed in the Indian literature in the *Arthashastra* of Kautilya and compared to is, Machiavelli's The Prince is harmless.[17] Although Kautilya proposed an elaborate welfare state in domestic politics, something that has been called a socialized monarchy, he proved willing to defend the general good of this monarchy with harsh measures. The *Arthashastra* is a treatise on statecraft and economic policy which identifies its author by the names Kautilya and Vishnugupta, who are traditionally identified with the Mauryan minister Chanakya. The traditionally identification of Kautilya and Vishnugupta with Mauryan minister Chanakya would date the *Arthasastra* to the 4th century BC. Most modern day historians are of the opinion that this document definitely dates back to the early Mauryan era. Many administrative terms used are similar to those used in the edicts of Ashoka. The Magadha kingdom under the Nanda dyansty is given as a case study. The language of many fragments is archaic. Certain inconsistencies may be explained by the fact that the document has probably seen many revisions by various authors at different times. It has been suggested that Vishnugupta was a later editor of the original work by Chanakya. However, certain affinities with smritis and references that would be anachronism for the 4th century BC suggest assigning the *Arthasastra* to the 2nd through 4th centuries CE. Thomas R. Trautmann and I.W. Mabbett concur that the *Arthasastra* is a composition from not earlier than the 2nd century AD, but based on earlier material.[18]

However, good governance is a contemporary notion which depends on other ideas like equality of opportunity, protection of human rights, gender equality and equitable sharing of resources. It does not make sense to trace the obligations and stipulation about such mode of governance in a monarchial set-up. Even though, most pre-modern societies and states had notions of righteous and virtuous rulers[19], they should not be compared with the present-day polities. *Arthshastra* is considered by historians as a manual on statecraft[20], dealing with what ought to be than what was. The text of this manual gives seven elements *(prakratis)* of sovereignty: the Swami or the monarch, the *Amatayas* or the group of advisors to the king, the *Janapada* or a specific territory, which included cultivable lands, forests, pastures, water resources in that region as well as mines, the *Durga* and *Pura* or fortified cities and trading centres, the *Kosa* meant treasury where revenue collected was deposited, the *Danda* refers to the coercive apparatus of state or force and finally the *Mitras* or allies and friends. The state carried out the executive role of collection of revenues or *Bali* and *Bhaga,* which became regular taxes as compared to pre-monarchial ritual offerings and gifts. It also maintained law and order and *dharma* or 'just ordering of society' or the meticulously articulated hierarchical *varna* system.[21] It was emphasized in Arthshastra that it was the *danda* and *dandaniti* on which the triple *Vedas* and *Vartas* depended. The triple *Vartas* were the agriculture, cattle breeding and trade that brought in grain, cattle, gold, forest produce or *kupya* and free labour or *vishti* for the king's treasury. It was claimed that there was never a better instrument than the spectre to bring people under control. The absence of a magistrate or wielder of *danda* *(dandadharabhave),* it was proclaimed in this text would lead to social anarchy and disorder expressed in the famous proverb of fishes *(matsyanyayumudbhavayati)* or how big fish eats the smaller ones. Speaking of duties of a king, *Arthshastra* depicts king as the *heda prasada* or the dispenser of both punishments and rewards or as a person in which powers of Indra and Yama were blended. The text also mentions the rebellious districts and wild tribes *(aranyacahara)* and need for special surveillance measures to track down the treacherous opponents of sovereignty. It was time of expansion of agriculture and *Arthshastra* advises the ruler to encourage steps to establish new settlements. In view of social cohesion, it further advised, not to settle people from same community or tribe in one place rather settle them in different *janapadas* so that they did not have the opportunity to congregate and conspire for a revolt.[22] Although, *Arthshastra* literally means the science of wealth but actually it was a work on polity concerned with increasing wealth and power of the ruler. The maximum collection of revenue and organization of an efficient law and order machinery was its main objective. In this sense, the economic thinking of Arthshastra can be compared to the seventeenth century Camaralist thinking in Germany, which also laid considerable stress on increasing tax revenue for the prince.[23] We may come across such statements in *Arthshastra* that "In the happiness of his subjects lies the happiness of ruler and in their welfare, his own welfare or that whatever pleases himself he shall not consider as good, but whatever pleases his subjects he shall consider good". However, Kautilaya's *Arthshastra* put the possession and use of power above ethical questions. Therefore, although there is advice and suggestion against oppressive fines, free labour and excessive taxes *(dandavishtikarabadhaih)*, simultaneously we also come across injunctions against actors, dancers, singers, drummers, buffoons *(vagjivana)* and bards *(kusiiava)* as they disturb the agricultural operations and get resources from villagers. The chief concern of state was to get maximum amount of agricultural surplus from the expanding agriculture. Apart from agricultural taxes, state also obtained produce from forests *(vana)* and herd of cattle *(vraja)*. The lands given to Brahmin for their subsistence were exempted from taxes and fines but the bulk of cultivable lands were occupied by taxpayers only for life *(ekapurusikani)*. Lands might be confiscated from those who did not cultivate them and given to others for cultivation or alternatively they might be cultivated with the hired labour *(gramabhristaka)* through leaders or *vaidehaka*. There are other references in the text of *Arthshastra* that points towards the existence of social hierarchy in the villages. There were *ardhasitikas* or tenants cultivating *vaptiriktam* or uncultivated lands on the basis of sharing the produce by half as well as *svaviryopajivinah* who lived by their own physical exertion and who received only 1/4th or 1/5th of produce as their allocation. The state also employed slaves, labourers and prisoners *(dandapratikartri)* to sow seeds on *sita* or crown lands. The marginalization and exclusion of certain social groups in the monarchial set-up comes out without a doubt because although there were references to cooperative ventures like construction of reservoirs for irrigation but personal physical labour was not required in such cases as the resourceful people could send their bullocks and servants. The state was also more and more trying to establish control over forest and other resources and such control might well have excluded the tribal people from entitlements to such common property resources. It was explicitly stated in the text of *Arthshastra* that that the king had the right of ownership in fishing, ferrying and trading in vegetables and the superintendent of forests collected timber and other products like medicines, animal skins from the forests. Particular attention was paid to exercise control over elephants as they were crucial in the battlefields for destroying the arrayed army of an enemy, its encampments and fortifications. The social conflicts arising out of expansion of cultivable lands might be the reason for apprehension expressed about the wild tribes and their activities and they foreshadows the stigmatization of these groups under colonial rule. The *Arthshastra* admonished the king not to take possession of any country which was liable to the inroads of enemies and wild tribes. This clubbing together of 'wild tribes' with enemies is understandable because the 'wild tribes', living under a leader and moving in the neighbouring forests had their own strongholds, they were numerous and brave and ready to fight in broad daylight and capable of seizing and destroying countries like kings. They could, therefore, cause problems for the stability and security of the kingdom.

What needs to be emphasized is that state emerged in highly differentiated economy and in stratified social formations; in our ancient history also state appeared as kingdoms and empires and it was the outcome of political processes in class structured societies. The transition from chiefdom to kingdom or monarchial system took place in North India in the middle of the first millennium BC while it came much later in the Southern parts of the subcontinent around sixth century AD. Once the state emerged, it subordinated the vis or peasantry. Social stratification created tensions between producers (ploughmen and tribes) and the agency that established its control over territories as the resources were required to carry out the managerial functions of the state. The good governance meant for the rulers how to get the maximum amount of agricultural surplus from the cultivators and how to control the social groups that existed on the fringes of settled agriculture. Romilla Thapar refers to anthropological concepts like lineage society and household economy to explain the hierarchically arranged *Varna* society.[24] She describes how Vedic literature is full of references to lineage terms like *gotra, vraja,* etc. and how lineage groups comprised of *rajanya* and vis and how the former group came to exercise greater control over the community resources leading to internal differentiation and dissolution of lineage based social organization during later Vedic period. Other contributing factors like environment, technology, extraction of social surplus from the producers, urbanization and ideology also paved the way for the making of state.

In light of above analysis of three different historical epochs, we may conclude that for a democratic restructuring of local administrative machinery, we need not turn to glorification of outdated monarchial ideals and norms. There is a need to specifically empower the marginalized and excluded sections of society and involve them in the process of governance. This is the only remedy that can save thousands of lives who are being lost in India's countryside through mass suicides due to the impact of deep-rooted agrarian crisis.

NOTES AND REFERENCES

1. For ideas and concepts of governance and good governance see Sam Agere, *Promoting Good Governance: Principles, Practices and Perspectives*, Commonwealth Secretariat, 2000; Commonwealth Secretariat, *Citizen's Governance Kit tool: Creating Change by Making People's Voices Heard*, 2005; Pani Niranjan, Santap S. Mishra and Bijaya S. Sahu, *Modern Systems of Governance: Good Governance vs E-Governance*, Anmol Publishers, 2004.
2. For a critique of World Bank type notions of governance see D. Parthasarthy, "From White Men's Burden to Good Governance: Economic Liberalization and Commodification of Law and Ethics" in Bernd Hamm and Russel Charles Smadyeh, ed., *Cultural Imperialism: Essays on the Political Economy of Cultural Domination*, Broadview Press, 2005, pp. 191-210 and Mortimer Sellers, *The New World Order: Sovereignty, Human Rights, and the Self-Determination of Peoples*, Berg Publishers, 1996, pp. 318-326.
3. For the nature of social inequalities in India see Andre Beteille, "Poverty and Inequality", *Economic and Political Weekly*, 18-24 Oct., 2003 and his other writings such as *Caste, Class and Power*, Oxford University Press, Delhi, 1996: *Equality and Inequality*, Oxford University Press, Delhi, 1983 and *The Idea of Natural Inequality and other Essays*, OUP, Delhi, 1987.
4. Claude Markovits, *Indian Business and Nationalist Politics, 1931-1939: The Indigenous Capitalist Class and the Rise of Congress Party*, Cambridge University Press, Cambridge, 1985 traces the growth of Indian capitalist class.
5. See Parnab Bardhan, *Political Economy of Development In India*, OUP, Delhi, 1999 and also Priyatosh Maitra's *The Globalization of Capitalism in the Third World Countries*, Praeger Pulishers, Westport, 1996 for the economic development of post-independence India.
6. Paul Brass makes this point in his famous work *The Politics of India since Independence*, New Delhi, 1990.
7. Recently D. Bandopadhyay has questioned the functional validity of retention of nonelective bureaucratic head of district magistrate at apex level even after introduction of Panchayati Raj Institutions for local governance in the new scheme of administration introduced with the passing of 73rd Amendment to our Constitution (1992). He argues that the post was created in the mid-19th century by the colonial rulers to manage their affairs of administration and revenue-collection and it creates

only a dichotomy between district administration and various self-government institutions at the village and district level. See D. Bandhopadhyay, "Is the Institution of District Magistrate Still Necessary", *Economic and Political Weekly*, 25 November, 2006, pp. 4847-4849.

8. For the changes in the demographic profile of populations and the impact of globalization on the world economies at the peripheries see the following works : Dorothy Stein, *People Who Count: Population and Politics, Women and Children*, Earth Scan Publications, London, 1995; UN Centre for Human Settlements, *Cities in a Globalizing World*, Earth Scan Publications, London, 2001; Barney Cohen, "Urban Growth in Developing Countries: A Review of Current Trends and a Caution Regarding Existing Forecasts", *World Development*, Vol.32, No. 11, 2004, pp. 23-51; and P. Panwalkar, "Upgradation of Slums: A World Bank Programme" in S. Patel and A. Thorner, eds, *"Bombay: Metaphor for Modern India"*, OUP, Bombay, 1996, pp. 121-142 and also see T.P.R. Calderia, *City of Walls: Crime, Segregation and Citizenship in Sao Paulo*, University of California, Berkeley, 2000 for the impact of globalization on the life of urban poor in a Latin American city, a life-experience which can be generalized to other displaced and dislocated people.
9. See Thomas R. Metcalf, *The New Cambridge History of India: The Ideologies of Rai*, Vol.111.4, Cambridge University Press, New Delhi, 1995 for an analysis of British ideologies and their impact on administrative policy in India.
10. See Dadabhai Nauroji, *Poverty and British Rule in India*. Delhi: Publications Division, Government of India. 1901 (1962); and Romesh C. Dutt, *Economic History of India: In the Victorian Age*, Volume 2, New York, 1904 (1969) for a sophisticated, moderate critique of colonial rule.
11. For the Nature of Colonial Forest Policies see D. Arnold and R. Guha (eds.), *Nature, Culture, Imperialism: Essays on the Environmental History of South Asia*, Oxford University Press, New Delhi, 1995
12. See Anand A. Yang, ed., *Crime and Criminality in British India*, Tuscan, 1985, p. 2.
13. See the following writings on the branding of indigenous communities: Y.C. Simhadri, *The Ex-Criminal Tribes of India*, New Delhi, 1979; Dilip D'Souja, *Branded by Law: Looking at India's De-notified Tribes*, New Delhi, 2001; Meena Radhakrishna, *Dishonoured By History : 'Criminal Tribes' and British Colonial Policy*, Orient Longman, New Delhi, 2001 and Sanjay Nigam, "Disciplining and Policing'the Criminal' by Birth" *Indian Economic and Social History Review*, Vol. 27, No. 2, 1990.
14. Some writings which draw inspiration from Kautilaya's *Arthshastra* include N, Shiva Kumar and U.S. Rao, "Guideline for Value Based Management in Kautilya's *Arthshastra*", *Journal of Business Ethics*, Vol. 15, No. 4, April, 1996, pp. 415-423; Charles Waldaner, William J. Zahka and Surendra Pal, "Kautilaya's *Arthshastra*: A Neglected Precursor to

Classical Economics", *Indian Economic Review*, Vol. 31, No. 1, pp. 101-108; Lazlo Zsolnai, *Spirituality and Ethics in Management*, Springer, 2004; Nicholas Cepddi, ed., *Business and Religion : A Clash of Civilizations*, M and M Scrivener Press, 2005 and Subash Sharma, "A Brief History of History", *Journal of Human Values*, Vol. 11, No. 2, 2005, pp. 123-137.

15. Amartya Sen, "Our Past and Our Present", *Economic and Political Weekly*, November 25-December 1, 2006, p. 4877.
16. *Ibid.* p. 4800.
17. Max Weber, "Politics as a Vocation", W.G. Runciman, *Selections in Translation*, Trans. Eric Mattews, Cambridge University Press, Cambridge, 1998, p. 220.
18. See Thomas R. Trautman, *Kautilya and Arthshastra: A Statistical Investigation of Authorship and Evolution of the Text*, E.J.Brill, Leiden, 1971, p. 185 and I.W.Mabbet. "The Date of Arthshastra", *Journal of the American Oriental Society*, Vol. 84, No. 2, 1964, pp. 162-169.
19. See N. D. Irani and Morris Silver, ed., *Social Justice in Ancient World*, Greenwood Press, Westport, 1995 shows how the idea of social justice was articulated and implemented in various ancient civilizations like Chinese, Babylonian, Iranian and other cultures. For ancient India, See M.G. Prasad, "Social Justice in the Ancient India" in Irani and Silver, eds., *Social Justice in Ancient World*, pp. 91-100.
20. References and citation for *Arthshastra* are based on 1915 Shamasastry's translation of Kautilaya's Arthshastra in our article.
21. See Vilho Harle, *Ideas of Social Order in the Ancient World*, Greenwood Press, Westport, 1998, especially the Chapters on 'Dharma and Caste as the basis of Social Order' (pp. 52-64) and 'The Wise King as the basis of Social Order' (pp. 111-128) to understand that there was nothing unique in the notions of Kautilya's *Arthshastra* and every society had its ideas about social justice as well as the proper social hierarchy and rules to be observed to maintain it.
22. See Jayant Gadkari, *Society and Religion From Rigveda to Puranas*, Popular Prakashan, Bombay, 1996, pp. 115-116.
23. See Ajit Kumar Das Gupta, *A History of Indian Economic Thought* , Routledge, 1993, pp. 28-41 for this interpretation.
24. See Romilla Thapar, *From Lineage to State: Social Formatioms in the Mid-First Milleenium BC in the Ganga Valley*, Oxford University Press, Delhi, 1984.

12 District Administration and Good Governance

Manjusha Sharma and *Monika Dara**

India is organised administratively into Union, states, districts, sub-divisions, blocks and villages. But today the district is the key unit of the state government in India. In fact, the district has always existed as the unit of administration in some form throughout the long history of our country. In Manu's time, about one thousand villages formed a district and was in the charge of separate official. Even today, the number of villages in a district is almost same. The Mauryas, who established the first historically identified empire in India had divided the administration into provinces which were further sub-divided into districts. Known as *ahars*, *vishyas* and *pradeshas*. Asokas's inscriptions refer to rajukas and pradeshika as officers charged with the welfare of the *janapadas* and pradesha or districts. Under the period of Guptas as well as their extensive kingdom was divided into province and provinces were divided into vishyas or mandals and the officer incharge of *vishyas* was called *ayukta* or *vishayapati*. The Mughal emperors continued to follow this system and divided their empire into provinces or subahs which were subdivided into sarkars or districts. Each sarkar was composed of a number of parganas and each pargana was a union of several villages.[1]

The East India Company after acquiring the 'Diwani'

* Reader and Research Scholar, Department of Public Administration, Kurukshetra University, Haryana.

rights from the Mughal emperors, appointed its own officials to collect revenue. The office of the collector was created in 1872 by Warren Hestings for the purpose of collecting revenue. Lord Cornwallis disapproved the system of concentrating executive, revenue and judicial powers in the hands of one individual and as a result collector ceased to be a judge of civil revenue courts and became the magistrate-collector as the district head. This system continued till India became independent in 1947.

After independence, the old priorities of district administration were suddenly gone and the role of administrative system changed in the context of three major factors, namely, democracy, development and decentralization. The Community Development Programme was introduced in the early fifties and three tier system at local level in the sixties.[2] The district administration is the key central position between the state government and the local people. It translates the policies of the government into actual practice and the problems of the local people are studied and are communicated to the state government. The district administration is the vital centre of operation by virtue of which we can measure the extent of success of governmental policies, plan and the different welfare programmes. It may be truly said that the district is the unit of administration with which almost every citizen comes into contact. So, a district can be described as the centre of political and administrative life.[3]

The role of the district administration can be classified into following six groups:

(1) Regulatory Role;
(2) Development Role;
(3) Tasks concerning with local bodies;
(4) Conducting fair elections;
(5) Emergency; and
(6) Residuary.

The first two roles are the most important roles. In

regulatory role of district administration covers maintenance of law and order; crime control and administration of justice; land administration in which there is assessment and collection of land revenue and taxes e.g. sales tax, forest and excise tax, income tax, etc; and control, regulation and distribution of food and other civil supplies.

The developmental role of district administration focuses on agriculture production, co-operation, animal husbandry and fisheries and welfare activities like community development programmes, public health, education and other social welfare activities like elimination of poverty and development of human beings and material resources.

The tasks concerning local bodies cover the functions which are concerned with the administration of local bodies. The district administration supervises and exercises control over municipal bodies and panchayats in urban and rural areas, respectively.

District administration also holds elections to the parliament, the state legislature and local bodies.

The fifth role is related to tackling of problems pertaining to emergencies and natural calamities. It takes immediate relief actions in case of scarcity conditions caused by natural calamities like fire, drought, and flood.

The sixth role is concerned with the functions relating to executive work done, which have not been defined precisely. Besides, it hears the complaints of the people and redress their grievances.[4]

Good Governance

Good governance ordinarily means looking after the welfare of all in all respects. According to Asmerenon and others, "Good governance is associated with efficient and effective administration in a democratic framework." Thus, good governance involves high level of organisational efficiency and effectiveness for responding in a responsive way in order to attain the predetermined desirable goals of the society. The concept of good governance is neither new nor static. It has been the gist and spirit of a very elaborate scheme of Kautilya in India and has always been present with some common variables in all the political systems of modern era. But this term has gained more popularity in recent past and a debate around good governance is going-on all round the world.[5] The World Bank's Document entitled Governance and Development (1992) put forward management and in this context, identified following four dimensions:

(1) Public sector management;
(2) Accountability;
(3) Legal framework for development; and
(4) Information and transparency.

Aedrian Leftwich have identified three features of Good Governance :

(1) Promotion of open, market-friendly and competitive economy,
(2) Democratization; and
(3) Improvement of human rights records.

In 1992, the World Bank's Document on Governance and Development stated that "Good Governance is central to creating and sustaining an environment which fosters strong and equitable development and it is an essential complement to sound economic policies. "[6]

Elements of Good Governance

People Participation

Both men and women's participation of good governance has been widely recognised. They are not only the beneficiaries but also the agents of good governance. Active and effective participation of people is necessary for achieving the basic goals of good governance. Such participation needs to be informed and organized. Citizen's participation always steer governance to the right direction and no governance can get success without involvement of the subjects. That governance is good which provides opportunities to the subjects in deciding future courses of action, monitoring and evaluation.

When we observe the participation of people in development of the district it is found that poverty does not allow the people to take initiative in the developmental activities of district administration. It has also been seen that most of the people are unaware about the significance of their involvement, therefore, they remain neglected. The attitude of district officials has also not been changed to the desired extent. Due to bureaucratic dominance and lack of strong political will, people participation has not proved its usefulness in the process of socio-economic transformation. It has been aptly observed: "As development went apace new plans and projects came to be implemented which gave boost to the burgeoning of bureaucracy in its wake. Over the years it has become an unmanageable and uncontrollable leviathan. With lack of controls, delayed disposal of cases and ultimate acquittal for want of evidence, corruption became more and more rampant. Nexus between politicians and bureaucrats and criminalization of politics further worsened the situation."[7] On the other hand, the Indian state does not appear to be serious to abolish the para-statal bureaucratic agencies like the District Rural Development Agencies.[8]

For effective people participation in decision-making process of district administration, awareness should be generated among the masses, the capacity of local body leaders should be enhanced through evolving appropriate training modules and there should be political commitment and proper publicity of government policies, effective implementation of programmes with the help of local government.

Rule of Law

Good governance requires such type of apparatus which can enforce impartially the rule of law. Not only this, it also requires full protection for human rights, particularly of those who are in minority. It is desired that the agencies responsible for the enforcement of laws are not biased and do not discriminate on the grounds of caste, creed, religion, area, language, etc. In other words, ensuring equal application of law or rule of law, wherever necessary.

Major obstacles of good governance in district administration are disruptive political practices and lack of social discipline. There is complexity of laws in the system and these laws are beyond the reach and understanding of common people. Also the administration is effected by the multiplicity of laws as everyday legislature frames number of laws for the betterment of democracy. On the other hand, these laws create obstacles for the implementing authority due to the overlapping of laws. The rules seems to be unrealistic perhaps the reason behind this is the discrepancies between reality and laws. To quote: "a country which for a whole generation practised a certain techniques of opposition to the government, it not easy to shift over to make people think differently. It may be their own government, but people still have the habit of opposing the government. Secondly, they are opt to adopt the technique, not rightly I think, but some variations of it, just to press on some complaint or something, which sometime opt to be nuisance." The answer to the loopholes in the district administration could be strict implementation of the laws by the bureaucrats on one hand and simplification of the laws on the other. Publicity of laws by government could also serve the purpose, pamphlets should be distributed among the common people to raise their awareness about laws. Those who are in the habit of going beyond the rules to please or acommodate someone should be brought to book.

Effectiveness and Efficiency

Good governance means that processes and institutions produce results that the needs of the society while making the best use of resources at their disposal. The concept of efficiency in the context of good governance also covers the sustainable use of natural resources and the protection of the environment.

It has been observed that in some of the districts, there is lack of efficiency and effectiveness in the functioning of district administration. The reason being most of the employees are not fully trained in applying the Information Technology in the management of their affairs. There are some of them who are not fully trained and are not skilful. Posts are allowed to remain vacant for years and in case, if some posts are not filled for particular period. The posts are abolished without taking into consideration the workload of the department working at the district level. The work is assigned to the available staff. They remain overloaded with work as a result of which both the quality and quantity are questioned. In such a situation we cannot make it sure that cent percent objectives are achieved.

It is suggested that for the purpose of effectiveness and efficiency, the efforts should be made to change the attitude of officials. Regular training should be made mandatory for all the employees in respect of their status. The government should immediately fill all the posts lying vacant in different departments of the district. Before abolition of any post, the need and relevance must be considered before going ahead. All the departments should ensure both quality and quantity of goods and services being provided through them. Those who attain or establish good performance should be suitably awarded.

Transparency

Transparency is another element of good governance under which working decision/actions taken are open to the citizenary, doubts can be cleared. Right to information, if implemented in letter and spirit, transparency can be achieved. Concealment of facts and delays causing corruption can be eliminated by transparency. The affected party may have accessibility to information freely and easily about the decisions or the actions taken or enforced.

Deliberate secracy of the government is a major drawback for the good governance. People do not know, what government is doing for them. It violates quality of transparency and accountability of the bureaucracy. Official and staff of district administration do not behave equally while performing their duties and responsibilities. In most of the cases they do not inform the people about the policies programmes at the right time. When the people came in contact with the officials to get their works done, generally, they are kept in dark and enormous delays take place which leads to wastage of time, money and energy.

For having a transparent set-up at the district level, citizen charters and Right to Information Act should be effectively implemented. E-governance can play important role. For effective implementation, freedom of information with appropriate record keeping and record management mechanism, allowing the citizens to have maximum access to governmental information should be done.

Accountability

Accountability of government institutions is a basic requirement for good governance. As no institution can be left unaccountable. The actions taken by the institutions can be checked so as to ensure accountability. Anyone who-so-ever is assigned any job should be made accountable to someone. In good governance, particularly at the district level, there is a great need to make the officials accountable to the people for their activities, tasks and responsibilities.

Now a days politicians and bureaucrats have nexus, they are busy to fulfil their vested interest. So the accountability of administration is not clear. According to the Constitution, bureaucrats are accountable to the ministers so the administration is indirectly accountable to the people but some time the civil servants and subordinates irresponsibly discharge their duties and responsibilities. Malpractices are going-on during the administrative activities. Thus, the bureaucracy is found unaccountable and irresponsible towards the duties.

The officials who do not work according to the constitutional spirit, should be strictly punished. Political parties must not issue ticket to such persons who are found indulged in corruption and criminal activities. If accountability is ensured, achievement of goals and objectives becomes easy through efficiency, effectiveness, probity and prudence.

Responsiveness

These days responsiveness is gaining ground that is why good governance requires that the institutions and processes should serve all the stakeholders within as reasonable time frame .[9]

Since the district administration is the basic unit to deliver goods and services to the people at local level, therefore, need of responsiveness is greatly felt at this level. There are scholars who feel that district administration is not responsive because it has not been placed under the elected representatives of the local self-governing bodies. The officials/officers at district level, it is pointed out "use government powers and for the commonman they are the government. Similarly, at the block and tehsil levels, even today, *Tehsildar, Thanedars, Girdawars* and *Patwaris* are the government personified for the common people. Their working style is inhuman, mechanical, heartless and formal. They take bribe, emphasise on paper work, and harassment of the people etc. are some of the prevalent practices in the administration at the cutting edge point." In Madhya Pradesh, the district government has been entrusted with the responsibility of all district level developmental plans and evaluation of activities and programmes, their supervision, monitoring and follow up to make government more responsive and democratic. Other states should also follow the suit for making district administration more responsive to the needs of the people.

E-Governance

Today, online government service is not thought while it is the revolution in information technology that makes it possible. E-governance helps in more participatory form of government. The use of e-governance can be powerful tool for good governance. Application of information technology to governance in rendering administrative services from ration cards, motor licenses, land records, health, education and municipal services, e-governance has profound efficiency in accomplishing such tasks at the doorsteps to the people. E-governance can play a significant role by aiding governmental activities, its efficiency, responsiveness and accountability.

E-governance is the commitment to utilize appropriate technologies to enhance governmental relationship, in order to advance democratic expression on, human-dignity and autonomy, support economic development and encourage the fair and efficient delivery of services. In simple words, E-governance can be said to be about the use of emerging information and communications technologies to facilitate the process of government and public administration.[10]

Honourable former President of India, A.P.J. Abdul Kalam expressed in his inaugural speech addressed at the International Conference on e-governance, (18 December 2003), He said that good governance is being recognised as an important goal by many countries across the world. They have taken up specific initiatives for open government. Freedom of information is being redefined and supported by detailed guidelines. The internet revolution has proved to be a powerful tool for good governance initiatives. An important dimension of the internet potential is the possibility of providing services any time anywhere. E-governance has to be citizen friendly. Delivery of services to citizens is primary function of the government. In India, e-governance should enable seamless access to information and seamless flow of information across the state and central government and local government in the federal setup.[11]

E-governance is capable in not only speeding up transaction but also allowing transparent functionary. Public life styles have totally changed with the spread of new information and communication technology, certain demands have also emerged touching the vital areas of government functioning, such as transparency in function, right to information and speedy decisions. E-governance has set goals before the governments worldwide to reinvent government systems in orders to deliver efficient and cost effective services, information and knowledge through information and communication technology.

Successful e-governance initiatives like *e-seva* of Andhra Pradesh, *Bhoomi* relating to computerization of land records in Karnataka, Sarita concerning land records in Maharashtra, Vahan used to signify permits in some states are some of the schemes are already in operation in some parts of India, to improve the services to the people. Himachal Pardesh has won the e-governance award thrice.[12]

The Right to Information and Good Governance

Public participation in the governmental process is at its

meaningful best when citizens have adequate access to official information. This access lays the foundation for good governance, accountability, transparency and participation. The fundamental right of freedom of speech and expression is meaningless. So a major step for improving administrative functioning has been set in motion by enacting the Right to Information Act, 2005, which came into force on October 12, the 120th day of Presidential assent to the legislation. The Act seeks to the end excessive secracy in the governance and strive for an open system with reasonable safeguards and empower the people in curbing corruption.

By implementing it the society and people access to information, the law seeks to eliminate delays, redress people's grievances and meet their aspirations and right to prompt service by official agencies and public servants.[13]

Public information officers have been appointed in all Central Government ministries and departments simultaneously with the enforcement of the law and a number of state governments, local bodies and organization substantially funded by the government have appointed public information officers to receive applications for information with a fee of Rs.10, but for the poor there is no such fee. They can have the information photocopied at the rate of Rs.2 per page and even electronically in compact discs, video cassettes or cassettes, certified samples and diskettes, tapes and floppies or the people can inspect official works, documents and record which are open to public and not secret information. The applicants can take notes of their own. Such information would be provided within 30 days of the application and if information concerns the life and liberty of a person or persons, such information will be deemed as refusal, but if there are genuine reasons for refusal of information reasons for such refusal will be given.[14]

No doubt, the Act can bring drastic change but its success through effective implementation largely depend on the dissemination of its knowledge and information to the people. Its effective implementation at district level and other lower levels may really expedite the developmental process and help in observing economy, efficiency and effectiveness.

We may conclude that there will be no effective implementation of policies in the absence of public participation, accountability, responsiveness, rule of law, transparency, efficiency and effectiveness at the district level. In the present scenario, to overcome the loopholes in the district administration, there is a need to implement the e-governance and right to information.

NOTES AND REFERENCES

1. Jayapalan, N., *Indian Administration,* Atlantic Publishers and Distributors, New Delhi.
2. Mishra, Bimla Kant, *Indian Administration : An Evolutionary Prespective,* Indu Prakashan, Delhi, 1996 p. 53.
3. Arora, Ramesh K., *Administration in India : Prespective on Change,* Aalekh Publishers, Jaipur, 1999, p. 132.
4. *Op. cit.,* Jayapalan, N., p.
5. Barthwal, C.P., *Good Governance in India,* Deep & Deep Publications, New Delhi, 2003, pp. 7, 8.
6. Ibid, p. 6.
7. Sudhir, R. L., "Reforming Bureaucracy", *Yojana,* August 2005, p. 45.
8. Dutta, Prabhat, "Development Administration: New Agenda," Arora R. K. (ed.), *Public Administration French Perspectives,* Aalekh Publishers, Jaipur, 2004, pp. 1, 4.
9. Barthwal, C. P. *Op. cit.,* pp. 9, 10.
10. See the *Employment News,* 27th March - 2 April, 2004.
11. Inaugural address at the International Conference on e-governance Hon'able President of India, A.P.J. Abdul Kalam, 18 Dec, 2003.
12. See the *Employment News,* 30th July - 5th Aug., 2005.
13. See the *Employment News,* 16th to 22nd July 2005.
14. See the *Employment News,* 3rd to 9th December, 2005.
15. For more details, see Mishra S.N., *et al* (Eds.), *Public Governance and Decentralisation,* Part Two, New Delhi: Mittal Publications, 2003, pp. 611-625.

13 District Administration and Good Governance

Ram Autar

Good Governance (GG) in District Administration (DA) has become equivocally indispensable in the age of Total Quality Management (TQM). The term TQM is pioneered by Deming, the father of Quality Consciousness, in an organization under the trio advents of Liberalization, Privatization and Globalization (LPG) of W.T.O. agreement series since January 1995. The annex-3 of W.T.O. legal text contains "the code of good practice for the preparation, adoption and application of standards" is the need of the hour. The substantive provisions for good governance for the district administration take a leading thrust by modernising. and re-structuring the operative mechanism at grassroot level. The macro system of governance provides the micro based at district level for the reflections, manifestations or illuminations of larger policies, programmes and perspectives of the government at the level of district for the cohesive, harmonious and effective delivery system of governance.

The historical perspective of GG is deeply embedded in Kotilya's four fold value system. *Artha* as eco political values, *Kama* as hedonistic values, *Dharma* as moral values and *Moksha* as spiritual values. Artha contains the seeds of Marxist perspective of proletariats, Dharma is the base of Gandhian moral value system in which politics should not

* District Food and Supply Controller, Rohtak, Haryana.

be divorced from honesty and integrity. Kama is the source of Freudian libidinal force of Id and Moksha is a sage, saintly or yogic way of life of Indian sadhus and saints. The whole gamut of GG stems from Aristotelian paradigm of "causes" i.e. the material cause, the formal cause, the efficient cause and the final cause. The efficient cause is the magna carta of good governance in Arisotelian parlance which is the base of Hegelian way of thinking i.e. ideas precedes the matter.

The concept of GG seems overtly innocuous and simple but covertly otherway round and complex. It is so demanding and challenging. Indeed a tough task to be tackled with utmost care and dexterity. The modicum of GG and DA demands the apt application of an adage "Think globally and Act locally". The first tenet of district administration and good governance focuses attention on global knowhow and its application at local level. To chalk out the local problems and seek their solutions. The requirement of good governance is an all time achievement at district administration and its integrated development approach towards realisation of aspiration of the masses under three tier system of Panchayati Raj Institutions (PRI). B.M. Sanyal says, "PRI as the long-term sustainability solution" for the effective management of panchayati raj system at grassroot level. 73rd Amendment of our Constitution puts a lot of emphasis on decentralizing the process of powers and policies at gram panchayat, panchayat samiti and Zila Parishad levels. B.M. Sanyal again says, "sustainable development" springs from the effective implementation of 73rd and 74th Amendments of Indian Constitution.

For good governance at district level requires how to root out the problem of proxy rule at three-tier system of PRIs. The women empowerment process through PRIs poses great problem for women folk as their kith and kin follow the home spun rule of governance by proxy. The *"Ghunghat Raj"* is still prevalent in Indian villages in general and at district level in Haryana particular.

To do away with such proxy rule becomes a formidable problem for district administration at good governance level. 33 per cent reservation of women in PRIs is not at ripe stage even today. The pitfalls and loopholes in PRIs due to proxy rule of men over women is common in Haryana at district level in PRIs. Bhiwani is the largest district comprising 462 gram panchayats, 10 panchayat samitis and 29 zila parishads members whereas Panchkula contains 162 GPs, 4 PSs and 10 ZP members for good governance. Panchkula becomes an easy task to a district administrator to tackle with and implement all Government policies and programmes at grassroot level in comparison to Bhiwani district.

The crucial problem of increasing population, its density, its literacy level, its decadal growth rate, sex ratio, rate of urbanisation, Male female literacy gap, the share of schedule caste population, the position of workers to total population, schedule caste literacy in districts, permanent houses conditions, social stability of the population in district, social mobility, inter-generational and intra-generational mobility of masses in the district, households with availability of electricity, tap water facilities, bathroom facilities, kitchens in houses, televisions, telephones, bank accounts, radios, cars/jeeps, scooters/motorcycles, bicycles, drainage of waste water, latrines, type of fuel as cowdung or fodder used, the users of LPG, the crime rate in the district, the law and order situation, the geographical locale of the district and topics galore constitute the labyrinth of district administration and good governance.

For example, the pressing demand of public distribution items at the district level becomes more complex for the district administration of Faridabad as compared to Panchkula. As Faridabad is at the top positions regarding population, density, urbanisation as compared to other districts of Haryana. Mahendergarh district attains top position in sex ratio as compared to Panchkula. The pressing demand of Total Sanitation Campaign (TSC) becomes need of the hour for the district administration of Mahendergarh where maximum households do not have latrine facilities as compared to Sirsa which is the best district from the angle of TSC. The revolution of IT (Information Technology) has benefitted Panchkula most whereas Mahendergarh is still lagging behind worst. Rewari district achieves the top position in schedule caste literacy whereas Fatehabad is the worst district in Haryana so far as literacy rate is concerned from all angles. For district administration the job of governance may become easy in top districts as compared to bottom districts at various levels. The job avenues are lesser in Bhiwani district for mechanics of scooter/motorcycle and bicycles in which the position of the district is at the bottom whereas Panchkula gets the top position in mechanical tools and operations. The use of LPG gas is common for the citizen of Panchkula district whereas the Kaithal district takes the bottom position in use of LPG. The distribution of LPG becomes a question of governance for the administration as per their positions in use of LPG. The use of cowdung is the most useful fuel in Mahengergarh district as compared to Panchkula. Mahendergarh may be a green pasture for LPG distributorship whereas the job of radio repairing in Jhajjar district becomes easy for the unemployed youth as Jhajjar has attained top position in having radios in households. The job of bicycles and its repair becomes a key question in Bhiwani which is at the bottom whereas Yamunanagar attains the top position in using bicycles. The proper study of people problems rivets our attention on various topics aforementioned.

The saving habits of residents of Rewari district are reflected through maximum bank accounts of the households in comparison to Sirsa district which is at the bottom having minimum bank accounts.

The public distribution system and public delivery mechanism attain most attention of the district administration at the level of governance. The targetted public distribution system beneficiaries should be benefitted their due share at a right time and at the best quality maintained at every cost. The consumer protection movement should be given proper thrust at the earliest. To maintain the public delivery system a viable and workable the role of district administration becomes crucial.

The priority based agenda for governance at district level get the top most attention for the speedy redressal of public grievances at all levels of administration. To identify the area of top priority and their proper implementation of Government policies become the pivotal point. The falling rate of girl child is an alarming and shocking question for the administration. The worst district is Panchkula which poses a potential threat to the sustainable growth of girl child for the harmonious position of social stability and mobility. To streamline the rotten system of female foeticide in Haryana again becomes a serious problem for coming generations. Where do we stand district-wise in sex ratio ? What is the remedy of this malady? To ponder over such issues and find out the viable solutions become the central question for the administration. Rohtak has 847 females over 1000 males, gets 14th position district- wise.

The effective growth of literacy at district level for the good governance always relates various questions district-wise. Ambala gets top position 75.31 per cent whereas Fatehabad is the worst district carrying 57.98 per cent literacy rate. Rewari district is the best literate district from the male point of view (88.45%) whereas Fatehabad is the worst carrying 68.22 per cent male literacy rate. Similar is the fate of female literacy, Ambala is the best and Fatehabad is the worst.

To inculcate the values of human development at the age of 0-14 the most formative age group of society where Sarv Shiksha Abhiyan may prove very effective in Fatehabad district where the literacy rate is the lowest at all levels. The narrowing the gap of male-female literacy becomes a key question for socialising the growth of society in a successful way. The role of micro finance and women empowerment may become easy in a district like Ambala or Panchkula where female literacy is the highest. But in Fatehabad district, such problems may be more difficult to be solved by the administration and may pose serious problems for good governance. The journey from marginalisation to mainstream for female folk becomes very tough in a district like Fatehabad. How to reduce the dropout rate of students in Fatehabad district, becomes a good study issue under S.S.A. The most vulnerable section of society is residing in Fatehabad district of Haryana in which S.C. population is the largest (27.43%) whereas Gurgaon has 11.32 per cent. The degree of vulnerablity poses the relative seriousness for the district administration and good governance. The child vulnerability in schools have come to light through infamous incident of rape of a girl child in Durjanpur village of Jind district, the Chudiana rape incident again put the question mark on the much achieved and ascribed positions of teaching community in Haryana. The labour vulnerability in Gurgaon district may pose big problem for administration in relation to good governance due to industrialization and liberalization.

How to overcome the unemployment problem of educated youth at village level in a district gets our serious attention for good governance. The district administration unveils a scalable and self-sustaining initiative in villages of the district to target at a rural educated unemployed youth. To aim at getting the benefits of information technology at grassroot level and how to reap the benefits of science and technology for the reduction of unemployment problem in villages. The district administration should know how to empower the rural unemployed youth "the son of the soil" to set a microsoft kiosk at every village level may become a viable solution in the coming age of computer. The rural sector has enormous potentials as 54 per cent of Indian GDP has its roots in villages. An icon of rural microsoft technology—Tarun Malik—may be a good example for unemployed educated rural youth. The rural kiosks would provide a mix of online and offline services to address a range of socio-economic needs by getting agricultural related information through e-governance and internet services. It may draw tremendous response in a village for the unemployed, educated rural youth who are now rendered aimless.

The proactive approach of district administration and good governance regarding health, hygiene, sanitation and social reformatory processes constitutes a good study material in Haryana. Open defecation is a health hazard for female in particular and children in general. Sirsa is the best district regarding sanitation, density of population and good condition of houses equipped with maximum latrine facilities. Thus the female lot in Sirsa is at best from this angle whereas Mahendergarh district contains the best housing facilities from social stability point of view. For good governance at the district administration level, for the implementation of Indira Awas Yojna, SGRY or employment assurance scheme, etc. would be more in demand in a district like Panipat where the condition of the houses is worst. The IAY scheme may be more useful in Panipat as compared to Pachkula. 41.61per cent population of Panipat District live under delapidated houses.

To provide life sustaining facilities to the people, the role of district administration for good governance becomes more crucial and challenging. The Human Development Report of India states that Haryana is at the fifth position. The life expectancy of the people, the gender ratio, the rate of literacy, the law and order situation, the PDS delivery, the grievances redressal system, the reduction of unemployment problem, to safeguard the vulnerable section of the society, to tackle the corruption in public life by minimising the nexus among "NETA, LALA, BABU, JHOLA and DADA(GUNDA) (N. Vittal)". The tendency of "craft for graft" (Gunnar Myrdal) and the rate of transparency in administration become the central points of concern for good governance.

14 Police Administration
A Reformative Look

*Jagbir Singh Narwal** and *Neelam***

The primary purposes of police department are the protection of life and property against crime, the preservation of peace and order, the safe movement of traffic and the production of emergency services. Police tasks of today differ widely from those of the colonial period, although the fundamental purpose remains the same. An additional problem facing the police today is based on the difficulty in overcoming public opposition to police authority when the police also demands protection from criminal elements.

The Indian Police can claim its origin from the ancient times. It is mentioned in Kautilaya's *Arthashasta* and in the memories of the early Greek and Chinese travellers. Despite continuing change in the political map of India and its restraint effect on the administrative apparatus the basic indigenous character of Indian police system, with appropriate local characteristics, continued till the advent of the British rule.

The police system in India had undergone numerous changes over the centuries since its ancient past. The British Government further modified it so as to meet their needs to consolidate their role and to reorganize the police administration on a more or less uniform pattern throughout the territories in India.

* Lecturer, Department of Public Administration, M.D. University, Rohtak.

** Research Scholar, Department of History, M.D. University, Rohtak.

In the period prior to 1860 they tried different experiments in different Provinces to have a police system suited for their purposes. In Bengal Presidency, the Mughal police system based on the principle of combination of military and civil functions was abolished. In its place, Cornwallis, who has a known dislike for the indigenous system, introduced the *daroga* system and the *zamindars* were divested of police responsibility and the police administration was placed under the control of European officers. The conduct of police was subjected to the control of the magistrate. In Madras Presidency, Thomas Munro, being an admirer of indigenous system, continued it. But, after the Torture Commission of 1855 had brought to light the numerous evils of the working of the Madras police, the Government re-organized it in 1859. The police force in the districts was brought under the effective control of the magistrates. In Bombay Presidency, like Munro, Mountstuart Elphinstone retained the indigenous police system. At the head of the police was the Collector and Magistrate, aided by the *Mamlatdars* who performed both police and revenue functions. But, in 1853, the police system was re-organized on Napier's model that had proved successful in Sind. Under the new system the police was placed under the control and supervision of a chief officer. The basics of the Sind model were adopted elsewhere in India. As a result, the police systems developed in the various Provinces were not exactly uniform but they had acquired certain similarities by the middle of the 19th century.

The need to develop an uniform police administration for the whole of British India, based on principles of efficiency and economy in expenditure, became the crying need of the hour following the Revolt of 1857. Accordingly, a Police Commission was appointed in 1860. On the basis of recommendations of this Commission the various police forces were re-organized into a single homogeneous force of 'Civil Constabulary' and a Police Act to regulate it was passed in 1861.

The Police Commission of 1860 evolved a hierarchical structure for the police organization in the Provinces of British India. That structure continues till today. In the four subsequent decades the British Government did not introduce any significant changes in the structure of the police. It attempted only to implement and perfect the reforms initiated in 1861.

The Police Act, 1861

The Police Act of 1861 imposed a homogeneous police system which replaced the innumerable forces of infinitely varying composition and efficiency that had in the past grown up in the absence of any uniform police policy in India. The Act regulated organization, recruitment, training and other allied matters concerning the imperial as well as the provincial police forces.

The Act of 1861 was a short legislative enactment comprising only 55 sections. Almost half of this Act dealt with the Constitution of the police force on provincial basis, duties, functions and judicial as well as executive powers of the police officers with regard to public assemblies and prescribed punishments for certain offences. It also contained provisions relating to the establishment of Police Superannuation Fund, deployment of additional police in the disturbed areas and payment therefore, servicing of all summonses and warrants and specified penalties for wrongful acts. This Act laid the basis of the police system which is still in force.

In 1902, another Police Commission was appointed by Lord Curzon to make a comprehensive inquiry into the subject and it resulted in the introduction of concrete reforms in the police administration for the whole of British India. The significance of this period lies in the fact that most of the measures adopted at that time still operate in our country. Above all it became the basis on which the subsequent character of the police administration in modern India has been continued. Entry into the Imperial Police was thrown open to Indians only after 1920 and the following year entrance examinations for the service were conducted both in England and India. Indianization of police service continued to be very slow despite pronouncements and recommendations of the Islington Commission and the Lee Commission. Till 1931, Indians were appointed against only 20 per cent of the total posts of Superintendents of Police. However, because of non-availability of suitable European candidates, more Indians were appointed to the Indian Police w.e.f. 1939.

During the period from 1905 to 1947, there started fervent political activity culminating in the struggle for independence for the country which naturally put great strain on the police. It was an irony of history that Indian policemen were pitted against their own countrymen struggling for national independence. This adversely affected police-public relations, because the people got an ever lasting impression that the police were never sympathetic to the aspirations of the people and the police continue to carry this dubious legacy.

The National Police Commission, 1977

Since independence several state governments appointed Police Commissions to improve the working and the image of the police. All these efforts finally culminated in the appointment of a National Police Commission in November, 1977 with wide terms of reference covering the police organization, its role, functions, accountability, relations with the public, political interference in its work, misuse of power, evaluation of its performance etc. This was the first Commission appointed at the national level after independence. The Commission produced eight reports between 1979 and 1981, suggesting wide ranging reforms in the existing police set up. Any arrangement for inquiry into complaints against police should be acceptable both to police and public as fair and just. The Commission therefore suggested arrangements, which would include enquiries conducted by departmental authorities and those conducted by an independent authority outside the police. The Commission felt that a large number of complaints against police should be looked into and disposed off by the supervisory ranks in the police hierarchy. The Commission however, recommended that a judicial inquiry should be made mandatory of complaints against the senior officers of police.

It recommended the establishment of special investigation cell in the police department at state level to monitor the progress of investigation of cases under the Protection of Civil Rights Act or other atrocities against Scheduled Castes and Scheduled Tribes. A composite cell may be constituted at the district level under the Sub-Divisional Officer to inquire into complaints emanating from Scheduled Castes/Tribes, particularly those relating to lapses in administrative measures meant for their relief.

An important cause for dissatisfaction of weaker sections of society is that the police sometimes do not take cognizance of their complaints of ill treatment at the hands of upper castes on the ground that complaints are non-cognizable and therefore cannot be investigated by them without orders from a magistrate. It emphasized that section 155 of the Code of Criminal Procedure should be suitably amended to facilitate appropriate and effective police response to non cognizable complaints in two categories of cases: (i) to protect a member of the weaker section from exploitation and injustice, or (ii) to prevent a possible breach of public peace that might result from absence of effective action on complaint of a non-cognizable offence.

A comprehensive legislation should be enacted setting out the procedure for the allotment of land to landless poor. Police officers from the local police station should be associated with act of handing over possession of land to the landless and a brief record of this should be kept in the police station records.

Sections 2(C) and 2(1) of the Code of Criminal Procedure (Cr.P.C.) should be amended to remove the emphasis on arrest in the definition of cognizable and non-cognizable offences. Moreover, Section 170 of the Code of Criminal Procedure should be amended to remove the impression that it is mandatory to make an arrest in non-bailable cases.

The Commission noted the non-availability of any imprest money in a police station to meet expenditure on several legitimate needs of the station. Therefore, the police stations should be provided with an adequate imprest amount to meet the contingent expenditure in day to day work. Adequate funds should be provided at station level to eliminate causes of corruption, which often engulf even the honest officers.

Victims of crimes are sometimes turned away from a police station on the mere ground that the reported crime has occurred in the jurisdiction of some other police station and it is for the victim to go there and make his complaint. This works to the disadvantage of ignorant people and weaker sections. So it has been recommended that an amendment to section 154 Cr. P.C. making it incumbent on a police station to register an FIR irrespective of the jurisdiction area and to transfer the FIR to the concerned police station. Later on the examination of witnesses should be conducted as far as practicable near the scene of offence or at the residence of witnesses concerned at some convenient place nearby.

To reduce the use of third degree methods, the Commission has recommended that :

- Surprise visits by senior officers to police stations to direct persons held in illegal custody and subjected to ill treatment.

- The magistrate should be required by rules to question the arrested person if he has any complaint of ill treatment by the police and in case of complaint should get him medically examined.
- There should be a mandatory judicial inquiry in cases of death or grievous injury caused in police custody.
- Police performance should not be evaluated on the basis of crime statistics or number of cases solved.
- Training institutions should develop scientific interrogation techniques and impart effective instructions to trainees in this regard.

It is recommended that women police should be strengthened and assigned investigation work in much greater measure in order to become an integral part of the police organization and to deal with crimes against women and children and in tackling the problem of juvenile delinquency. They should in due course share all the duties now performed by their male counterparts. They should be recruited in much larger numbers than at resent, particularly in the ranks of Assistant Sub-inspectors and Sub-inspectors.

Before promotion to the ranks of Superintendent of Police, DIG and IG, all IPS officers should be required to undergo specifically designed pre-promotion courses followed by an examination and an objective selection process. Those who are not able to qualify for the post of DIG and IG even after being given two more chances should be retired from service.

In large urban areas, crime and law and order problems develop rapidly, requiring a speedy and effective operational response from the police. .

During communal riots, adequate interest is not taken in investigation of heinous and serious crimes. For investigation of such cases, special investigating squads under the state CID should be set up comprising officers of proven integrity and impartiality. Vigorous investigation should be followed by prosecution to ensure different punishment to the offenders. Hence, withdrawal from trial of cases occurring during communal riots by the state governments with a view to promoting communal harmony often proves illusory and has to be discouraged.

The Commission has expressed its view against reservation of vacancies in the police for minorities and other weaker sections on the basis of their share in population. The Commission felt that it would fragment the force along caste and communal lines and it goes against the fundamental police philosophy that it must rise above caste and creed and act impartially as the agent of law and order. The composition of the force should reflect the general mix of communities as it exists in the society and thereby command the confidence of different sections of the society.

There should be continuous monitoring of the performance of the police forces in the country. The State Security Commission should have an independent cell to evaluate police performance. The annual administration report of the head of the police force and assessment report of the Central Police Committee will provide additional material to the State Security Commission to prepare a final report on the performance of the state police to be placed before the State Legislature.

The police functionaries individually as well as in groups should be sensilized to the idea of accountability to the police.

National Human Rights Commission

The National Human Rights Commission has taken many independent steps towards police reforms like : it is mandatory to report custodial deaths / rapes within 24 hours to the Commission and to the Police headquarters and a First Information Report (FIR) must be registered in the police station a fixed procedure must now be followed with regard to reporting extra judicial killing within 24 hours, provision to surprise visits to police lock-ups by its members to ensure that suspects spend not more than 24 hours in detention without seeing a magistrate, setting up human rights cells for better police-public relations.

Moreover, there is also a need to educate the people as the citizens are not aware of their rights and duties while interacting with the police, proper training to police officers about human rights.

The Ribeiro Committee on Police Reforms, 1998

The Ministry of Home Affairs, Government of India, set-up a Committee in pursuance of the Supreme Court's directions in 1998. The Committee was headed by J.F. Ribeiro, IPS (Retd.), a former D.G.P. of Punjab.

The terms of reference of the Committee were :– To review action to implement the recommendations of the National Police Commission, National Human Rights Commission, to suggest ways and means to implement the pending recommendations of the above Commissions/ Committee, to consider and make recommendations regarding any other matter which the Government may refer to the Committee or which the Committee considers necessary in this behalf. The Committee suggested in its report that :

- Setting up a Security Commission or Police Authority in each state and at the Centre.
- A prescribed procedure for the appointment of Police Chiefs.
- Insulating the investigation wing of the police from its law and order functions.
- A District Police Complaints Authority be set-up in each district as a non statutory body to examine complaints from the public of police excesses, arbitrary arrests and detention, false implications in criminal cases, custodial violence, etc.

- In every state, a Police Establishment Board should be constituted with the DGP and his four senior-most officer, borne on the IPS cadre of the state but who are immediately junior to the DGP, as members to monitor all transfers, promotions, rewards and punishments as well as other service related issues. The board should be given the legal authority to discharge its duties by amending the relevant Rules. rules should be framed by the government on transfers, tenures, promotions, rewards and punishments and the police authorities designated to administer these rules.
- The DG of Police will be selected by the Chief Minister of the state from a panel of three names prepared by a Committee headed by the Chairman of the UPSC and consisting of the Union Home Secretary, the Director of Intelligence Bureau, the state's Chief Secretary and the state's incumbent DGP.
- The old Police Act of 1861, needs to be replaced by a new Police Act.

The Padmanabhaiah Committee on Police Reforms, 2000

The Padmanabhaiah Committee on Police Reforms was set-up by the Government of India in January 2000. The recommendations of the Committee include :

- Raising the status of the constabulary and improving their service and living conditions.
- Preparing a new Departmental Inquiry Manual and a new Code of Conduct for the police.
- Filing of property returns both by gazetted as well as non-gazetted police officers.
- Improving the in house vigilance within the police department.
- Improving the accessibility of police officers to the public.

- Reviewing the record of arrests made by the police station staff.
- A Police Establishment Board, consisting of the Director General of Police as its chairman and four other members of the police department, should be constituted "to decide the transfers of all officers of the ranks of Deputy Superintendent of Police and above" to prevent the political interference.
- Recognizing the particular vulnerability of police officers, the Committee recommends that all complaints against police personnel should in the first instance be handled by the superior formations in the department itself.

Malimath Committee on Reforms of Criminal Justice, 2002

Government of India set-up a Committee under the chairmanship of Justice V.S. Malimath on reforms of Criminal Justice System. The Committee suggested that :

- The Investigation Wing should be separated from the Law and Order Wing.
- National Security Commission and the State Security Commission at the state level should be constituted.
- The post of an Additional SP may be created exclusively for supervision of a crime.
- Another additional SP in each district should be made responsible for collection, collation and dissemination of criminal intelligence, maintenance an analysis of crime data and investigation of important cases.
- Each state should have an officer of the IGP rank in the state crime branch exclusively to supervise the functioning of the crime police. The crime branch should have specialized squads for organized crime and other major crimes.

- Sessions cases must be investigated by the senior-most police officer posted at the police station.
- Fair and transparent mechanisms shall be set-up in places where they do not exist and strengthened where they exist, at the district police range and state level for redressal of public grievances.
- Police Establishment Boards should be set-up at the police headquarters for posting, transfer and promotion, etc. of the district level officers.
- The existing system of Police Commissioner's office which is found to be more efficient in the matter of crime control and management should be introduced in the urban cities and town.
- Deputy SP level offices to investigate crimes need to be reviewed for reducing the burden of the circle officers so as to enable them to devote more time to supervisory work.
- Criminal cases should be registered promptly with utmost promptitude by the SHOs.

Police Act Drafting Committee, 2005

Government of India has constituted a Committee in September 2005 to draft a new Police Act in view of the changing role/responsibility of police and the challenges especially on account of the growth and spread of insurgency/militancy/naxalism etc. The new Act is also to include measures for attitudinal changes of police working methodology to elicit cooperation and assistance of the community to reflect the expectations of the people. The use of scientific investigation methods to strengthen the criminal justice system, enabling the police to tackle futuristic trends and organized crime including cyber crime and technological additions in the hands of the criminals and to address the concern for human rights, weaker sections, women and the people belonging to Scheduled Castes/Scheduled Tribes.

Proposed Draft of New Police Act

The Police Act Drafting Committee, which was constituted on September 20, 2005 has had 27 meetings and took note of the deterioration in the functioning of the police due to, inter alia, lack of professionalism, undue interferences in police work, frequent arbitrary transfers of the police key functionaries, corruption and the nexus developing between police and mafia. It considered wider perceptions of public about police and has gone through the reports of the earlier Commissions/Committees. It also surveyed the legislations on policing abroad in both developed and developing systems like : England, Northern Island, South Africa, Pakistan and Sri Lanka, with a view to understand emerging policing needs and trends.

Moreover, the Committee had interactions with eminent personalities and experts from relevant fields.

(i) Issues : The Committee focused on a number of issues, including vexed ones, such as :

- Empowering police constabulary;
- Ensuring due attention for investigation work;
- Redefining superintendence and administration;
- Outlining policing patterns for metropolitan areas and the rural areas;
- New challenges of terrorism, organized crimes and extremism;
- Selection and fixing of tenure of key functionaries;
- Performance evaluation;
- Training and research, leading to needed attitudinal changes;
- Prevention of extraneous agencies/forces influencing policing;
- To make the police accountable to their deeds/ misdeeds;
- Improving working and living conditions of police personnel; and

- Emphasizing on care of vulnerable sections of society and on human rights.

(ii) Expected improvements : Some of the expected improvements in policing, envisaged through the proposed new Police Act, are as follows :

- Professionalism in police can be improved by adopting improved methods of investigation and maintenance of public order, with proper performance evaluation and accountability mechanisms;
- The police are re-oriented to be people-friendly and thereby enlist public participation in policing;
- Insulating the policing from undue pressures and interferences;
- Making policing proactive and thereby, effectively meet newer and emerging challenges;
- Mechanisms and methodologies are evolved for meeting the emerging challenges to policing, such as extremism, cyber crime, organized and international crime; and
- Empowering the police, especially the lower functionaries.

It shall be the responsibility of the state government to ensure an efficient, effective, responsive and accountable police service for the people. For this purpose, the superintendence of the police service throughout the state shall vest in and be exercised by the state government in accordance with the provisions of this Act. The state government shall also exercise its superintendence over the police service in such manner and to such extent so as to promote the professional efficiency of the police and to ensure that the police performance is at all times in accordance with the law. This shall be achieved through laying down policies and guidelines, setting standards for quality policing, facilitating their implementation and ensuring that the police perform their task in a professional manner with functional autonomy.

The administration of the police throughout the state shall be vested in the DG and in such ADG, IG, DIG and other officers as appointed under this Act. The administration of police in a district shall vest in the SP. Administration will mean the management of the police service, subject to law, rules and regulations; and will include framing of regulations; supervising the functioning of the police service at all levels; appointment to subordinate ranks of the police, deployment of the police; posting, transfers, and the requisite disciplinary action up to and including the rank of Inspector of police; and advising the government on the placement of officers of the rank of ASP/DSP and above. Provided that the state government may intervene in the exercise of the powers of administration by the DG or any other competent police authority only in accordance with the prescribed rules, regulations or in exceptional situations involving urgent public interest, reasons for which should be recorded in writing.

The Draft Committee proposed that there shall be one police service for each state. Members of the police service shall be liable for posting to any branch of the service including the armed police or any of the specialized wings.

Appointment of Director General

The state government shall appoint a DG who shall exercise such powers and perform such functions and duties and shall have such responsibilities and such authority as may be provided by or under this Act or rules made thereunder.

The post of DG shall be the senior-most position in the hierarchy of the police service of a state and no officer senior or equivalent in rank to the incumbent DG shall be posted to any position within the police organization to ensure that the unity of command is at all times maintained.

Method of Selection and Term of Office of DGP

(1) The state government shall appoint the DGP from amongst three senior-most officers in the police service empanelled for the rank.

(2) The empanelment for the rank of DGP shall be done through the Union Public Service Commission on the basis of following criteria :

- The prescribed length of service;
- The assessment of the performance appraisal reports of the previous 15 years of service on the basis of weightages assigned to different gradings, namely, 'Outstanding', 'Very Good', 'Good' and 'Satisfactory';
- The range of experience relevant to professional police work including experience of work in central police organizations;
- Clean record of service in terms of indictment of the officers in any criminal or disciplinary proceedings or on the counts of corruption or moral turpitude; and
- Due weightage being assigned to award of medals for gallantry, distinguished and meritorious service.

  Provided that the case of any officer against whom a prime facie criminal or disciplinary charge or a charge of lack of integrity has been made out and a trial/enquiry relating thereto is pending, shall be considered only after the disposal of such proceeding.

(3) The DGP so appointed shall have a minimum tenure of two years irrespective of his/her normal date of superannuation. Provided that an incumbent may be removed from the post before the expiry of his/her tenure by the state government through a written order specifying reasons, consequent upon:

- a conviction by a court of law in a criminal offence or in a case of corruption; or
- a punishment of dismissal/removal/compulsory retirement from service or of reduction to a lower post awarded under the provisions of the All India Services (Discipline and Appeal) Rules or any other relevant rule.

Appointment of Legal and Financial Advisor (LFA)

The state government shall appoint a LFA to assist and aid the DGP on legal and financial matters.

Police District

The state government, in consultation with the DG, may by a notification declare any area within the state to be a police district. The administration of the police throughout such district shall vest in the SP who may be assisted by as many Additional, Assistant or Deputy Superintendents as deemed necessary.

The state government may, in consultation with the DG and by notification, create as many police stations in a district as deemed necessary, duly keeping in view the population, the area, the crime situation, workload with respect to the law and order and the distances to be traversed by inhabitants to reach such station.

Tenure of Key Police Functionaries

An officer posted at Station House Officer in a Police Station or as office in-charge of a police circle or sub-division or as SP of a district shall have a term of a minimum of two years and a maximum of three years. Provided that any such officer may be removed from his/her post before the expiry of the minimum tenure of two years consequent upon.

- Promotion to a higher post;
- A conviction by a court of law in a criminal offence; or a punishment of dismissal/removal/discharge/ compulsory retirement from service or of reduction to a lower post awarded under the relevant Discipline and Appeal Rules; or
- Suspension from service in accordance with the provisions of the said Rules; or
- Incapacitation by physical or mental illness or otherwise becoming unable to discharge his/her functions and duties in the appointment.

Every state police organization shall have a State Bureau of Intelligence for coordination, analysis and dissemination of intelligence, and a State Bureau of Crime Investigation for taking up investigation of inter-state, inter-district crimes and other specified offences. The state government shall appoint any police officer not below the rank of IG to head such bureaus.

The state government shall establish a full-fledged Police Training Academy at the state level and as many fully-equipped police training colleges/schools as deemed necessary for ensuring efficient post-induction training of all directly-recruited police personnel in various ranks, pre-promotion training for all those promoted to higher levels and such thematic and specialized in service training course for police personnel of different ranks and categories as deemed necessary from time to time.

The state government may appoint any police officer not below the rank of IG to be the Director of the State Police Academy, and an officer not below the rank of DIG to head each College and an officer not below the rank of SP as the Principal of each Police Training School.

Procedure for Promotion of Police Officers

Promotion to each rank in the police service shall be based on merit which would include seniority, to be evaluated through a combination of the result of a qualifying examination and performance evaluation in respect of each officer. The DG shall frame the evaluation criteria in this regard for each rank and category of police personnel and have them approved by the state government. For the officers of the IPS, such evaluation criteria shall be framed by the Government of India.

Financial Management

The DG shall be responsible for submitting the budgetary requirements of the police service as a whole to the state government, sufficiently in advance in the preceding financial year. The budgetary requirements shall be carefully worked out on the basis of realistic needs of each branch, wing, unit and sub-unit of the police service, obtained from the unit officers concerned. The DSP shall take special care to ensure that the financial requirements of each police station in the district are worked out meticulously and adequately projected in the budgetary demands leaving no scope for the police stations to feel handicapped for meeting the legitimate expenditure on day-to-day police work.

The budgetary allocation made by the legislature shall be placed at the disposal of the DG who shall be vested with full powers to spend the amounts earmarked under each head of the budget. The financial powers of the DG shall be on par with those exercised by Principal Secretary to the state government. The DG and all the other police officers vested with financial powers shall observe utmost propriety and pragmatism in exercising their financial powers.

Role and Functions

The role and functions of the police shall broadly be:

- To act as upholders of the law, and to protect life, liberty, property and human rights of the public;

- To promote and preserve public order;
- To protect internal security, and to prevent and control terrorist activity, breaches of communal harmony, extremist violence, militant activities and other situations affecting internal security;
- To protect public properties including roads, railways, bridges, vital installations and establishments, etc. against acts of vandalism, violence or any kind of attack;
- To prevent crimes and reduce the opportunities for the commission of crimes through their own preventive action and measures as well as by aiding and cooperating with other relevant agencies in implementing due measures for prevention of crimes.
- To investigate all crimes and, where appropriate, to apprehend the offenders, and extend requisite assistance in the prosecution of offenders;
- To create and maintain a feeling of security in community, and to counsel and resolve conflicts and promote amity;
- To provide, as first responders, all possible help and succour to people in situations arising out of natural or man-made disasters, and to provide active assistance to other agencies in relief and rehabilitation measures;
- To aid individuals who are in danger of physical harm to person or property, and to provide necessary services and afford relief to people in distress situations;
- To facilitate orderly movement of people and vehicles, and to control and regulate traffic on roads and highways;
- To collect intelligence relating to matters affecting public peace, crimes including social and economic offences, communalism, extremism, terrorism and other matters relating to national security, and dessiminate the same to all concerned besides acting, as appropriate, on the same themselves.

Working Hours

The state government shall take effective steps to ensure that the average hours of duty of a police does not exceed eight hours a day. Provided that for exceptional reasons the hours duty of a police officer may extend up to 12 hours. In that event adequate compensation and facilities shall be provided to the police officers. The state government shall also ensure that the least one weekly off is provided to all police officer.

Supreme Court Judgement, 2006

The Hon'ble Supreme Court of India ordered to revamp the Indian Police Act, 1861. It has given its decision on the basis of the recommendations of National Public Commission, National Human Rights Commission, the Julio Riberio Committee and the Soli Sorabjee Committee. It was the Writ Petition (Civil) No. 310 of 1996, among the Parkash Singh and others versus Union of India and others.

On 22nd of September 2006, the apex court, in a historic judgement has given order to reform existing criminal justice system in order to establish a better rule of law in the country. It has ordered for some revolutionary changes in the Indian police administration to make it more accountable and over and above the political interference. The Court has issued directives to the Centre as well as states to immediately implement the 7-point directive e.g.

- The directive to separate crime investigation and prosecution process from the maintenance of normal law and order;
- To set-up a national security commission at the Centre and a state security commission at the state level;
- To set-up police establishment board and police complaint authority in every state and at the district levels;
- To restrict the politically interfered transfer and posting of officers when the government changes;

- To fix the tenure of DGPs, IGPs, DIGs and SPs for a minimum fixed tenure of two years;
- Introduce scientific research in crimes;
- The police establishment board will have the power of transfers, postings and promotion of officers below the rank of DSP;
- The National Security Commission will have the power for the selection and posting of chiefs of CPOs. It will take orders from Home Ministry;
- The State Security Commission will work under Chief Minister and DGP as ex-officio secretary;
- The state police complaint authority will work under a retired Supreme Court or high court judge.

Conclusion

The Nation's founding faith is the primacy of the rule of law and the police must be organized to promote the maintenance of rule of law and render impartial and efficient service to people with due concern for human rights and proper safeguards for the interests of vulnerable sections.

It is the duty of the state to provide a professional and service oriented police which has a paramount obligation and duty to function according to the requirements of the Constitution, the rule of law, and the democratic aspirations of the people. The functioning of the police needs to be professionally organized and service oriented, free from extraneous influences and accountable to law. It is expedient to redefine the police role, duties and responsibilities, by taking into account the emerging challenges of policing, the concern for security of the state, good governance, and human rights. It is necessary to appropriately empower the police to enable it to function as an efficient, effective, people-friendly and responsive agency and it is necessary for this purpose to consolidate and amend the law relating to the establishment and management of the police.

REFERENCES

Bhardwaj, R.K., *Indian Police Administration*, New Delhi : National, 1978.

Ghosh, S.K., *Police Administration., Organization and Procedure*, Calcutta: Eastern Law House, 1973.

Misra, S.C., *Police Administration in India*, Mount Abu : National Police Academy, 1970.

Report of the National Police Commission, 1977.

Report of the Riberio Committee on Police Reform, 1998.

Report of the Padmanabhaiah Committee, 2000.

Report of the Malimath Commission on Reforms of Criminal Justice, 2002.

Draft Outline of the New Police Act Drafting Committee, 2005.

Supreme Court Judgement, 2006.

15 E-Governance in the District
A Case Study of Gyandoot

*Navneet Kaur**

"That government is the best that governs the least"
—Mahatma Gandhi.

"Information Technology today is recognized as an effective tool for catalyzing the economic activity in efficient governance and in developing human resource. As the era of Digital Economy evolves, the concept of good governance assumes a greater significance. It is expected that in this context the Electronic Governance will result in improved transparency, speedy information dissemination, higher administrative efficiency and improved public services in sectors including transportation, education, power, health, water, security and the state administration and municipal services."[1]

Introduction

On January 1, 2000, Dhar district began the new millennium with a mass-based information revolution. Computers in 21 major centres in five blocks were connected through an Intranet network. These computers have been established in gram panchayats. They have been called *Soochanalayas*. From the *Soochanalaya*, user-charge based services are given to. the masses and at the same time the information technology

* Lecturer, Computer Science, Khalsa College, Patiala, Punjab.

related developmental needs of government departments and panchayats are met free of cost. This Intranet has been named *Gyandoot*.

The entire expenditure for the *Gyandoot* network has been borne by panchayats. The network has been set up at a total cost of Rs. 25 lakhs. The system is very cost-effective. In the *Gyandoot* scheme of things, the twenty-one centres where *Soochanalayas* have been established cater not only to the twenty-one villages proper but also to surrounding 25 to 30 villages. *Soochanalayas* have been established in the buildings of such gram panchayats which are located either at block headquarters or at prominent *haat bazaar* places or are prominent villages on major roads which are important from the point of the catching bus etc. Thus, each *Soochanalaya* caters to approximately 15 Gram Panchayats and about 25 to 30 villages. The benefits cover wide-ranging information needs of all villagers, not merely those belonging to co-operatives. Thus, the *Gyandoot* network benefits over half a million villagers living in 311 gram panchayats and over 600 villages.

All this has been completed in a short span of less than two months. The trial run of the system began on January 1, 2000 and the system was dedicated to the public by the Chief Minister of Madhya Pradesh, Digvijay Singh at the Deharisarai Soochanalaya on January 12, 2000.

Concept Development and Implementation[2]

In the month of November, 1999 Secretary, Information Technology, M.P. wrote a letter to all the District Collectors in which he asked them to prepare a project for establishing a computer network connecting villages, on the line of "wired villages" project of Warna in Kolhapur district of Maharashtra. After receiving the letter a meeting was called by the District Collector in which C.E.O (ZP), District Information Officer (DIO) and other senior officers were present. In the meeting it was decided that a network based system would be evolved which would connect villages with the district headquarter and initially 15 to 20 villages would be connected on a pilot basis. A core team consisting of the C.E.O (ZP) and others were given responsibility to actually implement this system. Thereafter, 3 meetings were conducted in different villages in which villagers were asked, what services they would like to have through such a network system. The villagers demanded information on *mandi* rates, copies of land records and system of lodging complaints. After these meetings, C.E.O (ZP) and other senior officers held a meeting in which they chalked out the basic design of the system and also about the services which would be provided. This was decided that the services would be provided on payment so that system can be viable and sustainable. Thereafter, Addl. Collector and DIO made of a visit of Warnanagar to learn from "wired villages" project. Learning from Warna were primarily on what should not be done rather than what should be done.

After returning from Warner, team listed out all the activities and probable number of days in which they would be completed. Most crucial among them were Hardware procurement, Software procurement, Land records data entry and operator (Soochak) selection. They also formed a basic team consisting of C.E.O (ZP), Addl. Collector, DIO, Data Entry Operators (DEO) of DRDA, programmer and such persons which were needed in various activities. It was decided to conduct a daily meeting of the basic team to monitor the programme of project implementation and to assign tasks on a daily basis. They fixed time limits for completion of each activities and the person responsible for ensuring completion. Data entry of land records, map digitization and Software development were the activities which had the potential to delay the project. *Gyandoot* is covering 3 tehsils initially which have a total of around 4 lakhs 78 thousand khasara entries. It was a massive data entry job. First they assigned the work to a data entry firm which developed the software for data entry and also entered the land record data for the villages where *Soochanalayas* are located and nearby 3-4 villages, so that project could be launch in time. The balance data entry work is now divided among the data entry firm and Soochaks. It is additional source of income for the Soochaks. For software development they decided on two firms. They provided them with all our requirements and formats for various software modules like complaint module, HMIS, PMTS, EMIS, Mandi rate module, etc. The software development work was finished in time. They launched the Gyandoot project on the beginning of the new millennium according to the schedule. So the project was completed less than two months.

GYANDOOT : A CRITICAL ANALYSIS

Components of Gyandoot[3]

Soochanalayas

Soochanalayas are 21 client sites I nodes working as rural cybercafe-cum-cyberoffices. Each *Soochanalaya* provides services to about 15 gram panchayats, 25 to 30 villages, 20,000 to 30,000 population. The intranet will cover 5 out of 13 blocks in the district and 3 out of 7 tehsils in the district in the initial phase. The *Soochanalayas* are located on the roadside and are central villages where people normally travel. These *Soochanalayas* cater to over half a million villagers in 311 gram panchayats and about 600 revenue villages.

Soochanalayas have telephone line connectivity to begin with. The hardware is procured and given to the gram panchayat under agreement with the zila panchayat. The gram panchayat in turn gives it for operation to the *Soochak* under agreement. The gram panchayat provides, readies and maintains the building where the *Soochanalaya* is housed. It also provides the telephone and electric connection as well as the furniture.

Soochana Kosh

Server/hub is a Remote Access Server (RAS) housed in the computer room in zila panchayat to be called *Soochana* Kosh.

Soochak

An important aspect of the scheme is that the person selected to operate the *Soochanalaya* is a local youth from the same village who was trained to run the *Soochanalaya.* These operators, called *Soochaks* have not been given any employment. Instead, they will run the *Soochanalaya* on commercial lines and generate income and livelihood for themselves. *Soochak* is not an employee but an entrepreneur. *Soochak* only needs maintenance and numeric data entry skills. He needs very limited typing skills since most of the intranet software is menu-driven. He is similar to an STD booth operator. Most of the youth selected for *Soochanalayas* had never seen a computer. They were all trained at the zila panchayat. They were given 7 days training in three stages at their own expenses by computer operators of DRDA. The *Soochaks* were selected interactively by gram panchayat along with representatives from the zila panchayat. Three member panels were selected who received training at their own cost at the zila panchayat. At the end of the training, the best trainees were selected as *Soochaks.* He/she will run the *Soochanalaya* at his own cost. He will be working according to an initial one year agreement with the gram panchayat. He will not receive any salary. He will bear the cost of stationery, maintenance and electric and telephone bills. He will pay 10 per cent of income as commission to the zila panchayat for maintaining the net. Each *Soochak is* expected to earn a net income of at least Rs. 24,000 per annum at conservative projections.

The relevant village level workers of various concerned departments, gram panchayat secretaries, etc. have also been given computer training. Meetings of panchayat representatives of all their tiers have been organised and they have been briefed about the facilities available. Various concerned district, tahsil and Block level officers have also been given extensive training.

Hardware[4]

A Pentium 111 Random Access Server (RAS) has been set-up in the computer room of the zila panchayat. The 21 *Soochanalayas* have been equipped with Pentium multimedia colour computer along with dot matrix printers. The entire intranet has a three-year guarantee period during which any complaints would be attended within 24 hours by the system engineer and if the problem cannot be solved the computer will be replaced with another standby computer. Full specifications are as follows :

Server : RAS P 111 450 MHz CPU, 128 MB ECC RAM, 2 × 9 Ultra SCSI HDD, 2 MB Graphic Controller, Card 15" colour monitor, 48 × CD-ROM Drive, 4 Port Serial Card, Keyboard, Mouse.

Clients : 19 Pentium Celeron 433 MHz CPU, 32 MB RAM, 4.3 GB HOD, 1.44 MB FDD, 4 MB AGP card,14" Colour monitor, 48 × CD-ROM with Multimedia kit, Keyboard, Mouse.

Modems : 19 + 5 (at server end) = 24 external modems 56.6 KBPS.

Printers: 19 132 column, 240 CPS, 9 pin DMPs.

UPS : 19 off-line UPS with 24 Volt Exide battery built-in 160 Volt AVR 120 Ampere Hour capacity sufficient for 5 hour back-up with printer 8 hour charging time.

CD Writer : HP 4×CD Writer/Rewriter

Software[5]

Aside from the software which has been designed for the

intranet and the internet, the following the pre-manufactured software have also been used —

Microsoft Windows NT Server
Microsoft Windows 98 Operating System
Microsoft SQL Server
Visual Basic
Java Development Kit
Microsoft Access
C-DAC's ISM fonts

Impact : Costs and Benefits

Costs for the initial system were around US $50,000, paid by the locall-village government units. This does not include the set-up costs of the kiosks since the first 20 soochaks funded these costs through bank loans; nor does it include the operational costs which soochaks are supposed to meet from the fees they charge. They should also pay 10 per cent of their income to the local government unit. The 18 later kiosks were set up as private enterprises, paying a US$100 annual license fee to the district government.

Overall, the Gyandoot system has not really worked as intended. It has delivered some infrequent transparency benefits. In the past, citizens often had to pay bribes in order to have public services performed; some groups (from lower castes, or the disabled) faced discrimination and the humiliation of being ignored or their applications rejected; and most faced the prospect of losing a day's wages plus paying transport costs each time they were forced to visit district headquarters. The Gyandoot system has—in a few places, at a few times, for a limited range of services—replaced this with a lower-cost, faster, and more transparent service. Corrupt "under-the-counter" payments to public servants have, occasionally, been replaced by transparent payments to private sector kiosk operators. Transport costs, wage losses and discrimination have been reduced on some occasions—a particular benefit for the poor. The public availability of welfare scheme lists has brought sporadic transparency benefits, enabling a few families to correct their omission from the lists.

A majority of Gyandoot's few users seem positive about it, but when asked—they see by far the main impact of the project as its improvement of their understanding of ICTs. There is a perception among many users that Gyandoot has reduced corruption, and improved transparency. Yet, at the same time, those users continue to see a need for bribes to be paid.

Live Work at Soochanalaya

In part this relates to the fact that some services have not been deliverable as initially intended. For example, it was intended that land records would be deliverable via the kiosk without needing to involve officials. However, since such records lacked an authorised signature, they were not accepted as an official document by banks and other agencies. The system has thus been adjusted. In some cases applicants merely apply via the kiosk and are then emailed with a date when they can travel to a government office to pick up their land record. In other cases, the record can be printed at the kiosk, but must then be signed by a government official. This may bring some benefits of reduced travel, but the intended disintermediation has not occurred. Indeed, there are complaints that adding the kiosk into the equation has merely added to the complexity and cost of the process.

A similar result has prevailed with public grievances — some are dealt with online, but in other cases the applicant must appear in person, in which case Gyandoot just functions as a system of complaint registration and appointment-making. There could be some improvements since speed of response to document requests, grievances, etc. is monitored by the government's management information system. In practice, though, 90 per cent of those submitting grievances via Gyandoot felt their complaint had not been satisfactorily resolved.

There has also been a growth in problems associated with Gyandoot over time, limiting even potential benefits still further. A number of kiosks lie idle for significant periods of time: around one-third appear to be permanently closed;

many others are closed for hours or days at a time. Lack of electricity is one cause, as are ongoing telecommunications problems. Limited income and, related, the commitment of kiosk operators is another cause of closure.When kiosks are open, service response times are often poor because hardware capacity is limited, and because several kiosks may attempt to access services at the same time when the electricity comes on.

In some communities, particularly those not close to district headquarters; this has led to a message of unreliability spreading about Gyandoot, further undermining use and sustainability of the service. This vicious circle is strengthened by the fact that some information on the system is not regularly updated. One quarter of users reported sustaining losses in their produce sales because they had based those sales on prices accessed via Gyandoot that turned out to be out-of-date. As a result, usage levels of the kiosks are incredibly low - typical usage levels are just one Gyandoot user every two-three days.

As a result of all these problems, some of the kiosk operators have lost confidence, since they depend on Gyandoot's proper functioning to earn their living. They are concerned about their lack of income and concerned that communities now suspect them of deliberately holding back information or services in order to try to extract bribes. As one *soochak* commented:

> "First of all Gyandoot should try to fulfil the promised services to the people effectively before going in for further additions, as due to the ineffective functioning of the present facilities and utilities the credibility of the project as well as ours *(the soochaks)* are at stake. People feel that we *[soochaks]* deliberately do not avail information in the right time, to earn extra from the community".

This reflects the way in which—when *Gyandoot* functions—the *soochak* partly replaces village or district officials as a key gatekeeper in the lives of villagers. This in itself, though, has led to problems. Some villagers have been unwilling to use kiosks where the operator was a woman; in two other cases, the *soochak* has barred lower-caste villagers from using *Gyandoot*.

Services Offered by *Gyandoot*

In all the *Soochanalaya* villages, three meetings each were organised with the villagers where in-depth participatory appraisal was done. The design of the services provided was a result of this interactive exercise and was based upon the advice and the felt needs of the villagers. In these meetings, it was learned that due to lack of information regarding the proper *mandi* rates not only in the local *mandis* but in the benchmark *mandis* (where the local *mandi* trader sells his own purchases), the farmers are unable to get the best price for their agricultural produce. Villagers also informed that copies of land records are difficult to obtain since the *patwari is* often on tour and one *patwari is* responsible for several villages. The villager needing a copy of the land records has to go out in search of the *patwari* who may or may not be available on that particular day at his headquarters. For small complaints or for giving applications, people had to go to block, *tehsil* or district headquarters which resulted in waste of time, money and potential livelihood earnings.

From the *Soochanalayas*, rates of grains and vegetables of nearly a dozen *mandis*, copies of revenue maps or *khasras* or B1 may be obtained. In addition, income certificates, caste certificates, domicile certificates, demarcation applications, applications for obtaining landholder's loan passbook (rin *pustika)*, etc. may be sent on-line. On the preparation of the desired certificate/*rin pustika,* the information will be sent through email to the concerned *Soochanalaya.* These will be prepared in a maximum period of 10 days although the attempt will be to provide them much earlier. Complaints regarding government schemes/programmes/institutions/employees may also be sent through the net and in a maximum period of seven days, preferably less, reply regarding their disposal will be sent back to the concerned *Soochanalaya.*

List of Services Offered by Gyandoot[6]

Sl. No	*Services and Prices*	*Description*
1.	Mandi Prices (Rs. 5)	The variety-wise current and prevailing rates of prominent cereal crops like wheat, gram, soybean, etc. at local and other prominent auction centres of the country.
2.	Income Certificate (Rs. 10)	Application made to local revenue court to certify the citizen's income.
3.	Domicile Certificate (Rs. 10)	Application made to local revenue court to certify the citizen's domicile.
4.	Caste Certificate (Rs. 10)	Application made to local revenue court to certify the citizen's caste.
5.	Landholder's Passbook (Rs. 10)	Application for getting demarcation done or for obtaining landholder's loan passbook ('*Rin Pustika*')

(contd...)

(contd...)

6. Rural Hindi E-mail (based on word length).	E-mail, in the regional language, with all the features and facilities of a state-of-the-art web based e-mail.
7. Grievance Redressal (Rs. 10)	Filing a complaint to the district administration, with assurance of reply within a maximum period of seven days. After redressal, response sent back at the Soochanalaya through e-mail. Complaints can be about drinking water, scholarship sanction/ disbursement, quality of seed/ fertiliser, employee establishment matters, queries, functioning of school, public distribution system, beneficiary oriented schemes, functioning of village committee etc.
8. Forms of Govt Schemes	Application formats for the villagers applying for schemes.
9. BPL Family List (Rs. 10)	The complete list of Below the Poverty Line families.
10. Employment News (Free)	Employment news for semi skilled employees.
11. Rural Matrimonial (Rs. 25)	Matrimonial service for the villagers to choose the right match for a prospective bride/groom. Every request is added to a centralized database with search facility on various criteria.
12. Rural Market (Rs. 25 to participate in auction and Rs. 10 to browse through)	Auction facilities for farmers and villagers for land, agricultural machinery, bullocks, equipment or other durable commodities.
13. Rural Newspaper (Free)	A local web-based newspaper catering to the rural people. The newspaper delivers micro-news about the happenings around the villages, with Soochaks as corres pondents.
14. Advisory Module (Free)	For farmers and villagers to inquire about latest techniques, advice for their problems, new technologies etc. from a group of experts

(contd...)

(contd...)

	pertaining to fields of agriculture, animal husbandry, health, or related to legal opinion.
15. E-education	Reading material for students containing syllabus of class X and XII, question banks developed by a team of experts and mailing facility to keep in touch with other intranet connected schools.
16. Driving License	
17. Khasra Nakal Avedan	Application for copy of Khasra needed by farmers.
18. Varmi Compost Khad	Application for fertilizer booking.
19. Board Exam Result	Results of examinations conducted by the State Board for V, VIII, X and X11 standards.
20. Information on International News	Summarized information on International news.
21. Naksha Test	

Expansion of Services

Brief profile of the Recent Additions to the Gyandoot Intranet[7]

Gram Daak: E-mailing software which is all set to become the Hotmail for villagers. Working in their local language, it has all the features and facilities of a state of the art web based E-mail. In addition to this, *Gram Daak* also has a client version which works locally at the Gyandoot *Soochanalayas* end has message queuing facility. On getting connected it transfers all the mails in the out-box to the Gyandoot server and receives the incoming ones stored therein. This reduces the burden on the perennially disturbed telephone connectivity.

Expansion in availability of rates for more *mandis* and more crops : State Mandi Board has begin supplying rates of wheat on the *Gyandoot* intranet for another 23 mandis over and above the initial 13 mandis whose rates were provided earlier for varieties and crops. The Board will be adding informatoin of rates of other varieties crops also soon for the new 23 mandis. Rates of 9 more varieties/crops have been added over and above the inetial 15. Thus, rate of 24 crops/varieties from 13 mandis and rates of wheat fron 36 mandis are now available.

Government sponsored loan project preparation and submission : Villagers who seek government sponsored loans may get a project report prepared for occupations in the approved shelf of loan projects at the nearyby *Soochanalaya* as and submit them their itself with necessary supporting documents for forwarding to banks/lending agency in case of the *Swarnjayanti Gram Swarojgar Yojana* (SGSY-the recast IRDP). The citizen need not hunt professionals for project preparation or chase files from extension workers to desks, offices and sponsoring committees. The correct project may be prepared, approved and forwarded to the banks/lending agencies with reply assured within two week by visiting a *Soochanalays* for a modest for a modest fixed fee of Rs. 25. It is planned to cover all other government loan schemes too. Shelf of 96 projects is already available on the intranet.

- *Information regarding government programmes:* Detailed Information regarding over a hundred government programmes is now available on the Gyandoot intranet.
- *Mandi Information Centre:* From 22nd June Dhamnod mandi has been linked with gyandoot. Besides hourly only mandi rates it will provide local weather report and information/documentaries of new techniques and technologies in agriculture/horticulture or allied activity will be available. The farmers can see them from a 29" television put up in the centre of mandi. It is estimated that around 800-1000 farmers will be benefited from this facility every day. The project will eventually link and create similar facility in Dhar, Badnawar and Rajgarh mandi as well.

Vaivahika : An online matrimonial application for the villagers to choose the right match for a prospective bride/ groom. Every entry from a *Soochanalaya* by a villager gets added on to a centralised Dhar database which when searched would provide accurate results. The program has been generated by keeping the parametres of the villagers in mind. The Patidar and Jain Samaj have already agreed to place their matrimonial here.

Developmental Benefits

Gyandoot describes a number of examples where farmers have been able to secure better prices for their crops by taking their goods to a local market offering the highest prices, and by cutting out local middlemen. Farmers in Bagadi village, for example, were getting a rate of 300 rupees ($6) per quintal from local traders for their potato crop. On getting the rate slip from their local Gyandoot information kiosk, they could not believe that the current rate in Indore market was 400 rupees ($8) per quintal. So they hired a truck to take their produce to Indore - one hour away (50 km).

- There has been increased awareness about computers and IT in rural areas, which resulted into *openings of new private computer training institutions* and the enrolment in such institution, has increased by 60 per cent. The effect has opened a totally new horizon of employment avenues for the rural youth. Demand for computer training has increased significantly.
- Results have been impressive: introducing *transparency and accountability* into the inner working of local government. The efficiency level in the functioning of the government departments has increased manifold producing better and prompt services to people.
- Self-Help Groups in the rural areas are getting more

organised and empowered due to transparency brought about in the government services and rural economy e.g. *Farmers' Association* in village Kod are demanding a new kiosk in the village.

- The *lower government functionaries have become computersavy*: This is apparent from increased number of applications for computer loans from Employees Provident Fund and increased number of officials who have joined computer-training classes.
- *Computer literacy has increased in the rural areas.* This is evident from the fact.

Perception of the people for Gyandoot[8]

Overall e-Governance Scores
(on a scale of 1 to 10, for each parameter)

Parameter 2005	*Score*
Ease of Use	9.5
User-ship	8.7
Speed of Delivery	8.8
Simplicity of Procedures	8.4
Time Savings Compared to Manual	9.6
Single Window Access to Many Services	4.5
Low Incidence of Errors	8.0
Speed of Rectification of Errors	6.4
Alignment with User Expectations	9.0
Affordable Cost of Service	9.1
Reduction in Corruption	8.6
Staff Behaviour	8.3
Staff Competence	8.6

The most important aspect is the citizen's perception towards the working of the Gyandoot project. This study was conducted by IIM Ahmedabad. Although the above table shows the excellent results of the project but the darker side is how many people have utilized these services.

Are they practically viable?

General Problems

Constraints/Challenges

- *Infrastructure.* This is a significant constraint in some parts of the district, particularly those more then 5 km from district headquarters. The UPS batteries have a charge-up time between four and eight hours. But in some villages, there is only an hour or two electricity per day, making Gyandoot operation only sporadic. There have also been connectivity problems with the intranet in some centres, combined with the problem of poor response times. The kiosk can easily get into a spiral of declining use and declining income that undermines its sustainability.
- *Rotation of senior staff.* An enthusiastic senior team is a critical success factor for e-transparency projects. However, in government service, staff are often rotated to another job after just a couple of years. This brings in a new team who will have far less ownership of, and thus perhaps less enthusiasm for, the projects started by their predecessors. When the District Collector and other key staff moved on, new incumbents proved less committed to a project they themselves had not initiated.
- *Process delays.* The Gyandoot system acts largely as a communication vehicle—it does not automate the core processes of creating documents, dealing with grievances, etc. These processes remain subject to the usual bureaucratic delays, corruption, and inconsistencies. This has also affected the updating of information for the Gyandoot system.
- *Financial sustainability.* The average Gyandoot—generated income for the kiosk operators is around US $35 per year. Their calculated breakeven point is nearer to US $100 per year. As a result, the soochaks

have been driven to attempt other income-generating ideas. In some cases, this has involved closure of their kiosks as they seek their fortunes in other ways.[9]

Recommendations

- *In-built e-Governance in all projects:* It is now critical more than ever to in-built e-Governance into all projects that have clear deliverables to the citizens. Rural Employment Guarantee Plan and the Right to Information would be an immediate case in point.
- *Even rural projects are reporting high ease of use:* Out of the projects visited, all were working well with power backups and connectivity options. While in some areas specialized technology solutions may be required, the emphasis should remain on functionality and what citizens want at the outset. At times too much focus is found to be given to the choice of technology very early on in the planning stage of a project diffusing focus from the really important issues.
- *Penetration is the key :* Less than a fraction percentage of the country's population is covered by such projects. While initiatives like Common Citizen Services Centers, etc. can play a major role in increasing accessibility; this does not diminish the importance of the domain ministries and local self-governance bodies getting computerized. There have to be services at the back end for the front end common service centers to deliver.
- *The spending on e-governance has to go up substantially:* Two per cent of the plan expenditure should be spent on the IT to enable the plan. While some such guideline already exists, it does not seem to be currently followed. This becomes increasingly important in light of the country's move towards outcome based budgeting.

- *Scaling and replication is a crying need :* Even with very good scores most of the projects evaluated by us so far would still qualify as only pilots. There are only a minuscule number of nationally rolled out projects. Speed of implementation would be another area requiring improvement as most such projects currently take forever to get implemented.

Evaluation : Failure or Success

Gyandoot was awarded the Stockholm Challenge Award for 2000 in the Public Service and Democracy category, and a Computer Society of India/Tata Consultancy Services National IT award for best IT usage in 2000.

These awards should be seen as justifiable recognition for design innovation, relevance and potential. However, longer-term evaluation shows that the project has fallen well short on all of its—admittedly over-ambitious—objectives. It should be described as largely unsuccessful. It has identified a model by which transparency of government information and services could be increased, and corruption, discrimination and other costs reduced. It has also made very occasional progress towards these ends. However, it faces a number of practical difficulties that have constrained the benefits delivered to date.

The details provided in this case are drawn particularly from an evaluation undertaken in 2002 by a team from Action Aid India, which visited the Gyandoot main centre plus three kiosks in outlying villages. Evidence has also been drawn from an even more comprehensive evaluation conducted in 2002 by a team from the Centre for Electronic Government, IIM-Ahmedabad. One main contrast the Action Aid India team found was between views about the project expressed by state officials, and those expressed by villagers.

The main reason why did projects like Gyandoot, which created so much of expectations and hype, fail to deliver? Is it poor conceptualization or poor implementation? Or is it the problem of technology or failure of people and process? However, it is not easy to ascertain the reasons for failures of these e-governance projects and give a generic explanation; mostly, it is the combination of some or all the factors mentioned here.

Many e-governance projects fail on account of improper conceptualization and subsequently, tardy implementation. Further, even if a project is sound on paper, it meets its waterloo on account of lack of stake-holder's involvement. The vested interest amongst the stakeholders also adds to it. Further, often IT departments or user departments, to show an immediate result, do not follow the proper life cycle of a project and they jump to a live project without even successful completion of a pilot project. Conversely, some projects do not go beyond the pilot stage on account of intrinsic problems associated with conceptualization of the project. And if a pilot project is scaled up to a live one-without achieving its critical mass—it is bound to reach its grave sooner or later.

Another problem with the e-governance initiatives is that most of them are driven by individuals and these projects lose steam after the e-champion leaves the individual department. Further, at times the objectives and goals set for these projects are so ambitious and diffused that it becomes impossible to achieve them and satisfy all the stakeholders.

NOTES AND REFERENCES

1. C-DAC
2. Ideasforgov.org
3. Department of Rural Development, Government of Madhya Pradesh.
4. Department of Information Technology, Government of Madhya Pradesh
5. Ibid.
6. A cost benefit evaluation study by IIM Ahmedabad.
7. Ibid.
8. Ibid.
9. Alok Kumar Sanjay and Vivek Gupta, e-government for development case study, Department of Information Technology, Govt. of Madhya Pradesh.

GLOSSARY OF TERMS

10 lacs=1 million Rs. 50 = USD 1

Civil Supplies Department: The government department responsible for the distribution of foodgrains and other supplies through fair price shops, to the citizens. It also issues ration cards to the citizens, wherein allocation of food grain is mentioned on the basis of the income of the family.

DRDA (District Rural Development Authority): The government department, which administers schemes oriented towards rural development and uplift of the rural poor.

Gram Panchayat: A 10-15-member council at the village level, with 15-20 villages in its jurisdiction. The state of Madhya Pradesh has a three-tier decentralized system of management in rural areas, with the gram panchayat forming the third-tier. Dhar district has 668-gram panchayats.

IAS: Indian Administrative Service: An elite stream of bureaucrats in the Indian government system. It was formally constituted in 1947. The IAS handles affairs of the government. At the central level, this involves the framing and implementation of policy. At the district level, it is concerned with district affairs, including development functions. At the divisional level, the IAS officers look after law and order, general administration and development work.

Janpad Panchayat : A decentralized council of 15-25 members, at the block (collection of 200-250 villages) level, forming the second-tier in the three-tier set-up. Dhar district has 13 Janpad panchayats.

Khasra: A paper document, issued by the district administration, and contains a description of the land parcel (stony, type of soil, etc.), ownership details, crop description and sources of irrigation for that piece of land. A unique survey number, given by the government, identifies each khasra.

Mandi: The agriculture produce market found in towns or districts of India. They are generally cooperatives and are autonomous.

Patwari: Government appointed village accountant.

Purdah: A veil, which covers the head and face of women. This centuries-old tradition is prevalent in certain parts of rural India today.

RTO (Regional Transport Office): The government department, which looks after the surface transport sector. It issues driving licenses, registers vehicles, collects vehicle tax, etc.

Sarpanch: Head of the gram panchayat.

Soochanalaya: A kiosk registered with the Gyandoot samiti. It has a computer and is provided connectivity to the Gyandoot Intranet server.

Soochak: The person who owns or manages the Gyandoot soochanalaya.

Tehsil: A group of 50-100 villages, which has an administrative control over these villages.

16 District Administration in 21st Century

*B.L. Sah**

Introduction

District administration constantly changes with changes in the philosophy of state, objectives of government and values of people. It is a dynamic apparatus of state, not a static instrument. Values of society have undergone drastic change and a new society and a new man with lofty ambitions and vaulting desires have emerged.

To be effective, public organizations will need to be increasingly more responsive. The key to responsiveness is organizational adaptability to change. The processes of social, economic and political change will continue to accelerate in the 21st century making it vitally important that organizations adapt themselves to changed conditions. The district administrators must learn to anticipate social, economic and political changes and capitalise on these. The administration at present has become an all-pervasive affair through political direction, economic management, social engineering and increased bureaucratization. However, there is growing public resentment and hostility towards increase in bureaucratization as reflected in the increasing demand for decentralization, democratization and public participation in administration. "Unless the administrative system is geared to keep pace with cultural transformation, social discontent, alienation and violence may ultimately lead to

* Reader, Kumaun University, Nainital, Uttaranchal.

the breakdown of the social fabric.[1] Besides, reflection on reinventing district administration in the 21st century is also necessitated by the changing socio-economic and political contexts and the new challenges facing the state and consequent onus of administrative responsibility to be borne by district administration.

As society progresses, the processes of societal change throw up new themes and challenges that widen the scope of district administrative studies. 'Environment and ecology', for instance, is a major concern calling for action at both international and national levels. Pollution monitoring and antipollution measures, conservation programmes for our forests, river and water bodies, and bio-diversity generally are important items today for imaginative policy and administrative responses.

Another important theme is the 'gender' issue in administration. Female participation in work force has been increasing over the years, calling for administrative changes in compensation and welfare policies and other related issues (e.g. sexual harassment at workplace). In the context of the developing countries, 'engendering' development by involving more and more women in development activities, has now been accepted as a general policy by the donor agencies and the recipient countries' governments. Again, issues like prevention and abolition of child labour, untouchability, bonded labour, and other obnoxious social practices are increasingly claiming administrative action.

Contemporary Developments

The relationship between administration and society has never remained static. Emergence of new social situations has always impacted on administration. For instance, the care of the aged is passed on to local government agencies or NGOs. Similarly, any new administrative attempt to influence or change social behaviour has often evoked varied responses from the society.

In recent times, two major administrative paradigms have opened up new relationship between administration and society. One the Neo-liberal vision-poses what is familiarly known as the State vs. Market debate. There has been a realisation of late in the developed. West that formal government has over the years taken upon itself more administrative burden than it can actually shoulder. This has resulted in big bureaucracy, more taxation, and overall governmental inefficiency. To get out of this 'governmental overload', the advocacy has been for lean and more performance-oriented government through 'downsizing' and 'privatization' of many of the government functions. The market is capable of working more flexibly and cost-effectively; hence, government should reorient itself as an 'enabler' rather than a 'doer'. The New Public Management philosophy that has emerged in recent times favours more market-driven development than state or government driven development. This is expected to release more social energy and allow for autonomous societal action.

The other paradigm that has gained currency is 'governance'. The totality of a country's ability to grapple with and solve collective problems is subsumed in the concept of governance. It is an amalgam of the formal government, the private sector and the non-government agencies. In this way, the ambit of district administration is sought to be enlarged. All the traditions and institutions of authority exercised in a society are thus put together to connote the total governing resource that is available to cope with the complex problems of collective problem solving. Also, the 'governance' besides extending the boundaries of administration, brings in additional dimensions of, 'accountability', 'openness', 'transparency', 'participation', and the notion of ethical administration. What is significant in this characterization of administration as 'governance' is the newly emerging administration society relationship under which formal administration is called upon to forge networked functioning to optimise administrative effectiveness. The trend now is thus to democratize administration, and make it more and more society-centric and citizen-friendly.

Another new development in this context that deserves special mention is a major on-going effort to create conditions to bring about a more 'inclusive' district administration, as against an 'exclusive' one. What it means is that there is a fairly widespread concern now to make government more 'decentralized', 'participative', 'gender-sensitive' and 'sensitive to the needs of the socially marginalized'. In other words, the traditional insularity of state apparatuses (e.g., bureaucracy) from the society is now under question and the trend seems toward closer state-society nexus in the interest of more effective and real democracy deeply embedded in society and faithfully serving its just causes.

Norms Governing the Interaction between Citizens and District Administration

In the field of development administration, the client is differentiated on the basis of target groups. There are projects that are meant for tribals, children and women, scheduled castes and other socially backward classes. Clientele differentiation increases the complexities of interaction between district administration and the public. In the developing countries, it is the poor and the underprivileged that constitute the majority of the population. National projects are implemented by the state concerned mainly through the district administration. These implementers/ bureaucracies treat the target groups as 'beneficiaries'. Such a top-down delivery system has, in most cases, failed to ameliorate the living conditions of the target groups, mainly because of hijacking of benefits and resources by the district elite.

The centrally planned projects have often disregarded

and misinterpret the local needs and conditions. Interaction between people and government, especially in dealing with poverty, has generally been looked at from the government's point of view, making the poor more and more dependent on the government for help. Field researchers are now forcefully arguing that developing people's capacity to improve their lot is what is needed rather than repeated governmental efforts to design newer and newer projects.

As Frances Korten has stated "The very ability of the poor to survive under the most unfavourable circumstances suggests that they are quite skilled in meeting their own basic needs even if only at standards intolerable to a socially conscious society. Too often the government programmes seek to improve their lot, not through interventions intended to strengthen their own capacity for 'self-help' action, but through doing for them, what they previously did for themselves—with the government making the decisions and providing the resources. As a consequence, the people's former self-sufficiency turns into dependence on the government leaving them even more vulnerable than before to the changes in the policies or lapses in the delivery systems."[2]

Participatory and people-centred development activities are now being advocated and actively undertaken for the real benefits of the people. It would also create good image of public administration in the minds of the poor and the underprivileged sections of the society. The relationship between district administration and the citizens raises a number of important issues regarding the role of the government machinery and its interactions with the public.

As Katz and Danet explain in their volume on Bureaucracy and the Public, the structure of bureaucratic organizations that subsume a set of guiding norms governing the relationships between the organization and the clientele.[3] These norms are identified as: (a) Specificity, (b) Universalism, and (c) Affective Neutrality. Specificity refers to the strictly limited zone of interaction between administration and the clients as formally defined by the organization. In a public transport the passenger pays the fare and the conductor assures him a travel up to a definite distance. Universalism stand for equal treatment of defined group as organizationally prescribed. For instance, every bus passenger will have to pay the same fare for the same distance and the conductor is duty bound to behave uniformly in each case. Affective Neutrality means exhibition of unbiased attitude toward the client, and by implication, non-display of the passions or feelings like anger, affection, etc.

Besides, a certain set of factors assume importance in any government-citizen interaction. These are : the 'manner', the 'procedures', and the 'resources' exchanged. Manner refers to the behavioural transaction in an interactional situation. How does the government officer talk to or receive a member of the public, say in a post office? Procedures refer to the administrative processes involved in an interaction. How many forms one has to fill up? How long does one have to stand in a queue before a bank counter, for instance? The Resources exchanged denote the outcome of interaction. Could a person ultimately withdraw money from his savings bank account? Did a person get the building permission from the municipality? The structural norms and the three dimensions of interactions are useful conceptualizations for empirical examination of bureaucracy-client relationships in specific situations.[4]

Environment and Citizens' Concerns

There is a worldwide recognition now that in order to survive on the planet Earth, it is very important that the delicate balance between the human beings and their natural habitat i.e., the environment should not be disturbed. Unfortunately, the modern human being is trying hard to be the master of the natural world. As a result, we have invited a host of problems like ecological imbalance, environmental degradation, depletion of flora and fauna and deteriorating human health. The environment includes water, air and land, human beings, other living creatures, plants, micro-organisms and property (Environment Protection Act, 1986). There is a need to choose appropriate methods and development technologies to reduce or eliminate environmental imbalances and adopt an alternative and sustainable development path to achieve this objective. This interdependence is a fundamental development, and it is essential to recognize it as integral to the desired transformation of the society.

The participatory approach to development should include women as equal stakeholders with the men. Rural women have to bear the brunt of drudgery as they are generally more dependent on forest resources. They have to meet many responsibilities like collecting and processing of the fuel wood, fodder, food, water, etc. These women, thus, have vested interests in conservation and improvement of the forest resources. If drought occurs, it is the women who face the consequences as a result of non-availability of drinking water, fodder, fuel wood, and local employment opportunities, more adversely than men who migrate into other towns and cities in search of livelihood.

Social participation to managing forest-land resource or Joint Forest Management (JFM} has drawn the attention of multilateral donor agencies. The World Bank's forestry projects that are providing substantial support include the important component of social participation. The major features of these projects are:

- Equal representation of women in decision-making,
- Equity in representation of all sections of the society and a special provision for the underprivileged,
- Demarcation of JIM area,
- Legal status to the social groups and the powers delegated to there; and
- Equal distribution of user-rights amongst all the

sections. If the agencies concerned to implement the environmental laws fail in doing so, citizen have the right to sue the polluter in the form of three civil remedies,

- A common law tort action against the polluter,
- A writ petition to compel the agency to enforce the law, and
- A citizens' suit to enforce statutory compliance.[5]

Public Interest Litigation (PIL) has opened a new era in judicial administration. Through PIL, even citizens who are not directly affected by pollution can file a law suit in the public interest. In this regard, the role of the higher judiciary i.e, the High Court and the Supreme Court has undergone a radical and creative transformation. The Supreme Court, in this process has interpreted the Right to Life and Personal Liberty to include the Right to a Wholesome Environment. The apex court has even gone to the extent of appointing expert committees, and based on their findings, has given direction for closure of the polluting industries, and so on.

District Administration has to contribute substantially to environmental protection by undergoing necessary attitudinal changes, facilitating institution building and people's participation, adopting holistic and long-term perspective to prevent negative ramifications in the human sphere and on future generations, preparing in depth and environmental feasibility studies on prospective legislation and ensuring an effective feedback to analyse environmental implications.

Gender Issue

The issue of 'gender' has been late entrant to public administrative studies. Though the Minnowbrook Conference in 1968 did talk of the pertinence of equity, values and social justice, the emphasis on gender issues was not specifically highlighted. In the 1980s, however, women's issues were recognised as an empirical and theoretical area of concern in public administration. The approaches to women's empowerment have been undergoing a substantial change. The shift in policy approaches towards women, from 'welfare' to 'equity' to 'anti-poverty', as categorised by Buvinic and Greeley,[6] to two other approaches, which have been categorised as 'efficiency' and 'empowerment' has mirrored the general trends in Third World development policies. The equity approach, it has been observed, recognises that women are active participants in the development process. This approach meets strategic gender needs and links development with equity. As such, the approaches aim at a redistribution of power.[7]

The 73rd and 74th Constitutional Amendments Act, 1992 have a direct impact on the role of women as they aim at making them more participative in respect of local democracy in both rural and urban areas. This has ensured the political presence of the women in panchayati raj bodies and the municipal institutions. They have moved into a position of power, and this has surely enabled them to participate in local government decision-making, a sphere that effects their lives the most. It has given them political administrative visibility and the opportunity to learn politics and local governance. Inherently, it has made them aware, conscious and confident. In terms of absolute numbers, according to the Statistical Abstract (Government of India, 2003), as far as grassroots democratic institutions that is the panchayati raj and local bodies are concerned, these amendments have helped to a great extent.

Recently adopted National Policy for Empowerment of Women (2001) is being translated into action. Among other steps in the direction of empowerment, it includes: (i) Creating an environment through positive economic and social policies for the development of women to enable them to realise their full potential, (ii) Providing equal access to participation and decision-making in socio-political spheres, health care, education at all levels, career and vocational guidance, occupational health and safety, as well as social security; (iii) Changing societal attitudes and community practices by active participation and involvement of both men and women; and (iv) Building partnerships with civil society, especially women's organisations, corporate and private sectors.

Future Administrator : Role to Play

The future administrator needs to have not only efficiency and integrity but also a human approach to all problem. He must have a spirit of service to the community. He must also have the following :

(1) He should possess a broad outlook on public affairs.
(2) His only aim should be to help the public rather than getting bogged down with rigid and mechanical implementation of rules and regulations.
(3) He should have the capacity to judge advice rendered to him and take decisions promptly.
(4) When a decision is taken, the administrator should inspire and motivate his staff at all levels to execute it effectively. Every successful administrator should be result-oriented and prompt in meeting the demands of the public. What is needed is not a procedure - oriented bureaucracy but a performance-oriented one.

According to Richard L. Chapman and Frederic N. Cleveland;

(1) The future administrator will be more of a moral leader, mediator and coordinator than mere issuer of order;

(2) He will learn to be a tactician and politician as he will be subject to vastly increased political processes; and

(3) He may also be called upon to act as an agent of change.[8]

The future administrator has to know as much of management, economics, sociology, history, law and politics. The increased complexity of social change and administrative arrangement will make the work of administration more demanding. They are adaptable and knowledgeable and perceptive and good readers of men and situations.

Variable of Successful Administration

Variable of successful administration and by extension administrator are[9]:

(1) To recognise new solution rather than modify old ones;

(2) Reformulate problems in new terms to elicit new responses and initiatives;

(3) To turn crises to advantages, use deviation and conflict in problem solving to generate self-transformation with minimum alienation;

(4) Deal with uncertainty and fluidity and absorb change, instability, and interdependence;

(5) Tolerate deviation, conflict and confrontation without over-reading or losing sense of proportion in inter-disciplinary problem-solving;

(6) Encourage error-correction, initiative and creativity and learn from mistakes;

(7) Learn from experience and uncertainty; and

(8) Remain human and humane under stress.

Role of an administrator, according to M.A. Muttalib, has

to be sorted out by reinterpreting public interest which is the corner- stone of administrative value system as the persons in authority often get intoxicated with power and money in the absence of adequate checks and forget the distinction between public interest, political interest and personal interest.[10] Further, Muttalib holds that values of district administration are at the threshold of revolution. The basic sources of administrative values, namely power, discipline and knowledge have been undergoing change with the changing social, political and professional values.

His Multiple Roles

Public administration today has broken away from its stereotype image of a rigid, conservative, inept and impersonal entity and the administrator has assumed the new image of a humane, innovative and responsive being. In this context, he has acquired a multiplicity of roles and responsibilities as follows :

(1) Crusading reformer intent on transforming some aspect of community life according to preconceived notions of the ideal society;
(2) Proactive policy formulator, ready with possible strategies to meet the unknown;
(3) Social change-agent ready to accept new ideals and to push others into accepting them also;
(4) Crisis manager, slow to burn out but quick to react and brilliant at immediate improvisation;
(5) Dynamic programme manager able to show new courses and adapts on-going arrangements;
(6) Humanitarian employer, treating staff with respect and meeting out even-handed justice;
(7) Political campaigner, responsive to public needs and champion of public causes;
(8) Competent administrator ensure effective performance with minimum political embarrassment;

(9) Interest broker, choosing among competing interests and reconciling all parties to the outcome;
(10) Public relations expert, adept at building up support, showing his area to advantage;
(11) Speedy decision-maker, oriented to assume responsibility and clear instructions;
(12) Constructive thinker, not easily led astray by others who would want to make up his mind for him; and
(13) Optimistic leader, not easily discouraged in adversely but able to command attention and emulate subordinates.[11]

The future would call for a resetting of the goals of district administration in the wake of the changing demands of the future civilization as follows:

(1) Human rights;
(2) Human development;
(3) Empowerment of people;
(4) Gender equity; and
(5) Care for non-humans and concern for future generations.

Summing Up

Any discussion on reinventing district administration for the 21st century is indeed a thought-provoking. A futuristic study of this nature suffers from the drawback of speculative predictions and extrapolations based on the past and the current. However, we could reasonably conclude that the district administration for the next century calls for rethinking, reorienting and refocusing on priorities, goals and strategies. District administration has endured by conceding and adapting to the changing time. It has evolved and readjusted with the changing nature of the state. It has risen to the challenges of modern times, such as overpopulation, poverty, resource crunch, illiteracy, economic imbalances, etc., by undergoing necessary structural and attitudinal changes. District administration, however, has suffered from afflictions and drawbacks which have been highlighted by thinkers from time to time as public maladministration. District administration of the 21st century should gear itself to human development, economy, performance-orientation, empowerment of the people, advocacy, technocracy, cultural-specificity and women-oriented structures and should have the lofty objectives of human rights, empowerment, gender-equity, care for nonhumans and concern for future generations.

NOTES AND REFERENCES

1. Gerald Caiden, 1971, *Dynamics of Public Administration*, New York, Holt, Rinehart, pp. 290-91
2. Korten, Frances F, 1981, "Community Participation: A Management Perspective on Obstacles and Options" in David C. Korten and Felipe B. Alfanso (Eds.), *Bureaucracy and the Poor*, McGraw Hill, New York.
3. Katz, Elihu and Brenda Danet, 1973, "Introduction" in Elihu Katz and Brenda Danet (Eds.), *Bureaucracy and the Public*, Basic Books, New York.
4. Bhattacharya, Mohit, 1987, (2nd Edition), *Public Administration, Structure, Process and Behaviour*, World Press, Calcutta.
5. Rosencranz, Armin, 1992, *Environmental Law and Policy in India: Cases, Materials, and States*, Book Review Literacy Trust, New Delhi.
6. Buvinic, Lycette and W. Mc Greevey, 1983, *Women and Poverty in the Third World*, Johns Hopkins University Press, Baltimore.
7. Ostergaard, Lise, 1997, *Gender and Development*, Routledge, London.
8. Gerard Caiden, *Dynamics of Public Administration*, *op.cit*.
9. M.A. Muttalib, 1994, "Towards the Nuclear Theory of Values". *The Administration Man in Action*, Vol. XI : No. 4, p. 614.
10. Gerard Caiden, 1971, *op. cit*
11. David Osborne and Ted Gaebler, 1992, *Reinvesting Government : How the Entrepreneurial Sprit is Transforming the Public Sector*, Reading, Addison- Wesley.

17 District Administration and Good Governance

Reforms in Local-Governance

*Rajesh Kumar**

Introduction

In the ancient Indian polity, a series of administrative reforms were brought about by monarchs such as Chandragupta Maurya and Ashoka and the rulers of the Gupta dynasty. Treatises such as Dharmashastra, Arthashastra, Shukraniti are full of guidelines for improving the competence and responsiveness of the politico-administrative system. Muslim rule in India witnessed significant administrative reforms during the periods of Akbars (1556-1605). Mughal administration which was the result of well-designed administrative reforms introduced over a period spanning a century and more.

During rule of the East India Company and British Crown, a series of reforms were introduced in the administrative system which continue to have an impact even on the present-day administrative system.

District Administration in India : Perspectives on Change

Good governance and management requires clarity about responsibilities, access to information about how the government works and using competition to achieve value

* Reader, Department of Public Administration, Kurukshetra University, Kurukshetra.

for money in service delivery. The elements of accountability, transparency and contestability are required to be reflected in the governance and management structures and processes of the city. Therefore, the test of good governance lies in the goals and objectives of a government; in its policies and programmes. The concept of "governance" is not new. It is as old as human civilization. Simply put "governance" means: the process of decision-making and the process by which decisions are implemented (or not implemented). Governance can be used in several contexts such as corporate governance, international governance, national governance and local governance.

Local Government : Conceptual Framework and Significance

The term 'local government' originated when India was under the British rule. At that time Indian did not enjoy any self-government either at the Central or State levels. When British Government took a decision to associate Indians in administering the local affairs, it meant a slice of local government for the people. The term 'Local Government' or 'Local Self-government' means the government by freely elected local bodies, which are endowed with power, discretion and responsibility to be exercised and discharged by them, without control over their decisions by any other higher authority. Their actions are, however, subject to the supremacy of the national government. Thus local inhabitants representing local body possessing autonomy within the limited spheres, raising revenue through local taxation and spending its income on local services constitute local self-government.[1]

Local government has been a part of the system of government in every country. The nature of local government depends upon the political philosophy of the country. In the contemporary period, generally there is three tier system of government namely, Central government, state government and local government. Local government has been an integral part of the three tier system of government in India also, the other two tiers being the Union government and state government.

The scope of the jurisdiction of local government has been limited to a specific area and it has been responsible for providing civic amenities to the local population within its jurisdiction. A local government operates within the provisions of the law according to which it has been set-up.

The institutions of local government have been subordinate to the state or provincial government, which exercises control and supervision over these institutions. The activities and functions of local government have constantly been increasing due to the population pressure and commitment to the philosophy of a welfare state. Various activities which regulate the conduct of the citizens such as provision of public transport, construction of houses for the poor, supply of electricity, health centres, parks, playgrounds etc. fall in the domain of local government. In fact the institutions of local government have been playing a greater role in daily life of a citizen than the state or central government.

State government transferred some of its powers to local units to render public services to their residents. While due to the fact that it is the welfare state in which functions of local governments have increased after the implementation of 73rd and 74th Constitutional Amendments Act, 1992. This leads to the serious problems of imbalance between their expenditure and revenue. The municipal governments are supposed to provide more and more services to their residents while, on the contrary, the state governments impress upon the local governments to raise the revenue resources, viz. restriction on property tax rates, and restriction on the raising of debts.

The Problems of Local Bodies

No doubt, the urban governments revamping efforts through

74th Constitutional Amendment Act (1992) reflect the genuine concern of the governments, both centre and states, about the democracy at grass-root level. But it is disheartening to see the dismal performance of the local urban institutions even after structural changes and providing these bodies a constitutional status. Several studies and reports make us feel that the urban local bodies have failed to achieve the desired objectives of turning the municipal governments into genuine democratic institutions and rendering them into effective instruments for making the cities worthy of decent living and fulfilling the hopes and aspirations of the urbanities.

Meaning of Good Governance

The word 'good' is derived from the word 'God' which means an ability to distinguish between right and wrong, just and unjust. A judgment is good if it is just, right and moral. In the context of good governance it is taken in public interest and service the public interest. While in India we believe in *'Sarva Jana Hitaih Sarva Jana Sukaiah'*, which implies welfare of all and happiness of all.

The Concise Oxford Dictionary defines it as an "act or manner of governing" and "the office or function of governing,"[2] governance, state or provincial governance or local governance. It is recognized that governance is about how an organization steers itself and the processes and structures that are used to achieve its goal. Andrian Leftwich, who has already been referred to above, gives three defining features of good governance (i) to promote open, market-friendly and competitive economy; (ii) democratization: and (iii) improvement of human rights record. The World Bank, for the first time in 1989, highlighted the concept of good governance. By good governance it meant sound public management and in this context, identified four dimensions: (i) public sector managements; (ii) accountability: (iii) legal framework for development; and (iv) information and transparency. In 1992, the Bank's document Governance and

Development said, "Good governance is central to creating and sustaining an environment which fosters strong and equitable development and it is an essential complement to sound economic policies."

Pai Panandikar sees good governance as it pertains to a nation, which handles its people to lead peacefully orderly, reasonable, prosperous and participatory lives.

Why Good Governance?

The Human Development Report 2002 has identified a few reasons for having good governance. However, describing the features of good governance from the human development perspective it is identical to democratic governance. Democratic governance means that :

(1) People's human rights and fundamental freedoms are respected, allowing them to live with dignity.
(2) People can hold decisions, which are accountable.
(3) Private and public spheres of life and decision-making. The needs of future generations are reflected in current policies.
(4) Economic and social policies aim at eradicating poverty and expanding the choice choice that all people have in their fives.[3]

Elements of Good Government in Local Government

These elements should be reflected in the local governance and management structures and processes of the city. Good government requires:

Participation

Participation by both men and women is a cornerstone of good governance in local government participation could be either direct or through legitimate intermediate institutions or representatives. It is important to point out that representative democracy does not necessarily mean that the concerns of the most vulnerable in society would be taken into consideration in decision-making. Participation needs to be informed and organized in the local government. This means freedom of association and expression on the one hand and an organized civil society on the other hand.

Rule of law

Local government and good governance requires fair legal frameworks that are enforced impartially. It also requires full protection of human rights, particularly those of minorities. Impartial enforcement of laws requires an independent judiciary and an impartial and incorruptible police force.

Transparency through Good Governance in Local Government

Transparency means that decisions taken and their enforcement are done in a manner that follows rules and regulations. It also means that information is freely available and directly accessible to those who will be affected by such decisions and their enforcement. It also means that enough information is provided and that it is provided in easily understandable forms and media.

Responsiveness

Local government and good governance require that institutions and processes try to serve all stakeholders within a reasonable timeframe.

Consensus Oriented

There are several actors and as many view points in a given

society. Good governance requires mediation of the different interests in society to reach a broad consensus in society on what is in the best interest of the whole community and how this can be achieved. It also requires a broad and longterm perspective on what is needed for sustainable human development and how to achieve the goals of such development. This can only result from an understanding of the historical, cultural and social contexts of a given society or community.

Equity and Inclusiveness

A society's well being depends on ensuring that all its members feel that they have a stake in it and do not feel excluded from the mainstream of society. This requires all groups, but particularly the most vulnerable, have opportunities to improve or maintain their well-being.

Effectiveness and Efficiency

Good governance means that processes and institutions produce results that meet the needs of society while making the best use of resources at their disposal. The concept of efficiency in the context of good governance also covers the sustainable use of natural resources and the protection of the environment.

Accountability

Accountability is a key requirement of good governance. Not only governmental institutions but also the private sector and civil society organizations must be accountable to the public and to their institutional stakeholders. Who is accountable to whom varies depending on whether decisions or actions taken are internal or external to an organization or institution. In general an organization or an institution is accountable to those who will be affected by its decisions or actions. Accountability cannot be enforced without transparency and the rule of law.

Contestability

Contestability is about using competition to achieve value for money in service delivery. There is greater evidence to suggest that services provided by the public sector are more expensive than those provided by the private sector. Contestability means choice in the provision of services through open competition between potential providers. Let us start on our home ground first. How did Indian administration get scant of 'good governance'? It was felt that it was necessary to take corrective measures to arrest the present drift before it becomes too late. In the agenda note titled 'For an Effective and Responsive Administration in India.

Decentralize Power in Local Government

There is every case for a wholesale review and decentralization of political power in a genuine system of governance down to the lowest grassroots levels. With a large number of smaller states and a four-tier system of governance, it may be possible to involve various groups in governance more closely.

The imperative need was for governments at all levels to reinvent themselves and redefine their roles and responsibilities and bring about reforms in all areas which have an impact on the lives of the people. It was, therefore, decided that steps should be taken to restore people's confidence in the capacity and fairness of administration.

The test of good governance lie in the goals and objectives of a government in its policies and programmes in the manner of their execution, in the results achieved and above all, in the general perception of the people about the quality of functioning of its various agencies, their attitudes and behaviour towards the public, their sincerity, honesty and commitments towards public duties. It is also important to see that there is no undue concentration of power.

Bureaucrats, Judges and Politicians

The three pillars of governance-edifice-do not bother about deadlines (they all want to hog headlines and bylines) because they deal in other people's money, time and morale. For the last named category, there are particularly no morals; they live in the present "Raat gayee baat gayee." These three, in 'joint venture' with the other three, namely, economic-financial mafias, underworld dons and trade unions/vested interest lobbies, have made mincemeat of good governance.

Constitution Amendment

An urban local government (ULG) is a public institution concerned with community welfare, social justice and economic prosperity of its people through the 74th Constitutional Amendment Act, 1992. The urban local body is supposed to manage resources in public trust and (among all tiers of government) is closest to the people. These two aspects play a prime role in deciding the quality of the urban life and thereby the level of urban productivity. It has to be efficient, transparent and accountable to the public. The objective of 'good governance' is not only philosophically relevant but has become a compelling necessity for urban local bodies.

The decentralized system of elected governance has certain inherent advantages, e.g., it will bring efficiency as decision makers, who live locally are likely to know about local conditions and would be in a position to match resources and needs more precisely. Secondly, it will also bring accountability in the sense that the decision makers live and work in close contact with the users and as such are exposed more effective scrutiny and greater pressure to deliver the goods.

In many states, local bodies have become weak and ineffective on account of a variety of reasons, including prolonged suppressions and inadequate devolution of powers and functions. As a result, urban local bodies are not able to perform effectively as vibrant democratic units of self-government.

Strengthening the local bodies, which "are the backbone of the development process of the bottom areas, can make a beginning. These institutions are already under pressures owing to rapid urbanization and lack of political and social will to make course corrections. The mode of governance of the local bodies is also outdated.[4]

Empowerment of Local Government

The presently, all the states are dilly-dallying in empowering local self-governance and the Union Government has taken up the matter with all the states and has further sought information in this regard as to what has been done so far on this front. The Union Government has reached to the conclusion that even after ten years of these amendments to the Constitution, most states have not given powers to the local self-governance.

The problem being faced by the authorities concerned is that no department is ready to dilute its authority by handing over powers to these urban and rural officials feel that these departments might be closed once powers are handed over to these bodies. Examples are being cited in this regard.[5]

In addition to the political support and commitment, at the administrative level review and changes are essential in the following areas :

(1) The provisions of the Municipal and Panchayti Raj Act, 1992.
(2) Administrative set up and decision making process.

(3) Human resources policies including training and rewards.
(4) Cost saving measurers.
(5) Systems and procedures and use of automation wherever possible.
(6) Optimum utilization of human assets (numbers and skills).
(7) Optimum utilization of non-movable assets.
(8) Billing and recovery/collection system, identification of areas of revenue leakage and suggesting measurers to eliminate the leakage.
(9) Accounting systems and MIS.
(10) Resources mobilization from non-tax sources.
(11) Introduction of quality control systems in all service.

Consclusion and Suggestions

The term 'good governance' has continuously evolved with the development of human civilization. It has acquired much broader meaning recently in the wake of globalization, economic liberalization and corporatization. Good governance is a broader notion than good government. It involves governments and also civil society (citizens, civic institutions, etc.).

For democracy to be successful at the national level, the grassroots organizations have to be strong. The local authorities have to respond to the felt needs of the people. The citizens have to have faith in the efficacy of the administrative system so that the distance between people and the government is reduced.

Suggestions

Strengthening to Governance

The governance needs to be strengthened by vigorously pursuing the centralization initiatives envisaged in the

Constitution. In regard to executive system,, functional domain, intra-city decentralization and authority to the governments to set their own tax rates and charges. It is also imperative to inject into the governance process elements and attributes of good governance, including participation of the civil society.

The following measures need to be taken to improve and strengthen to governance :

Democratic Decentralization

- Empowennent and strengthening of the governments by devolving powers and authority as required by the Constitution.
- As per the provisions of the Constitution Amendment formulation of realistic and effective integrated development plans incorporating resource mobilization plan be ensured.

Improving Service Delivery

- Develop incentive structure to encourage local self-government in efficient and responsive service delivery.
- Replace incentives that produce a negative effect and act as constraints to efficient service delivery by those that encourage reform and improve the delivery of services.
- Constitution of technical support groups should also be constituted in every government to supervise the works at the local level.

Facilitating Private Sector and People's Participation

- Development of proper relationship and systems for interaction with and participation of NGOs, CBOs, Residents associations, professional groups,

industries and other organs of the civil society in local governance.
- Promotion of initiatives for privatization, contacting out of civic services to .private operators and producers and communities development societies.

Local Self-government

Those aspiring for good governance believe in democracy and democracy is epitomized by a system of local self-government. Although local government institutions have existed in our county even prior to independence somehow these did not function well because of their being considered as mere appendages of the respective state governments. The 73rd and 74th Constitutional Amendments have somewhat tried to remedy the situation yet in many states. The new leadership that has emerged at the local level is qualitatively no better. A qualitative change is therefore required.

Role of NGOs

People need some outsider for help organizing themselves so that they could also become active participants in good governance. The role of organizing people can be most effectively played by the NGOs. These can help in bridging the gap between the local community and local administration. The central issue in good governance such social mobilization can done only by the agencies are not bureaucratic. In this task, the NGOs have a crucial role to play and as such they become agents of change as well. The NGOs can also be helpful to newly created PRIs institutions under the 73rd Constitutional Amendment.

Taking Socio-Economic Problems

We should also try to tackle our socio-economic problems.

Even today, after more than sixty years of independence, our basic problems on the socio economic front are the same that were there at the time of independence in 1947, viz., poverty, illiteracy, backwardness, population explosion leading to overpopulation, shortages of food, drinking water, etc. Unemployment has reached alarming proportions.

NOTES AND REFERENCES

1. Harris, G.M., *Comparative Local Government*, London, 1948, p.9.
2. Oxford Reference Dictionary, 1995.
3. Tiwari, R.S., Good Governance : Populist Democracy to Quality Democracy, *Indian Journal of Public Administration*, Oct-Dec 2002, Vol. XLVIII, No. 4, pp. 584-85.
4. Economic and social policies aim at eradicating poverty and expanding the choice that all people have in their lives.
5. Progress reports sought from states — Empowerment of Panchyats, an article as published in *The Tribune*, July 11, 2003.

18 Restructuring the District Food and Supply Department
A Look at Haryana

*S.S. Rana** and *Anita Kharub***

The Food and Supply Department, Haryana is mainly assigned the task of procurement of foodgrains as well as supervising the working of the targeted public distribution system. For this purpose, the department has established circle offices called as the District Food and Supply Controller (DFC) office at district headquarter. The DFC as the central figure, the pivot around which, the entire food and supply organization revolves. He is the head of the food organisation in the circle. His most important function is to plan, organise and supervise the process of purchase, receipt and storage of the foodgrains reserve, coordinates and monitors the supplies and distribution of essential commodities within the circle under the public distribution system and ensures the enforcement of various control orders issued under the Essential Commodities Act, 1955. He is assisted by field and office staff. It is on his initiative, executive ability, guidance and supervision that the efficiency of a circle office depends to a large extent. He ensures by frequent inspections that his staff understands and acts in accordance with instructions, issued to them. He has to carry out the procurement policy of the government and has to account for and store the grain

* District Food and Supply Controller, Ambala, Haryana.

** MA, Ph.D. in Public Administration and District Food and Supply Officer, Ambala, Haryana.

and other miscellaneous stock articles. He undertakes that the foodgrains purchased or received are removed to godowns without avoidable loss of time and in particular that no wharfage or demurrage accrues to the extent practicable. He ensures that adequate godown accommodation is available and foodgrains are stored in godowns which are suitable for storage and have been properly repaired, cleaned and treated. He has also to see that all avoidable loss to the grain during storage is avoided.

He also ensures that foodgrains which are less fit for long storage are issued for consumption in preference to those which can stand prolonged storage. He also sees that grains and stocks are kept in proper custody under a system of double locking; that arrangements of watch and ward are satisfactory and that all issues from the stocks are made under orders of the competent authority and after due realisation of price as fixed by government. He is to examine that all outstanding claims are speedily settled and realisations are promptly made and credited to government account. He has to pay greatest possible attention to ensure that the grain supplied is always of the right quality. In short, the DFC has to discharge multifarious duties of a responsible nature and he spares no pains to make a success of them. The office of the District Food and Supplies Controller has two distinct branches:

(a) General Branch
(b) Accounts Branch

General Branch

The head clerk is the immediate incharge of this branch which is responsible for all items of work not specifically allotted to the supplies or the accounts branch. The general branch deals with—

(i) the receipt and issue of dak;
(ii) general correspondence;
(iii) all establishment work;
(iv) contingencies;
(v) regulation of supply and distribution of essential commodities.

Accounts Branch

The section officer (finance) or the accountant is immediate incharge of this branch and is responsible for the maintenance of proper accounts of—

(i) receipts and issues of all grains and other stock articles into or from the provincial reserve;
(ii) payment and realisations in connection with (i);
(iii) Discrepancies between quantities allocated or purchased and received in godowns, quantities received and issued, quantities issued and payments realised, write off of shortages, if any, loss in cleaning of grains and, in short, all other items relating to the scheme; and
(iv) submission of various periodical returns to head-quarters.

Relationship between the District Food and Supplies Controller and Deputy Commissioner

The Deputy Commissioner (DC) is the head of the district and the DFC is to assist the DC in the administration of food matters in the district. He, therefore, keeps the DC informed of all important developments on the food side, and acts on his advice. As, however, the hands of the DC are already too full, DFC needs not worry him in all matters connected with the day to day administration of food work unless they are of more than purely food significance.

Besides, the office of the DFC at the district headquarter, there are *provincial reserve centres* the number of which vary from district to district according to the size of the district.

Organization of the Provincial Reserve (PR) Centre

A centre is the smallest unit of provincial reserve organization. The Assistant Food and Supplies Officer/senior most Inspector, Food and Supplies, is incharge of a centre. There are, however, also other Inspectors and Sub-Inspectors attached to each centre for supervision of their work. Purchases in the *mandis* are made under the supervision of the Inspector Incharge of the concerned mandi by an approved commission agent. The Inspector has also to test weigh, transport and store in the provincial reserve godowns, all foodgrains purchased or received and has to maintain proper accounts.

All issues from the centres are the direct responsibility of the concerned Inspector who should see that no issue is made without proper authority. It is the provincial reserve centres which have to bear most of the brunt of the DFC's field work, it is the heart of the DFC's organization. All purchase, receipt, storage and issue of foodgrains are concentrated at the centre. It is here that the entire initial accounting of stocks—both foodgrains and miscellaneous articles, is maintained, as also of all expenditure and income and all claims and realisations. The DFC pays detailed attention to the proper setting up of each of his centres and to the posting of efficient and honest staff at each centre. He inspects each centre at regular intervals thoroughly which covers a detailed checking of the accounts of foodgrains, stock articles and funds.

The general control of the whole organization is maintained by headquarters staff which issues instructions regarding quantities of grains to be purchased, purchase rates, movement, storage and sale of PR stock and which deals with all matters of accounting and audit. Besides this, the PR centres ensure the smooth supply and availability of essential commodities in their area and keep a vigil over the distribution of essential commodities under the targeted public distribution system.

Functions of the Food and Supply Department in the District

The department of Food and Supplies is engaged in :

(A) the procurement of various foodgrains namely wheat, mustard, bajra and paddy;
(B) the distribution of foodgrains and other essential commodities to various categories of consumers at reasonable price; and
(C) the enforcement of various Control Orders issued under the Essential Commodities Act, 1955.

(A) *Procurement of Various Foodprains—Wheet, Mustard, Bajra and Paddy*

With a view to extend the benefits of price support scheme to the farmers, the purchase of rabi and kharif crops commences every year in the months of April and October respectively. For this, wheat, mustard, paddy and bajra are procured on minimum support price fixed by the Government of India in various regulated mandis of the state in consonance with the directions issued by the government from time to time.

Infrastructure for Procurement

For the smooth procurement of various foodgrains following infrastructure is being provided by the department:

(1) *Mandis and allocation thereof* : During the current rabi marketing season, 352 mandis operated whereas in case of kharif marketing season, 172 mandis functioned for the purchase of paddy and 41 mandis for the purchase of bajra. It is ensured well in time that these mandis are well equipped with basic amenities such as drinking water, electricity, pucca platform, sheds, parking place, etc. The concerned heads of the procurement agencies in the state and in the districts ensure that all mandis are inspected and cleared well before the commencement of season so as to facilitate uninterrupted procurement operations. No farmer has to travel more than 10 kilometers to sell his produce in Haryana.

(2) *Procurement Agencies* : Six procurement agencies effect the procurement of foodgrains namely Food and Supplies Department-28 per cent, Hafed-35 per cent, FCI-10 per cent, HAIC-9 per cent, HWC-9 per cent and Confed- 9 per cent. The staff of the procurement agencies remains present in the mandis on the specified days allocated to them and effect purchase of foodgrains in the event of market price falling below the minimum support price.

(3) *Cash Credit Limit and Payment to Farmers* : The state government is committed to make the payments to the farmers within 48 to 72 hours. For this sufficient cash credit limit for the purchase of foodgrains is arranged from the Reserve Bank of India.The Food and Supplies Department places sufficient funds at the disposal of the DFC for this purpose. All possible efforts are made to ensure that there is no distress sale by the farmers.

(4) *Communication System* : The Food and Supplies Department starts functioning control rooms at the state headquarters well before the commencement of the season. Similarly, the procurement agencies also set up their own control rooms at their state

headquarters as well as district headquarters. The procurement agencies ensure to communicate information about the procurement to the control rooms of Food and Supplies Department on day to day basis. The Food and Supplies Department, in turn, communicates the procurement information to Government of India on day to day basis.

(5) *Laboratories* : About 35 laboratories for the maintenance of quality have been set up in all the districts of the state.

(6) *Packing Material* : The state procurement agencies and FCI make necessary arrangements of packing material such as gunny bales, polythene covers, tarpaulins, fumigants, wooden crates, etc. The procurement agencies ensure stocking of packing material particularly the gunny bales at the strategic points and the mandis, well before the commencement of the season to avoid difficulty when the actual procurement starts.

(7) *Billing-cum Payment Agents* : Billing-cum-payment agents (BCPAs) in all the mandis are appointed before the commencement of the season. They collect the bills from all the *arhatiyas* and prepare one bill of each day and submit the same to the DFC or to the concerned heads of the procurement agencies for payment. Ths BCPAs ensure timely payment to the farmers through *arhatiyas*, proper weighment of foodgrains, maintenance of proper accounts of foodgrains purchased, lifting the stocks from each kacha *arhatiyas* shop and storing the same at storage points. They are paid a commission of 0.15 paise per 50 kg bag.

(8) *Labour and Transportation* : Committees have been constituted in each district under the chairmanship of D.C. to finalise contracts for labour and transportation well before procurement. The tender committee ensures that the contracts are finalised

strictly in consonance with the guidelines and the schedule. Ths concerned agency and district administration ensure that the appointed contractors function smoothly during the year and bottlenecks, if any, are removed promptly.

(9) *Deployment of Staff*: Each Procurement agency deploys sufficient staff in the mandis allotted to them to resume procurement operations as and when warranted by the situation.

(10) *Rice Millers* : The number of functional rice mills in the state is about 856. The millers may buy leviable paddy as well as doing custom milling, of paddy purchased by the procurement agencies. The rice millers doing the levy/CMR work are under obligation to adhere to various terms and conditions and guidelines issued by the government.

(11) *Milling Committee* : The state government has constituted a milling committee under the chairmanship of DC. for every district. The district heads of procurement agencies and two members of rice millers, nominated by the Rice Millers Association are its members and DFC is its Member Secretary. Further, an officer from the headquarters of one of the state procurement agency also participates in the proceedings of the committee. This committee meets from time to time for allocation of paddy to the millers and reviewing the progress of custom milling of paddy. The committee also ensures that the time schedule for the custom milling of paddy, the delivery of CMR and levy rice to central pool and other terms and conditions of the agreement are adhered to.

(12) *Mandi Level Committee for Determining Correct Prices of Foodgrains* : A committee consisting of Inspector, Food and Supplies/AFSO, Secretary market committee or any official of the market committee representative of BCPA, representative of the growers

and local representative of FCI., Hafed., HWC, HAIC and Confed is constituted in every mandi to determine the quality of foodgrains especially in doubtful cases and to settle disputes connected therewith.

Procedure of Procurement

Allotment of the Mandis

All the mandis are allocated to different agencies as per their share. All the procurement agencies ensure that their staff enters in the mandis allotted to them on the commencement of rabi/kharif marketing season. Farmers bring their produce to the nearest regulated mandi.

Entering the Arrivals in Record

The arrival of foodgrains in mandis is entered in the record of the Haryana State Agriculture and Marketing Board (HSAMB) and concerned procurement agency.

Auctioning of Stocks

The auction of heaps is undertaken everyday from both sides of mandis at 10-00 a.m. and 3-00 p.m. simultaneously. The offices of the market committees also remain open on all holidays i.e. Saturdays/Sundays and gazetted holidays during procurement seasons. It is ensured that auctioning of heaps take place regularly and any violation in this regard is not allowed to take place. If price tends to fall below the MSP, government agencies purchase as per specifications laid down by Government of India.

Purchase of Foodgrains (Wheat, Mustard, Paddy and Bajra)

(i) The purchase of paddy, *bajra,* wheat and mustard is

made by agencies on MSP strictly as per parameters/specifications issued by the government from time to time. Procurement agencies ensure that the farmers do not in any way get price lower that the MSP and the farmers do not resort to any distress sale of their produce. In case, however, any stocks arrived in mandis do not conform to specifications, the same is got improved by cleaning or blending with good quality of grains. In this connection, the farmers are advised/educated by the staff of the market committees as well as the procurement agencies.

(ii) The procurement agencies ensure that the purchase of foodgrains is made as per specifications and by carrying out proper visual inspection of stocks. The laboratory staff i.e. head analyst and junior analyst are associated while effecting its purchase. To ascertain moisture contents in foodgrains, moisture meters are increased according to need.

(iii) For the convenience of the farmers, two boards in Hindi indicating specifications of Paddy/*Bajra* as laid down by Government of India and the price payable are displayed at prominent and conspicuous places in each mandi. In case of big mandis the number of such boards is increased according to need.

(iv) Procurement agencies ensure that representative samples of foodgrains are properly drawn everyday in each mandi and analysed in order to determine its proper quality. While ascertaining the quality of foodgrains, it is to be ensured that the interest of the farmers are fully protected.

(v) Procurement agencies exercise strict supervision and control at all stages of operations so as to ensure that there are no malpractices or manipulations in transactions of the procurement.

Method of Sampling/Analysis

The representative samples of foodgrains are drawn/

analyzed daily to determinants quality. For this purpose, a register, is maintained in each mandi in which such sampling together with the results is entered. The register contains the columns such as date, time of drawing the sample, name of the *arhatiyas*/farmers, etc. This register is maintained in each mandi/purchase centre which can be inspected by any visiting officer. A report giving details of the samples so drawn is also sent daily to the Headquarters of the Food and Supplies Department.

Cleaning arrangements in Mandis

It is mandatory for every *arhatiyas* to have an electric fan/ jharnas, sufficient labour, wooden crates, polythene covers etc. This facility can be availed by the farmers to bring his produce upto the prescribed specifications. The staff of the Market Committees and procurement agencies ensure that every arhtia in the mandis has made arrangements of this cleaning facility.

Check Against Un-necessary Rejection of Foodgrains and Coarsegrains in Mandis

Samples of all rejected stocks are drawn and analyzed in the Food Grains Laboratory of the DFC. A report about the rejected stocks showing *inter alia* the name of centre, number of heaps along with quantity, name of farmers along with proper address and results of analysis may be sent on day to day basis to the Additional Director, Food and Supplies Department, Haryana by name.

Filling of Bags

The foodgrains are filled in 50 kg and properly stitched as per standing instructions of headquarter issued on April 17, 1984. Thereafter it is delivered to FCI or stores.

(B) Distribution of Foodgrains and Other Essential Commodities through TDPS

Public distribution system evolved as a major instrument of the government's economic policy for ensuring availability of foodgrains to the public at affordable prices as well as for enhancing the food security for the poor. It is an important constituent of the strategy for poverty eradication and is intended to serve as a safety net for the poor who are nutritionally at risk. The Targeted Public Distribution System (TPDS) has been implemented in the state of Haryana with effect from May 1, 1997.

The state government has covered the people below poverty line (BPL) category and 'the poorest of the poor' families under Antodaya Anna Yojana (AAY) category and special cards of yellow and pink colour for BPL and AAY families respectively have been issued. Under the TPDS 35 kg wheat to AAY families is being provided at subsidized rate of Rs. 2.10 per kg. per family per month whereas the BPL families get 25 kg wheat @ Rs. 4.84 per kg and 10 kg rice @ Rs.6.40 per month. The scale of issue may vary as per scale of foodgrains fixed by the Government of India from time to time.

Monitoring and Regulation of PDS

Strict Vigilance System

(i) Inspectorate staff carries out inspection of all the fair price shops under their jurisdiction whereas AFSOs check eight such shops every month and DFO and DFC each inspect two ration depots per month besides the surprise checking carried out by the officers of headquarter.

(ii) Every DFC submits to the headquarters a monthly PDS diary highlighting details of distribution of essential commodities in the district. The PDS diary is critically examined and appropriate action is taken accordingly.

(iii) Information such as allocation, lifting and distribution position of various essential commodities, and report on action taken against offenders under the PDS Control Order 2002 etc. is sent in prescribed proforma to the Government of India on monthly basis.

Transparency

Vigilance committees have been in existence since the inception of the rationing system. Following PDS vigilance committees are active in the state of Haryana at various levels:

(i) *State Food Advisory Committee* has been set-up under the chairmanship of Food and Supplies Minister which meets every three months. It comprises official as well as non-official members. It reviews the price and availability of essential commodities.

(ii) *District Food Advisory Committee* has been constituted under the chairmanship of DC. The DC and its members review the position of essential commodities every month.

(iii) *Sub-Divisional Food Advisory Committee* is composed under the chairmanship of Sub-Divisional Officer (Civil). Apart from MLAs, local people are its members.

(iv) *Village/Ward Level Committee*: To keep a watchful eye on the distribution of essential commodities, following village/ward level committees have been set-up. MLAs, MPs representatives of trade union organizations, housewives, SCs/BCs and consumer bodies are included in the committee. They review the availability position of essential commodities, their price and other related matters. The essential commodities are distributed to card holders in the presence of these committees which certify the proper distribution of the essential commodities.

The Constitution of the committees is as follows :

Urban Committee	Rural Committee
Member Municipal Council/Committee	Sarpanch
EX-member Municipal Council/Committee	Harijan Panch
One female member of the locality	Village Patwari/
nominated by the SDO(C)	Anganwari Worker

Detailed guidelines were issued by the Central Department of Food and Public Distribution in June, 1999 for greater involvement of Panchayati Raj Institutions (PRIs) in the functioning of TPDS and to bring in a more transparent and accountable system of distribution as a measure of social audit. Accordingly, the state government has ensured the involvement of PRIs in the following spheres:

(i) Opening of new fair price shops
(ii) Making additions/deletion in ration cards.
(iii) Proper distribution of PDS items.
(iv) To hear and settle local complaints regarding PDS Profit of a depot holder.

The responsibility of fair distribution of essential commodities under the TPDS mainly lies with the depot holder. If the profit of the depot holder is not sufficient enough to provide him a decent living, it can become a hindrance in the smooth working of TPDS. On an average 600 ration cards, if he lifts the entire allocation/quantity, he earns a profit of Rs.1960 in urban and Rs. 2260 in rural areas. Margin of the depot holder is calculated as under:

Commodity	*Cards*	*Quantity*	*Amount of Margin (in Rupees)*
Wheat	100 (BPL/AAY)	35-00 qtl	@Rs.I 8 per qtl= 630.00 Cost of Bag = 420.00
			Total =1050.00
Sugar	100 (BPL/AAY)	2-50 qtl	@Rs.19.38 = 48.45 Cost of Bag = 29.60
			Total = 78.05
Rice	————	————	————
K/oil	300	1.80 kg	@ Rs. 165/KL = 297.00
Total			=1425.05
If he iifts APL Wheat	110	38.50	@ Rs.18 = 693.00 Cost of Bag = 462.00 =2580.05

Details of Expenditure (Rs.)

	Towns	*Villages*
(i) Rent of Shop	500-00	200-00
(ii) Elce/Water Charges	70-00	70-00
(iii) Stationcry	50-00	50-00
	620-00	320-00

Note: Manual labour/wages of a depot holder are extra.

(C) Enforcement of Various Control Orders Issued Under the EC Act, 1955

These include enforcement of various control orders issued under the EC Act 1955, spreading consumer awareness, preparation of ration cards, etc.

(i) *Enforcement of Various Control Orders :* In order to check the rise in the prices of essential commodities and to check the black marketing, hoarding and adulteration, etc., the district administration enforces the provisions of various control orders issued under the EC Act, 1955. Action taken under the Act includes registration of reports with police, suspension/ cancellation of licenses of fair price shops/kerosene oil wholesalers and brick kilns etc, forfeiture of security and goods thereof, etc.

(ii) *Checking of Petrol /Diesel/LPG/Brick kiln* : All the petrol pumps in the district are checked to detect adulteration and short measurement/delivery of petrol and diesel in such a rotation that every petrol pump in the district is checked once in a quarter. Similarly, LPG agencies and godowns are also checked. Periodical raids are conducted to check the misuse of domestic cooking gas by the commercial and industrial users. Strict vigil is kept on the availability of bricks for governmental development works in the district and general consumers at reasonable rates. In cases of irregularities, action is taken under various control orders issued by the government in this regard.

(iii) *Citizen Charter for TPDS and Right to Information (RTI)*: The Citizen's Charter was issued by the Government of India in November, 1997. It is an important milestone in the ongoing efforts of the government to provide services under the PDS in a more transparent and accountable manner. In pursuance, the state government has also issued the same. It contains essential information viz. entitlement of BPL families, fair quality of foodgrains, information regarding FPS, procedure for the issue of ration cards, inspection and checking, right to information, vigilance and public participation. The Citizen's Charter is available in all the districts and the DC and DFCs are engaged in implementing its provisions meticulously.

Under the Right to Information Act 2005, the state government has nominated DFC and DFSO as Information Officer and Assistant Information Officer respectively.

The DFC is the member of various district level committees like committee for mid-day meal, committee for enforcing various provisions for prevention of child labour, committee for ready-to-eat items for the school children, committee for senior citizens. He also represents the department at the meeting of the district grievance redressal committee and open house sessions held for the general public.

(iv) *Preparation of Ration Cards :* The department issues three types of cards,viz. APL cards, BPL cards, AAY cards and their colour is green, yellow and pink respectively. The list for BPL and AAY ration cards is issued by the ADC on the basis of survey conducted for the purpose.

To get an APL ration card for the first time, the consumer (card holder) will apply in the prescribed form either in the office of DFC/Assistant Food and Supplies Officer/Inspector, Food and Supplies in whose jurisdiction his residence falls. These application forms are available in the office of DFC/AFSO/IFS.

He (consumer) will submit two attested photos of passport size of his family along with the application form and will give an affidavit declaring that he has not got prepared any ration card anywhere in India earlier and name of the members of his family are included in any of the ration card. He will also declare his permanent address. He will also disclose his place/places of residence during the last five years. He will also undertake that if any information is found false he would be liable for action as specified in the rules/act. The consumers will get a slip indicating the date as to when he should contact the concerned office for fee which will be Re. 1 (Re One only). This will be normally two weeks after the date of submission of application form, the Inspector/Sub Inspector will verify the particulars by physically visiting the residence of the applicant and making necessary enquiries and he will also consult vote list/ census record while making reco-mmendation. After considering the recommenda- tion the DFC/AFSO will issue the ration card and paste one copy of photograph on the same. The ration card can be collected by the applicant from the office of DFC/ AFSO/IFS where he submitted his application.

BPL ration card will be issued to those families, whose name are in the list of BPL families which is already surveyed by ADC/DRDA office through different departments with the help of village panchayat and municipalities. AAY ration card will be issued to those families which are surveyed by village panchayat and municipalities as per direction of ADC/DRDA office.

Some Recent Changes in the Mode of Orders/ Functionaries

The concerned agencies have introduced the following changes:

(i) Prior to April, 2005, the Release Orders for foodgrains to be distributed under the TPDS were being issued by the FCI But for quite sometime, the need to vest the state government with more powers under the TPDS had been felt. As a step forward in this direction, the Government of India declared Food and Supplies Department, Haryana as designated agency for delivery of foodgrains under TPDS and other welfare schemes in the state instead of FCI w.e.f. March 2005. Now, the DFCs issue Release Orders of foodgrains for TPDS and other centrally sponsored schemes in their respective jurisdiction.

(ii) Haryana government has already issuing wheat flour to BPL/AAY w.e.f. November 2003. But, there have been several complaints about the inferior quality of wheat flour being supplied through the FPS and the dubious role of flour mills selected for the purpose. So after a serious reconsideration, it has now been discontinued w.e.f. April, 2005 and it is decided that now wheat is being supplied in grain form only.

(iii) The Government of India has made allocation of grade A rice to BPL and APL families in Haryana at the scale of, 10 kg per month w.e.f. August 2005. The scheme has got good response in terms of lifting.

(iv) The Government of India has considerably curtailed the allocation of wheat for APL families in Haryana w.e.f September 2005.

(v) *Computerization*—For a long time the need for computerization of records of procurement of foodgrains and PDS had been felt. For this purpose, the Government of India has decided to implement the Integrated Information System for Foodgrains Management (IISFM), which aims to put in place an on line Management Information System (MIS) which will give the stock position of foodgrains kept in Central Pool in any depot at any given point of time and with view to improve the accuracy of the data being generated, quicker analysis and timely reporting thereof.

With a view to achieve the above objective of implementing the IISFM project, FCI has entered into agreement with the state government procuring agencies in October 2006. In this regard, National

Informatics Centre (NIC) is acting as the overall consultant of IISFM project on turnkey basis. The state government has agreed to provide suitable site/ premises with requisite furniture and has already identified 57 locations throughout the state for installation of computer systems in Haryana and the project is likely to be completed within the next six months or so.

Limitations in the Working of the Field Staff

The field staff faces certain problems in its working like:

(i) *Problem of Groupism*— India being a welfare and agrarian state, the foremost concern at the time of procurement of foodgrains is to watch and safeguard the interest of the farmers and avoid any glut in the mandi. The procuring staff remains very vigilant during the procurement operations and takes all steps to ensure that the farmers are not exploited in any way. But, whenever the procurement staff rejects. The foodgrains which do not conform to the specifications issued by the government in this regard, the farmers present in the mandis form a group and try to influence and threaten the procurement staff using abusive and foul language, and try to impress upon the visiting officers like the DC, officers from the headquarters of various procurement agencies, MLAs ministers, etc. that the procurement agencies are unnecessarily harassing them. They make allegations that such stocks are purchased by the traders at very low rates and then passed on to the procurement agencies the next day or after a few days at the procurement prices which is not always true and puts the procurement staff in at tight spot making their integrity doubtful. Such situations really affect the working of the procurement staff.

(ii) *Storage Losses*—As already stated, there is a pressure on the government agencies during the procurement seasons to purchase all the grain coming into the mandis, government agencies generally succumb to the pressure and many a times foodgrains not falling into the specifications have to be purchased. If the government agencies insist on the specifications, there is bound to be unrest among the farmers leading to disturbance in the procurement operations and glut in the mandis. The foodgrains purchased under the pressure may have high moisture content than the prescribed one or the quality of the grain might be inferior. This results in shortage of weight during the storage. Moreover, the bags containing grains are double machine stitched contrary to the earlier practice of hand stitching when the norms of giving excess on the stored grain were fixed. Therefore, nowadays the required excess weight/gain does not come during the storage and the officials/officers of various agencies have to bear huge recoveries on account of not giving excess as per the norms fixed by the government. Resultantly, the inspectorate staff engaged in the procurement is under constant stress of delivering the stored stock as per norms till the foodgrains are lifted by the FCI. This may tempt them to indulge in overweigh met at the time of purchase so that they do not have to suffer storage losses. There have been cases of suicide by the inspectorate staff fearing recoveries on this account. Keeping in view the above conditions, the norms of taking assured gain/excess on the stored grain need to be reconsidered.

(iii) *Lack of Conveyance Facilities*—The field staff has multifarious duties to perform besides the procurement duties, the inspectorate staff has to carry out 100 per cent inspections of the FPS falling in their area and ensure the distribution of various essential commodities at all the shops in their presence only. They have to check and verify the stock of commodities as and when delivered by the confed at the FPS. Moreover, they need to conduct surprise raids to check the misuse of domestic cooking gas cylinders at the hotels, restaurants, dhabas, sweet shops, industries, etc. where commercial cylinders are to be used as per law. It is quite a tedious job which needs frequent movement within the area of their jurisdiction. But, the officers and officials posted at the various Provincial Reserve Centres do not have any conveyance facility and have to manage on their own. As a result, they find it difficult to discharge their duties effectively and efficiently. There is a dire need of one government vehicle at every PR centre in the district.

(iv) *Power to take action against Petrol Pumps and LPG Dealers*—The control orders issued in this regard do not empower the district officers to impose any penalty on the offenders other than to register cases with the police or to refer the matter to the respective oil companies who are always reluctant to take action against their dealers. Therefore, there is a need to vest the district authorities with more powers under the EC Act, 1955 so as to maintain quality and quantity of these commodities.

(v) *False Allegations of Corruption*—Some people having contacts with power groups want that their work should be done on priority basis setting aside all the rules and regulations. They try to pressurize the department by getting themselves recommended on telephone. Some carry the visiting cards of VIPS and boast of their links with them to impress the officials/ officers. If they are asked to complete the formalities, they make a lot of hue and cry. These vested interests sometimes level false allegations of demanding bribes and extortion against the employees in order to exert pressure to get their illegal work done. This disturbs the peace of mind of the sincere employees and makes the working environment tense and strenuous.

(vi) *Problems Faced During Inspections, Raids, etc.*— Periodic raids are conducted by joint teams of officers of the oil companies, Food and Supplies Department and the police to check the misuse of domestic cylinders. The cylinders found to be misused at the hotels, dhabas, restaurants, tea stalls, railway stations, sweet shops, vehicles, industries, etc. are forfeited and sometimes cases are registered with the police against the defaulters. Thereafter, these defaulters and their relatives run from pillar to post to get back the forfeited cylinders. They even start lobbying in the offices and try to influence the employees in all possible manners. They threaten the employees with dire consequences if they do not cooperate with their unjustified demand of getting back the forfeited cylinders. The employees have to undergo a living hell to bear with the mob and sustain the pressure.

Suggestions for Restructuring

Fixation of MSP

There is considerable difference between the price of wheat in the open market and that fixed by the government. Due to higher price of agricultural produce in the open market than the procurement price offered by the government, the farmers prefer to sell it to the private traders instead of the government agencies. These private traders and dealers take advantage of the situation and offer a slightly higher price than that offered by the government but it is definitely lower than the actual market price. Recently, foodgrains prices have increased at a faster rate than prices of other commodities but very few farmers have benefited from this rise in prices because most of them sell their produce soon after the harvest in the local mandis. Their financial constraints do not allow them to store the foodgrains and wait for the right time to get higher price for their produce. Moreover, they do not have ample storage facilities and are compelled to sell it in distress only a few big farmers who can manage to store their foodgrains for a few months after the harvest get good price for their produce. Therefore, the MSP should be rationalized keeping in view the cost of cultivation including the cost of agricultural inputs, the hard labour put in by the farmers and prevailing market prices.

- *Government Purchase of Other Agricultural Commodities*—Government purchase is restricted only to a few commodities like wheat, bajra, paddy, mustard, etc. It should be extended to other crops like cotton, pulses, oil seeds, etc.
- *Food Articles Control Order*—The removal of licensing requirements, stock limits and movement restrictions on specified foodstuffs was ordered in May 2002. Now, any dealer may freely buy, stock, sell, transport, distribute, dispose, acquire, use or consume any quantity of wheat, paddy/rice, sugar , edible oils, etc. without taking any licence from the government. It has encouraged the private traders and dealers to hoard huge quantities of foodgrains during the season. Such hoarding leads to soaring prices. In the absence of any control order to check hoarders and black marketeers, district authorities find themselves helpless in controlling the situation. Therefore, the food articles control order must be revived to check hoarders and black-marketeers and keep the prices of foodgrains under control.
- *Position of Buffer Stock*— Food stocks are maintained

by the Central Government to (i) meet the prescribed minimum buffer stock norms for food security, (ii) for monthly releases of foodgrains for supply through the PDS/welfare schemes, (iii) to meet emergent situations arising out of unexpected crop failure, natural disasters, etc. and (iv) for market intervention to augment supply so as to moderate the open market prices. There has been a dwindling trend in the buffer stock of the Government of India recently and the government had to import wheat to meet the domestic requirements during the year 2006-07. The cause of this trend is not only the higher off-take of foodgrains for PDS but due to fall in procurement of foodgrains by government agencies. It affects the Public Distribution System adversely. Recently, the government curtailed the allocation of wheat for the APL category of consumers. Moreover, the government earlier used to release wheat under the Open Market Sale Scheme (OMSS) to stabilize the market price during off season. However, now it has issued very less quantity of wheat under OMSS. People are compelled to buy from open market which further leads to spurt in prices. Sincere efforts should be made to fulfil the domestic requirement from within the country rather than to resort to imports. This is possible only if the MSP is enhanced keeping in view the market conditions as now, even the MNCs have entered the foodgrains sector.

- *Security of Wheat Stocks*—Past experience has established that the services of the permanent *'chowkidars'* employed by the department are not reliable and up to the mark. On some occasions, their carelessness and negligence resulted in pilferage and shortages in the stocks of foodgrains stored under their custody and the government had to suffer huge financial losses. As the stocks to be looked after run into crores of rupees, the arrangements of watch and ward should be made through some private security agencies which can be held liable in case of any shortages in the stock.

- *Labour and Transportation* — The basic rates of labour and transportation have not been revised for a long time. At the time of finalization of tenders, the main criteria is to award the tender to the lowest bidder irrespective of the fact that the rates quoted by him may not be rational enough to complete the work satisfactorily. Even if the tender committee feels that the rate quoted by the lowest bidder are not practicable, it is bound to award the tender to him only because otherwise it might lead to litigation and can also make the integrity of the committee doubtful. It may raise the questions why the committee wants to offer more rates when the work can be done on lower rates. But, on many occasions after getting the tender one finds it difficult to complete the work during the season and leaves in between at the peak of procurement season . The concerned procurement agencies, then, have to face a lot of difficulties in making alternate arrangements as the *mandi* is to cleared on a day-to-day basis to make the procurement operations successful. In order to prevent such critical situations, the basic rates of the labour and transportation should be revised and rationalized by the government at the earliest possible.
- *Problem of Finance for Depot Holder*—Under the present system, it is required to make advance payments against the quantities to be lifted in a particular month. As the depot holders are not financially very sound, they generally lift one commodity at a time and sell it and then lift the other commodities one by one. It results in the consumers making two–three rounds to the FPS to get all the commodities. They

should, therefore, be provided with some interest free or low interest credit facilities by the government so that they can lift all the commodities together. The purpose of TPDS is definitely welfare considerations rather than profitability. Providing easy finance to the depot holders will not only benefit the consumers as they will not have to come again and again and but will also make it easier for the vigilance committees and inspectorate staff to supervise the distribution of essential commodities in one go. Thus, it will definitely be a step forward in the strengthening and streamlining of PDS in the state.

- *Profit Margin of Depot Holder*— As highlighted in the foregoing pages, the margin of the depot holder is meagre. A depot holder dependent solely on the ration depot for livelihood is unable to make both-ends-meet. As a result, he is likely to take recourse to unfair means like overcharging, under weight delivery of commodities, making fake supply entries in the ration cards with a view to divert commodities for sale to the open market. It leads to complaints against him from the consumers and in order to avoid action against him, he runs to his political patrons to save his depot from being suspended/cancelled. If we do not allow reasonable commissions to him we can never expect him to function fairly. To ensure fair distribution at the FPS, adequate quantities at reasonable commissions must be supplied to the depot holders so that the temptation for malpractices may be low. Even after that if anyone resorts to malpractices, stringent action under the PDS control order can be taken against him.
- *Role of Vigilance Committees at Village/Ward Level*— Many times, ration depot holders come and complain that the members of these committees make undue demands from them . If they do not listen to them,

they complain against them at various levels and make it difficult for them to work honestly. Therefore, such complaints must be verified by some independent agency.

- *Scale of Issue of Kerosene Oil*—One of the objectives of TPDS is to insulate the poor from rising open market prices. A poor person would be worse off in a dual market system if he gets only a small proportion of his requirement through TPDS. Presently, the non-LPG consumers in the state are supplied kerosene oil at the scale of 6-6.5 litres per family which is not sufficient from any angle for the household needs of a family of 5-6 members. As the government has stopped the sale of free sale kerosene oil also, these consumers face a lot of difficulty to arrange for alternative fuel for their kitchen. Therefore, the scale of kerosene oil distributed through the PDS needs to be raised at least upto 10 litres per family.
- *Levy Sugar* — Levy sugar at the scale of 235 gm per unit per family is being distributed to BPL/AAY categories of consumers. A family of four gets just 940 grams sugar in a month, which is not sufficient at all. Also, such quantity is difficult to weigh on the traditional weighing scale normally available with the depot holder. Moreover, it is difficult for the illiterate consumers to calculate the cost of such a quantity. The scale of issue per month per unit should be at least one kilogram so that the beneficiary gets an adequate quantity of sugar and is also easier for him to calculate the exact amount of the quantity he has purchased.
- *Rice*—Under the PDS, 10 kg rice per month is being provided to BPL and APL categories whereas there is no such provision for the AAY category. Rice should be allocated for AAY category as well.
- *APL Wheat*—The government has withdrawn a

considerable quantity of wheat from the allocation of wheat under the APL category. The present allocation is insignificant; hence, there is almost no lifting of wheat in this category. As the price of wheat in the open market is quite high, there is definitely demand of wheat from this category of consumers. The remedy to check diversion of foodgrains does not lie in withdrawing the allocations, but in finding ways and means to strengthen the PDS.

- *Fixation of Price of Various Essential Commodities*—Kerosene oil is being sold @ Rs.9.07 per litre, AAY wheat @ Rs.2.10 per kg, BPL wheat @ Rs.4.84 per kg, BPL rice @ Rs.6.40 per kg, APL wheat @ Rs.6.86 per kg and APL rice @ Rs. 9.15 per kg. On the present scale of commodities, the cost of AAY wheat comes to Rs. 73.50, BPL rice Rs. 64, APL wheat Rs.171.50, APL Rice Rs. 91.50 and Rs. 45.35 for 5 litre kerosene. Thus, The prices of all these commodities offer an opportunity to the depot holder to overcharge. He, on the pretext of non-availability of change, generally overcharges. To check this tendency, prices of all commodities should be rounded off so that the revenue so collected at least goes to the government as otherwise also it is not going to the consumers.
- *Addition of Essential Commodities*—The TPDS is one of the instruments for improving food security of the poor who suffer from persistent poverty and malnutrition. There is an urgent need to provide the essential commodities of daily consumption necessary for a nutritional diet as the aim of TPDS is to improve the welfare of a specific group of target population. Just as the state government has focused its attention on the mid day meal scheme to provide nutritional diet to the school children, similar efforts need to be taken under the TPDS also as a substantial number of poor families do not send their children

to school in spite of the best efforts made by the government. Also, such nutritional food is required for the parents also who work day and night to afford two square meal a day. Therefore, the state government should revise the list of essential commodities keeping in view the soaring prices of commodities like pulses, edible oils, the prices of which have increased manifolds in the past few months and which have become out of reach of the poor people.

- *Lack of Awareness of Panchayati Raj Institution* (PRIs)—It is a welcome step to strengthen the democracy at the grassroot level that PRIs have been empowered to contribute in the smooth functioning of TPDS at various levels. But the dark side is that a majority of them are unable to perform this role effectively due to lack of awareness and training required for the purpose. Following are some of the problems which hamper the smooth working of the PDS.

(i) *Allotment of New FPS*—Village panchayats have been empowered to pass resolutions in favour of the person interested in running a fair price shop in the village. Many times what the panchayats do is that after passing the resolution in favour of one person want to change it in favour of another person even before the depot is allotted. They start visiting the office telling their intention of changing the resolution saying that the earlier person is not liked by majority of the villagers and villagers have revolted against the panchayat. They do not even know that under the Panchayati Raj Act, 1994, the resolution once made cannot be changed before the expiry of ninety days. Their frequent visits disturb the working of the office. Therefore, the members of PRIs be given proper training by the institute like Haryana Institute of Rural Development, Nilokheri to create awareness among the members.

(ii) *Problem of Women Sarpanches*—Where there are women sarpanches, they are being reduced to rubber stamps only and have no knowledge of the working of the PRIs and the important role they have to play in the supervision of distribution of essential commodities in their village. So, the district administration should deal strictly with the proxy players in order to ensure a greater participation of women members in the working of PDS and other welfare schemes.

(iii) *Complaints of Unfair Distribution*—Many a times sarpanches make false complaints of unfair distribution against the FPS owner just because he does not belong to his caste, group or political party and he wants that it should be run by a person of his personal choice. They even get the thumb impressions and signatures of villagers on the complaint without telling them what they are actually signing. At the time of inquiry, the villagers tell that they had been told something else and they have no complaint against the FPS owner. Further, the members of panchayats be encouraged to work above the party lines.

(iv) *Identification of Target Population*—Identification of target groups falling under BPL and AAY categories suffers from many difficulties and limitations. Economically weaker sections of the population are to be identified by using the criterion of a specific level of household income. Use of these criteria is biased and rich and well to do find place in the list. PRIs have been associated with the responsibility of identifying the poor based on household specific characteristics (possession of various household items, annual income of the family, widows etc.) But, contrary to what was expected, PRIs included in the survey team influence the identification process and families having political affiliation with them find place in the survey list irrespective of the fact that they do not conform to the parameters set for the identification. Consequently, the benefit of the centrally sponsored schemes does not reach the needy and poor. Therefore, there is need for much more transparency in the mode of survey to list the beneficiaries.

(v) *Degeneration of Moral Values*—The government has stopped the supply of kerosene oil for LPG owners as they are already taking benefit of the subsidy given on the domestic cylinder. But, the people want to avail both the benefits by hook or by crook. For this, they get separate ration cards made even if they are living under one roof. They get one ration card stamped for gas and take kerosene oil on the remaining cards. In a number of cases, separate ration cards are got issued for the widow mother or widower father. The curiosity to know the reason for this behaviour brought out the fact that kerosene oil instead of diesel is being used by the villagers to run their engines in the fields. In the towns and cities, it is used in autorickshaws. When enquired that it could damage the engine, it was told that it was cheaper even after paying for the repair of the engines. So, such malpractices be curbed by the concerned departments working at the district level.

(vi) *Ration Cards for Other Purposes*—Ration cards are being issued for the purpose of ration only by the Food and Supplies Department, but these are being used mainly for the purpose of identification. Although the government has issued directions in this regard, still even many government departments insist on the production of ration cards for the purpose of identification. The passport offices do not accept the application for passport without the ration card. The number of people rushing to the Food and Supplies Office for the ration card just because they need it for purposes other than rationing. The government must do something on its end to stop this routine so that the time spent on making unnecessary ration cards can be usefully devoted to some other useful works of the department.

(vii) *Old Guidelines and Instructions*—Panchayati Raj manual of the Department has not been revised ever since it was written. It carries designations like District Food Controller, Distribution and Supply Officer, Assistant Food Controller, Foodgrains Supervisor etc. which are no longer used and have been redesignated. Many instructions and guidelines have lost their signi-ficance in the light of changed circumstances. So, there is a need to amend the manual at the earliest.

(viii) *Low Pay Scales*—Just like the guidelines, the pay scales of the district officers/officials are not in tune with their duties and responsibilities and need to be enhanced in view of the complex nature of their jobs and heavy responsibility they carry on their shoulders. It will act as a morale booster.

REFERENCES

Provincial Reserve Manual, Part-1, Department of Food and Civil Supplies, Reprinted on August 1998.

Citizen's Charter, Food & Supplies Department, Haryana.

Guidelines for Procurement of Rabi Marketing Season and Kharif Marketing Season 2006-07

Guidelines for making Ration Cards.

19 Imperative Need for Improving the Working of the District Administration in India

A Study of the Aizawl District in Mizoram

*Lalneihzovi**

Today India consists of 593 districts (Census of India, 2001) and each district consists of nearly thirteen hundred villages on an average. Average area covered under a district is nearly eleven thousand square kilometers. While some of the districts cover an area as large as fourty thousand square kilometers, there are some districts having areas as small as a few hundred square kilometers only. There are 5,470 sub-districts, 5,161 towns and 638,588 villages in the country. District, hence as a unit of administration, is neither too large nor too small an area to enjoy competence/autonomy. It is just the "optimum unit" that can draw sufficient resources and the technical know-how that are needed for the efficient administration, and to maintain the right balance between homogeneity and diversity that is needed for sustaining an active elite group. It is the first level in the country where the officials try to implement the planned programmes. Therefore, district is the level at which the government machinery is represented in its totality. It is the cutting edge of the administrative machinery since it implements all the policies formulated by the government departments at the State and the Central Government level. The formulations

* Reader, Department of Public Administration, Mizoram University, Aizwal.

of all the plans and the policies at the State and Central Government level requires huge amount of data which can be collected and compiled most effectively at the district level due to its optimum size and the fact that each and every department of the government is represented at the district level. District is also the first level in the hierarchy of administration in India at which the administrative machinery of the government (both the Central and the State Government) comes in direct contact with the people. It is the level at which the image the government is formed. Any inactivity on the part of the district administration is directly manifested in the form of decrease in the popularity of the government. Thus, every village and town in the country forms part of the district. S.S. Khera has defined that "district administration is the total functioning of government in a district; that total and complex organisation of the management of public affairs at work, dynamic and not static in the territory of a geographically demarcated district-district administration includes all the agencies of government, the individuals officials and functionaries, public servants-all institutions for the management of public affairs in the district, all the bodies corporate such as the panchayats of different kinds-all advisory bodies associated with the administration."[1]

It is at this level that the policies of the government are made into practice and the problems of local people are studied and communicated to the state government. It is in the district that the big and complex administrative machinery of government is in operation and it is by its accomplishments at this vital centre/unit that the extent of success of governmental policies, plans and programmes are measured.[2] A district is normally placed under the charge of a district officer called Deputy Commissioner or District Collector who virtually acts as the eyes, ears and arms of the state Government. Thus many state functionaries like the Superintendent of Police, Assistant Registrar of Cooperative

Societies, District Agricultural Officer, District Medical Officer, etc., are located at the district headquarters and their jurisdiction extents to the district. The district thus, has a multiple organizational units having a galaxy of officers for administering the affairs of the government.[3]

District has always existed as the administrative unit in some form throughout long history of the country. For instance, the code of Manu describes the general form of administration which starts with the village as the basic unit. He describes the village as a more or less self-contained republic, a social group in a state of stable economic equilibrium, a political group running its own affairs as a community in a state of balance. The Mauryas, Guptas and others established the historically identified empires/ kingdoms in India to administer their huge dominions efficiently and effectively. They divided the empires/ kingdoms into provinces, which were further divided into districts, known as *'ahars'*, *'vishyas'* and *'pradeshas'*. The Mughal emperors had divided their kingdoms into provinces which were sub-divided into 'sarkars' or districts. Each sarkar was composed of a number of 'parganas' and each pargana was a union of several villages. When the British came to India and acquired territories, through conquest or otherwise, they needed a machinery to collect the revenue from the areas acquired by them. They created a new office of District Collector. The Collectors were appointed "to supervise the revenue collections and to preside in the courts" following the historic decision of the East India Company to "stand forth as diwan and to take upon themselves, by the agency their own servants, the entire care and administration of the revenues". Thus, the office of the Collector of today was for the first time in India created by the Government of Warren Hastings under the regulations of May 14, 1772 which provided for the appointment of such an officer in each district in their acquired territory. Since independence, the district administration has acquired a new dimension. An efficient administration is the backbone of any organization. The government is concerned about the needs to tone up the administrative machinery with a view to make available quality services, medical care and other services to general public expeditiously.

In the present age of development administration, the districts do face a change in the ecology of administration; those incharge of the district, in turn, face a challenge in their new role as change agents. A part from this it has even assumed greater significance in the light of the growing emphasis on development planning and the implementation of welfare and development programmes through process of democratic decentralization. Consequently the problems relating to district organization and the efficient functioning of administration have increased tremendously, and these have at times defied adequate and appropriate solutions. By the close of the seventies and beginning of the eighties, district administration got added dimensions so as to function as a real and effective instrument of change and development. This perhaps has been reflected in the policy statements of successive governments and constitution of various committees and commissions to achieve the goal of decentralized planning and decentralization of democratic institutions up to the grass-roots level. Behind all these efforts the main concern had been to make district administration action and development oriented and to make it responsive to the hopes and aspirations of teeming millions in the countryside. The vision and expectations of the founding father of the nation,.......could not get the proper hearing........... and only a lip service was given to decentralization and responsive district administration. As a result, after independence instead of adopting the bottom-up approach to all the developmental activities at the district level, the policy planners and implementors opted for 'top-down' approach and trickle down theory which resulted in dismal performance at the development front.[4]

The paper gives an account of the historical evolution of District Administration in Mizoram and presents imperative need for improving the working of administration in the Aizawl District.

District Administration in Mizoram

The district administration in Mizoram (then Lushai Hills) began in the year 1891 when the territory was divided into two administrative wings, viz., the North Lushai Hills District, part of Assam, and the South Lushai Hills District, a part of Bengal. The Political Officers[5] were an incharge of the districts with administrative control. Prior to 1891, there was no regular administrative set-up. But the 1891 status lasted for only seven years. The British rulers in 1898, decided to merge the two areas (districts) into one Lushai Hills District, as a part of Assam for administrative convenience. The same year marked the beginning of settled administration in the district. J. Shakespeare, who was till then Political Officer of the North Lushai Hills district, became the first Superintendent[6] of the newly amalgamated district. The last was Satyendra Nath Barkatoki, who was the first Indian to be appointed as the Superintendent.

The new amalgamated district (Lushai Hills) started functioning from April 1, 1898 under the provisions of Assam Frontier Tract Regulations, 1880 and the Scheduled Districts Act, 1874. Under Rules for the Regulation of Procedure, 1937, the administration of the Lushai Hills was vested in the Chief Commissioner of the then composite Assam, the Superintendent of then Lushai Hills, his Assistants and in the Chiefs and the Headmen of the villages. The Chiefs were responsible for the behaviour of their people and the Superintendent and his Assistants were to uphold the authority of the Chief to the best of their ability.

Since there was a single line of administration in the district, the Superintendent was the real authority and also the official head of all departments in the district. The Chiefs, in turn, had supreme power in the village administration. Briefly, the Superintendent and the Chiefs used to rule over the people as virtual dictators. The political system was such that no one could dare speak against their activities or criticise any act of their.[7] The British Superintendent neither liked the Mizo people to develope political consciousness nor allowed them to come in contact with Indian nationalism and freedom movement.

This status of the Superintendent continued till the Indian Constitution came into force in 1950, but there was a gradual change in the powers of the Superintendent and the Chiefs in accordance with the gradual changes in the British India. With the introduction of the Mizo Autonomous District Council in 1952 and the Pawi - Lakher Regional Council in 1953 (Pawi, Lakher and Chakma), the designation of the Superintendent was changed and the district administration was put under a Deputy Commissioner (DC) and the Chief Executive Members (CEMs) of the District and Regional Councils with much curtailed powers after Independence. Since 1952, the head of the district administration began to be called Deputy Commissioner. The name of the Lushai Hills district was changed to the Mizo Hills district. The exploitative institution of the chiefship was abolished by both the Mizo Hills District Council and the Pawi- Lakher Regional Council on April 1, 1954 and April 15, 1954 respectively. The village administration in Mizoram was vested in the democratically constituted Village Councils, which later started functioning in the respective jurisdictions of the Councils. The Mizo Hills district was elevated to the status of Union Territory of Mizoram on January 21, 1972 under the provisions of the North-Eastern Areas (Re-organisation) Act, 1971 with the Legislative Assembly. The Mizo Hills District Council stood abolished. The Pawi-Lakher Regional Council was trifurcated into the Lai District Council, the Mara District Council and the Chakma District Council. The

Government of Union Territory of Mizoram reorganised the district administration. As a result, the Aizawl, the Lunglei and the Chhimtuipui districts were set-up. Their headquarters were respectively Aizawl, Lunglei and Saiha. The three Deputy Commissioners headed these districts, representing the state government. The Chief Executive Members of the three District Councils represent their Councils. Thus, both the functionaries worked independently of each other having no coordination. Mizoram was elevated from the status of Union Territory to Statehood on February 20, 1987. The three Deputy Commissioners with their Assistants carried out the district administration in Mizoram.

Administration in Aizawl District

The Aizawl district is the biggest of the three districts of Mizoram, the 23rd State of the Indian Union which covers an area of 12,588 sq. kms., a little over 59.71 per cent of the total area of the state. With a set-up of a Union Territory of Mizoram under the provisions of the North-Eastern Areas (Re-organisation) Act, 1971, the Aizawl district headed by the Deputy Commissioner came into existence who was assisted by Additional Deputy Commissioner and Sub-Divisional Officers with other Officers and the staff at the district headquarters. The Sub-Divisional Officer is assisted by one Sub-Divisional Magistrate at the Sub-Divisional headquarters, the Block Development Officers at the Community Development headquarters and the Administrative Officers in certain selected centres. Till 1998, the Aizawl district covered more than half of the areas of the state of Mizoram. To have an effective administration as well as to implement various developmental schemes in the larger interests of both the rural and the urban people, the Aizawl district was divided into five districts viz., Aizawl district, headquarters at Aizawl; Champhai district, headquarters at Champhai; Mamit district, headquarters at Mamit; Kolasib district, headquarters at Kolasib; and Serchhip district, headquarters at Serchhip. The operational/functional jurisdiction of the Deputy Commissioner owing to the division of erstwhile Aizawl district was reduced, no doubt, but the powers and functions of the Deputy Commissioner remained the same and unchanged. It may be said that the district administration has not yet been decentralised and as a result, the Mizo people have no political participation in decision-making and implementing processes, though the district administration is an important feature of Indian decentralised democratic governance. Therefore, efforts should be made to make district administration perfect in all respects keeping in view that on its perfection depends to a large extent the perfection of Indian democracy.[8]

The administrative structure and functioning of the Aizawl district are still based on the colonial rules, regulations and acts even after fifty nine years of Independence. Briefly, the district administration in the state has not yet been democratized and decentralized. It has centralized governance making the office of the Deputy Commissioner more powerful compared to his plains counter parts which contradicts the constitutional provisions. The Aizawl district has both structural and functional problems. Therefore, it is suggested restructuring the existing administrative structures of the district in view of the constitutional changes in order to make it responsive, goal and result oriented.[9]

Concluding Observations and Remarks

The Deputy Commissioner derives his powers and functions from the rules framed by the Governor of Mizoram under section 92 of the Government of India Act, 1935 and numerous standing orders like the Rules for the Regulations of the Procedure of Officers appointed to administer the Lushai Hills, 1937. The Rule 1-A of the Rules of 1937 says that the district administration in Mizoram is vested in the Governor, the Deputy Commissioner and his Assistants (ADCs) and in Chiefs and Headmen of villages. The Deputy Commissioner, thus, discharges multiple functions like those pertaining to collectorate, magisterial, public distribution system, revenue, arms, elections, maintenance of law and order, implementation of government orders, development functions, relationship with the police, coordination between various technical departments in the district, public press, elected representatives and administration of Inner Line Regulations. Besides, he has the most important power of judicial administration.

Rules for the Regulation of the Procedures appointed to administer justice in the Lushai Hills (now Mizoram), 1937 empowers the Deputy Commissioner and his Assistants to exercise criminal and civil justice. The Deputy Commissioner is also empowered to carry out executive functions. Thus, he combines in himself both executive and judicial powers which may lead to violation of justice by encouraging partial, arbitrary and biased decisions in criminal and civil cases, enjoying more powers than his counterparts in plain districts of the country where there have been a seperation of executive and judicial powers following the enforcement of the Directive Principles of State Policy. Since judiciary is a corner stone of democratic government and upon it is built the superstructure of civil liberty.[10] It is suggested to bring about a seperation between executive and judicial functions of the Deputy Commissioner which is an imperative need without delaying further. It has been further suggested that the powers of deciding criminal and civil cases need to be vested in the District and Session Judge or Judicial Officers, who are Law graduates. The combination of the two powers of the Deputy Commissioner in the district also contradicts the federal feature of the Indian Constitution which is an independent judiciary to decide issues/cases concerning criminal and civil justice.

So to make an impartial, efficient and healthy justice available to the people of the district, to check arbitrary decisions and to maintain the principles of checks and balances, the government of Mizoram has taken certain steps to transfer control of subordinate magistracy or judicial powers to some authority other than the Deputy Commissioner. But the steps taken by the government are not made effective till today. Thus, seperation of the Deputy Commissioner's judicial powers from his executive powers/functions by way of immediate repeal of the Rules of 1937 and extension of the Criminal Procedure Code, 1973 will definitely fulfil a long avoided constitutional obligation.[11]

It is also suggested to streamline/strengthen the revenue and personnel administration in the district to have effective and efficient revenue administration, there should be a proper arrangement of maintaining land records to avoid land litigations. It is also suggested that the Land Revenue Acts, Rules, Regulations, and Agricultural Acts/Rules and Regulations which have been enacted by the erstwhile District Council and adapted by department need to be changed or amended keeping in view of fast changing in the revenue and land administration. The government should initiate land reforms measure and Land Ceiling Acts to prevent a fast individualisation of land which results in producing a large number of landless, agricultural labourers and share croppers. To avoid confusion in respect of Village Council's role in revenue administration in rural areas as well as in urban areas, it is suggested that the implementation of the provisions of Part IX and Part X of the Constitution relating to panchayats and nagarpalikas to ensure proper land administration in the state.[12]

In view of the growing problem of crime and its sophistication there is an urgent need for modernisation of law and order administration through incorporation of modern techniques of administration as well as new technology needed for the maintenance of law and order.

The process of computerization should be extended in a big way so as to keep the information relating to crime and criminals upto date. There is also the need for decentralization of power and devolution of authority from the state police headquarters to the district level and down to the lower level of law and crder administration. Better public relations would not only ensure effective functioning of the police administration but also meaningful public relation programmes which would provide necessary public support to the police to enable them to render better and more acceptable service.[13]

It may be further suggested that our legislators need to think a great deal keeping in view a frequent breakdown of the law enforcement in several states and the partisan law-enforcement policy. If there is any danger, it is not from the law-enforcement officers but from the politicians who either due to ignorance or personal or party interests, might take delight in the muddle of many forces and the many organizations. It is necessary to remember that an efficient law enforcement machinery of any nation forms the keystone in the structure of a democratic government.

It has been emphasised that restructuring and revitalising of the Aizawl district administration for decentralized democratic governance in the larger interests of the people especially the rural and the urban areas by implementing the provisions of the 73rd and 74th Constitutional Amendment Acts. This grassroots democratic decentralised polity by introducing/making Panchayati Raj Institutions and Municipalities appears to be an instrument of rural and urban local-self governments. Therefore, it has been suggested to introduce the provisions of the 73rd and 74th Constitutional Amendments Act, 1992 by a suitable enactment to have a local-self government institution in the district/state. Because the village council is not a local-self government institution. So the concept of democratic decentralistion hardly operates in the state. The Village

Councils have very limited functions and mostly administrative and judicial powers of petty nature. Development functions to bring about socio-economic transformation in the rural/urban Mizoram are beyond the scope of Village Councils. Not to allow the operation of the 73rd and 74th Constitutional Amendment Acts, 1992 is not in keeping with the national goals democratic decentralised governance and decentralised planning processes for both rural and urban developments.[14]

Inner Line Regulation, (ILR) 1873 framed and introduced in the then Lushai Hills/Mizo Hills district (now Mizoram) by the British rulers and continued to be enforced by the government of Mizoram (Deputy Commissioner of the Aizawl District) has been losing its relevance after post independence period owing to the adoption of the capitalist model of modernisation or capitalist-market economy by the country. As a result, the tribal economy has already been exposed to capitalist economy.

It is suggested that the ILR needs to be liberalized/ modified to have competition in the market for the all round developments of the district and of the state, as regards the generation of revenues/growth of economy to fulfil the growing needs of the people. No faster development is possible if the territory is to remain a closed community and shut its door on the people from outside the state. So there is a great need of relationship between the Mizo people and the outside elements in trade, commerce, administrative works and socio-economic development spheres.[15]

There is also need to improve the field administration of the development departments in the district to promote optimum delivery of public services. There is also the need to build complete transparency and openness in public transactions and insist on the requirement along the line of 'citizen's charter' of response time and regard to various public transactions/performances.

The administration of the Aizawl district, whose structure and functioning are still based on colonial rules, regulations and acts even after more than five decades of independence. Briefly, the district administration in the state has not yet been democratised and decentralised. So the people have no democratic participation in the governance of the district. Thus, the district has both structural and functional problems/defects.

Therefore, this paper strongly proposes to suggest restructuring the existing administrative structure of the district in view of the constitutional changes in order to make it responsive, goal/result oriented supported by political masters/policy makers with strong will.

As has been experienced, the district, which exists today, suffers from various problems and ailments such as structural or organisational inadequacies, administrative process and problems thereof viz, planning, information collection, unity of action, control and coordination, motivation, mobilization of personnel and human resources development, behavioural inconsistencies involving district collector and other officers and the general public, elites, representatives, party functionaries, organised groups, press correspondents, social interests, economic interests of industries, professional groups of doctors, engineers, lawyers, contractors, forest lessees, administrative classes, police officers, judges, magistrates, attorneys and procedural hurdles and bottlenecks, red tapism, delays in justice, "preferred justice" civil procedural hurdles.[16] Undoubtedly, this pivotal administrative unit and office of the collector have experienced ups and downs during the course of their long history. The decline in authority and prestige of the District Collector/Deputy Commissioner is not an isolated phenomenon but is part of an all-round decline of institutions and professions caused by the steady erosions of the value system. Despite, it also remains true that by whatever Constitution, India may be ruled, no government will be able to do without the district and its district officer. It may be further added that district, before 1947, was indeed, an image of total government writ small. Professor Richard L. Park says that, "It is not very surprising that independent India saw little reason in 1947 to develop a new organization. The old administrative pattern was accepted more or less intact."[17] All essential welfare activities for the people are undertaken/ performed at the district level. With the introduction of planning and development functions, the district administration has become overburdened, no doubt, but it has been trying to develop/build the country from below. Briefly, since independence, the district administration has acquired a new dimension. An efficient administration is the backbone of any organization. The government is concerned about the needs to tone up the administrative machinery with a view to make available quality services, medical care and other services to general public expeditiously. In this context the level of administration that needs to be reformed and restructured if necessary is the District level administration where the implementation of all policies and programmes is vested with. This has to be taken care keeping in view of the socio-economic changes that has taken place in the era of LPG in today's world. This may necessitate restructuring and reforming of the whole administrative structure/system in the country.

NOTES AND REFERENCES

1. S.S. Khera, *District Administration in India,* New Delhi, National Publishing House, 1979, p. 78.
2. Lalneihzovi, *District Administration in Mizoram : A Study of the Aizawl District (1972-1995),* (unpublished Doctoral Dissertation), p.17.
3. R. B. Jain, T. N. Chaturvedi, *District Administration,* New Delhi, Volume 1, Indian Institute of Public Administration, p. vi.
4. Sweta Mishra, District Administration and Panchayati Raj Institutions, in, S. N. Mishra *et al., Public Governance and Decentralisation,* New Delhi, Mittal Publications, 2003, pp. 631-632.
5. Singh, B.P., *The Problem of Change : A Study* of *North-East India,* Delhi, Oxford University Press, 1987, p. 107 (cited in Arvind K. Sharma, District Council in the North-East, New Delhi, *Indian Journal of Public Administration,* July-September, 1997, p.784). The District Officers of

the hill areas carried designations different from those of the Assam-plains' Deputy Commissioners (those in the hills were called Political Officers/Superintendents) and they had far larger discretion than their plains' counterparts .....

6. *Ibid.*
7. R.N. Prasad and Lalneihzovi, Analytical Study of the Judicial Powers of the Deputy Commissioner in Mizoram, *in,* R.N. Prasad and P Chakraborty, *Administration of Justice in MIzoram,* New Delhi, Mittal Publications, 2006, p. 44.
8. Lalneihzovi, *qp.cit.,* p.145
9. R.N. Prasad, *Public Administration in North-East India,* New Delhi, Vikas Publishing House, 1998, p. 18.
10. Lalneihzovi, *op. cit.,* pp. 51-52
    Notification of the Revenue Department, Government of Mizoram No. K *15013/69/99-Rev/Dated* Aizawl, the 26th September, 2005.
11. Jaytilak Guha Roy (ed), *Policing in Twentyfirst Century,* New Delhi, Indian Institute of Public Administration, 1999, p. 98.
12. Lalneihzovi, *op.cit.,* pp. 55-61.
13. *Ibid.,* pp. 151-153.
14. R. N. Prasad and Lalneihzovi, Perspectives on Democratic Decentralised Governance for Rural Development in Mizoram, in E. Vayunandan and Dolly Mathew (eds), *Good Governance in India,* New Delhi, Prentice Hall of India, 2004, p. 130.
15. Lalneihzovi, *op. cit.,* pp. 148-149.
16. R.D. Sharma, (ed.), *District Administration in India : Problems and Prospects,* New Delhi, H.K. Publishers and Distributors, 1990, pp.17-18.
17. *Ibid.,* p. 17.

20 Role of IT in District administration
A Case Study of District Sirsa

*Raj Kumar Siwach** and *Balraj Singh***

The truly revolutionary impact of the Information Revolution is just beginning to be felt...

—Peter F. Drucker[1]

Introduction

Transformation is a rudiment law of nature, everything has changed with the passage of time. But the innovations of new technologies in 21st century have enhanced the speed of transformation marvelously. Among these technologies, the Information Technology emerges as a powerful tool for delivery of services in the public sector, private sector, education, training and numerous fields of the transport, communication, trade, banking, education and governance. But its effects in the field of governance for improving transparency, efficiency and effectiveness has been ushering a new era. So, it becomes pertinent to understand the meaning and definition of IT.

Macmillan Dictionary of Information Technology defines IT as, "The acquisition, processing, storage and dissemination of vocal, pictorial, textual and numerical information by a

* Lecturer, Public Administration at Ch. Devi Lal University, Sirsa (HARYANA) (E-mail:R.Siwach@rediffmail.com)

** Ph.D. Scholar, Department of Public Administration, Ch. Devi Lal University, Sirsa (HARYANA) (E-mail:siwach.b@ rediffmail.com) micro-electronics based combination of computing and telecommunications."[2]

Wikipedia, the Free Encyclopedia defines, "IT is the technology required for information processing. In particular the use of electronic computers and computer software to convert, store, protect, process, transmit, and retrieve information from anywhere, anytime."[3]

P.K.Mehrotra a practicing administrator opines, "Information Technology is as electronic means of capturing, processing, storing and communicating information. It is basically a combination of computer hardware and software and communication networks.[4]

So, it emerges from above definition that IT embraces acquisition, processing, storage, transmition and retrieve information for desired one with the help of computer hardware and software and communication networks.

The Ministry of Information Technology, Government of India emphasises its importance in following words, "The advent of Information Technology as a highly leveraged enabling tool for delivery of services in the public and the private sector has by now been universally recognized. This has redefined the fundamentals and has the potential to change the institutions as well as the mechanisms of delivery of services forever."[5]

When IT is used by governmental organisations for improving the governance process then it is known as E-Governance (electronic-governance). Adoption of E-governance brought a massive change in approach of government procedures and work, style. Different authors have defined E-governance as following—

According to Sameer Kochhar and Dhanjal, "Electronic delivery of government services (that are actually received) to citizens, businesses and other external consumers of such services in a reliable, timely and transparent manner."[6]

In the views of INTOSAI, "E-Governance is the online

exchange of government information and the delivery of services to citizens, business and other government agencies."[7]

The Gartner Group describes E-governance as, "The continuous optimization of service delivery, constituency participation, and governance by transforming internal and external relationships through technology, the Internet, and new media."[8]

Another succinct definition of E-governance comes from OECD. The OECD defines, "E-governance as the use of information and communication technologies, and particularly the Internet, as a tool to achieve better government."[9]

H.M. Rajashekar defines, "E-governance is as an application of IT to the processes of government functioning to bring out responsible, efficient and transparent governance."[10]

The World Bank defines E-governance as, "The use of information and communication technologies by government agencies to transform relations with citizens, business and other arms of the government."[11]

Jasmeet Kaur Egan defnes, "E-Governance is the application of information in the functioning of governmental activities/ services and allowing direct participation of the citizens in policy making, policy implementation, decision making."[12]

P.C. Hota Committee defines, "E-Governance is the use of Information and Communication Technologies (ICT) to transform government by making it more accessible, effective and accountable."[13]

P.K. Mehrotra defines, "E-governance is the name given to the information technology driven public and development administration system which essentially means delivery of government services and information to the people using electronic means."[14]

Renu Budhiraja defines, "Electronic Governance as giving citizens the choice of when and where they access government information and services channel view. This would mean using more and more of Electronics Information Technology in many of the government functions."[15]

An analysis of above definitions reveal that E-Governance is a process requiring provision of hardware, networking, software and re-engineering of the procedures for better delivery of services. It is the application of Information Technology to the processes of government functioning in order to bring about Simple, Moral, Accountable, Responsive and Transparent (SMART) governance.

Initiatives and Objectives of E-Governance in India

In India, for keeping in view far reaching benefits of E-governance many initiatives were taken at the governmental level. Though globally we are lagging far behind as the status of India is ranked 43rd out of 60 (EIU 2002), 54th (IDC 2001), and 34th (Global Technology Index, 2002).

The Prime Minister while reiterating the importance of IT on August 15th, 2002, said "Government would implement a comprehensive programme to accelerate E-Governance at all levels of the government to improve efficiency, transparency and accountability at the government-citizen interface".

India has become one of the most preferred destinations for sourcing software and IT enabled services. In comparison to other low cost locations, India ranks high in several critical parameters, including level of government support, quality of the labour pool, english language skills, project management skills, entrepreneurial culture, strong customer relationships and exposure to new technologies. India's strength has been enhanced by the industry's strong focus on quality software and processes.

The software and services industry continues to be the dominant factor in the overall growth of the Indian industry. The total value of software and services export is estimated at Rs. 55,510 crore (US$ 12.2 billion) in 2003-04, an increase of 20.4 per cent in rupee terms and 28 per cent in dollar terms. This segment will continue to show robust growth in future also. Indian IT, Software and Services industry is expected to account for 2.64 per cent of India's GDP and 21.3 per cent of exports during 2003-04 and, is projected to account for 7 per cent of India's GDP and 35 per cent of exports by 2008. The Nasscoin McKinsey Report of June 2002 has reiterated that despite recent slow down the IT Services (ITS) and IT Enabled Services (ITES), the industry is poised to meet its long term export potential of US$ 57-65 billion for the Software and Services sector by 2008. This means a share of 6 per cent of the global market. International Institute of Information Technology (IIIT), Hyderabad is a new generation institution set-up to produce manpower and new technologies to power the IT industry. It has already become a prime destination for student in India seeking high-quality education in IT.

As an IT institution, IIIT Hyderabad has tried to combine education in Computer Science with Electronics and Communications. This is the age of convergence of hardware and software. In this institution computer scientists are also taught electronics, while electronics engineers learn software development too.

National Institute of SMART government: The National Institute of Smart Government (NISG) at Hyderabad was set-up by the Department of Administrative Reforms and Public Grievances and the Department of Information Technology, Government of India and some private agencies is an institution for promoting public private partnerships in the area of E-Governance. The NISG has taken up a number of E-Governance projects both at the Centre and the states. Though this is a good beginning, one NISG is not likely to make a significant impact on the problems facing E-Governance in the country. After evaluating the performance of the NISG more such institutions should be set-up in different parts of the country so that conceptualization and implementation of E-governance projects are taken up on a Mission Mode.

National Informatics Centre: The National Informatics Centre (NIC) is the foremost agency under the Department of Information Technology which is in charge of the hardware and software aspects of E-Governance in the states and Central Government. The NIC has undertaken large scale investments to lint; different districts in the country and push through E-governance initiatives in a number of areas. Many state governments are struggling with the same or similar problems without being aware of the successes achieved by other states in same area. Since NIC is present in all states of the country, it could function as a vehicle for disseminating best practices right across the country.

The Department of Administrative Reforms and Public Grievances and the Department of Information 'Technology have instituted awards for exceptional E-governance initiatives. The National E-Governance Conference is organized to highlight the achievements of such initiatives in various part of the country.

The Government of India has approved the National E-Governance Action Plan for implementation during the year 2003-2007. The Plan seeks to lay the foundation and provide the impetus for long-term growth of E-Governance within the country. The plan seeks to create the right governance and institutional mechanisms, set-up the core infrastructure and policies and implements a number of Mission Mode Projects at the center, state and integrated service levels to create a citizen-centric and business-centric environment for governance. The National E-Governance Action Plan was presented to the Prime Minister on 6th Novermber, 2003. The Plan has been approved in-principle and endorsement has been given to the overall program content, implementation approach and governance structures. However, for budgetary outlays separate approvals from Planning Commission/Ministry of Finance are envisaged.

Objectives of E-Governance

In India, the objectives of E-Governance could be enumerated as under :

(1) Ensuring better service delivery to citizens;
(2) *Transparency in governance:* E-government can be used to reduce opportunities for petty corruption at the point of service delivery; and provide mechanisms to create more accountability and transparency in the pubic sector;
(3) *Empowerment through Information:* Information is a critical ingredient for development. The more information that the poor possess, the greater their sense of empowerment;
(4) Empowered citizens can more readily hold governments accountable. With greater information the poor also better able to organize and take actions to improve their quality of life;
(5) To bring efficiency and effectiveness in governance;
(6) Services at any time and any where; and
(7) Elimination of delays, harassment, red-tapism in administration.

E-Governance Programmes in India: Some Experiments at the State Level

Government of India and state governments have implemented some E-Governance programmes. Here, it will be pertinent to explain some of very successful programmes. These are;

Suwidha : Suwidha centers in rural Punjab are providing a single window for 24 services in 120 flavors. These include all kinds of licenses certificates, passports, approvals, pension cases and ration cards, etc. There are 18 suwidha centers-one each for every district in Punjab. These are now planned to be rolled out to 72 sub-divisions by the end of this year

(2005). Most of these services that used to take days earlier are now available in a matter of hours.

Rajiv Computer Literacy Program in Assam *(RCLPA)* : is already implemented in 400 schools covering 1, 50,000 students in places even as remote as Majuli, a remote island in Brahamaputrarry. Students are taught Physics, Chemistry, Mathematics and English using computers. The facilities in Majuli were as good as those in Guwahati so were the students aspirations. While a students in Guwahati wants to be becomes an engineer, a Mishing tribal girl in Majuli is planning to become an airhostess thanks to her English lessons.

E-Seva : In the case of the rural E-Seva project in the West Godavari belt of Andhra Pradeah the original project began just as a facilitation centre, to allow citizens to get their income and other certificates in one place. Now, it is used to pay bills, to allow children to get computer-enabled education, people are even selling traditional product like lace through the system. The most interesting point is that while utility bill payments were being made through the system, the users of it even, bid to become meter readers and won the tender? The original project began with 46 such centers and has scaled to over 200 centers and 2 million transactions till date.

Citizen Information Centre : In remote Temi village of *South Sikkim*, the Citizen Information Centre (CIC) housed in the Panchayat Ghar is their window to the outside world. From examination results, to downloading all kinds of government forms, looking for jobs, Internet banking and commodity prices, the citizens aged 6 to 60 are finding good value in the service. There are 40 such centers spread over the state.

IT in Judicial System

While one of the solutions being worked in to reduce the pendency of cases in the country's courts is to increase the number of benches, a computerization project in the Supreme Court saw the pendency of cases come down from 152,000 in 1996 to around 29,000 today. To curb cases on the basis of 'points of law and once this was done, and a judgment given on one point of law, automatically a whole host of other cases got decided as well, E-Governance is successfully implemented in the *Supreme Court and 18 High Courts*. Today, for courts like the Supreme Court and the Delhi/Rajasthan High Court, case status can be got on the internet, judgments since 2001 are available on the internet, and a pilot project has been done already to have digitally signed copies of orders available immediately after an order is dictated.

Apart from doing video-conferencing with under trials in the jails itself (with the judges in their chambers), an attempt is being made to speed up things with 'virtual' benches. Similarly, while it took litigants up to 6 months sometimes to get certified copies of judgments, this is now available within half an hour. Indeed, in Delhi, judges have been given laptops and training in ICT techniques. A lot of the time taken by for instance is to study precedents in similar cases now all this can be done much faster using ICT technology.

WARANA : Cooperative complex is an example of successful integrated rural development resulting from co-operative movement through people's participation. It comprises of 25 co-operative societies in the field of sugar, milk, poultry, house construction, etc. The primary objective of the project is to demonstrate the effective contribution of an IT infrastructure in the accelerated socio-economic development of a cluster of 70 contiguous villages around Warana in the Kolhapur and Sangli Districts.

SETHU : Is an initiative of the Government of Maharashtra which provides for citizen satisfaction through its services. The facilitation centre offers one stop counter services for all certificates, permits, etc., time bound clearance of applications across the counter, public grievance redress, availability of information relating to all administrative processes, the pendancy of applications and such other details.

FRIENDS : Janasevana Kendram is a Citizen Friendly

Service Centre set-up by the Department of Information Technology, in association with the Thiruvananthapuram Corporation. The Integrated Service centre called FRIENDS (Fast, Reliable, Instant, Efficient, Network for Disbursement of Services) at Saphalya Complex of TRIDA at Palayam has 20 computerized counters which work on the principle of "Collect And Remit" and "Receive And Forward" methods to offer services such as KSEB Bill Payments, KWA Bill Payments, Property Tax, Professional Tax, Traders License Fee, Building Tax, Basic Tax, Revenue Recovery, fee for new —ration card, Motor Vehicle Tax - and so on. FRIENDS Centre will be linked to the server of the concerned departments for updating of data on a real time, once the computerization of the departments are completed.

BHOOMI: Government of Karnataka Bhoomi is a comprehensive Land Records Computerization System with fully online system to carry out mutations on land records data, finger print biometrics to ensure fool proof authentication and enforce non-repudiation. The system envisages land records centre in each taluk offce. It provides facility to scan the field mutation order passed by revenue authorities, notices served, etc. Interfaces for synchronizing with field work as also providing information through touch screen kiosk has been implemented.

STAR : Simplified and Transparent Administration of Registration (STAR) of the Government of Tamil Nadu, is a large scale computerized services of land records transactions such as issue of encumbrance certificate, certified copies, computerized registration process, property , valuation, registration of marriages/societies, firms, chits, etc. with archival facilities for scanning, storage and retrieval of records.

GYANDOOT : Project of the government of Madhya Pradesh in Dhar district is a computer network connecting rural cybercafes. It caters to the everyday needs of the masses in providing information and transacting services relating to Commodity/Mandi Marketing Information System, Income Certificate, Domicile Certificate (*mool niwasi*), Caste

Certificate, Landholder's passbook of land rights and loans (*Bhoo adhikar evam rin pustika*). Rural Hindi e-mail, Public Grievance Redressal (Shikayat Nivaran), Forms of Various Government Schemes, Below Poverty Line Family List, Employment News. Rural Matrimonial (Vivah Sambandh), Rural Market (*Gaon ka Bazaar*), Rural News Paper (Gram Samachar), Advisory Module (Salahkar), E-education, Driving License, Khasra Nakal Avedan, Varmi Compost Khad Booking.

E-Governance in Haryana

IT Policy 2000 of Haryana Government: This policy seeks a deep impact initiative by the state government in encouraging replacement of traditional delivery system of public services by IT driven system of governance that works better, costs less and is capable of serving the citizens' needs with case. This policy further seeks to facilitate private domain initiative in e-transition of Haryana by providing critical infrastructure, systems framework and enabling environment.

The IT Vision is sought to be realized by achieving the following objectives:

- Upgrading the standard and quality of administration, particularly in social and public services sector through a process of modernization and rationlisation of the administrative set-up;
- Providing public centred, efficient and cost-effective government;
- Extensive percolation of IT literacy and education in the state;
- Promoting investments in IT industry;
- Encouraging private sector initiative in IT related infrastructure and services;
- Increasing the share of IT in State Gross Domestic Product;

- Generating IT related employment opportunities; and
- Enhancing earning capacity of the residents thereby ensuring a better quality of life.

The state shall undertake intensive re-engineering and administrative reforms, redefining its role, and recasting the structure and functioning of its administrative departments to facilitate adaptation to IT.

IT Budget: Each Department, Board and Corporation shall earmark 5 per cent of its budget for IT applications. The allocated budget shall be spent on procurement of hardware, systems software, establishing IT centre, networking, web technology, development of applications software, training and technical consultancy, etc.

Besides this, the state shall establish backbone network Haryana State Wide Area Network (HARNET) for voice, data and video transmission and dissemination. Many other improvements for better plantation of IT techniques in public services.

Presently, the state government implements 25 projects in different departments. These in brief, are written here as under;

E-Governance Projects Implemented in Haryana

Sl. No	*Project Name*	*Name of Organisation*
1.	HALRIS — Haryana Land Records Information System	Directorate of Land Records. Revenue Department, Haryana
2	E-Gram Vikas Net	Secretariat of Chief Minister, Haryana
3.	On-line Treasuries Information System (OTIS)	Treasuries and Accounts Directorate Finance Department Haryana
4.	House Tax Assessment and Collection System	Department of Urban Development (Local Government), Haryana
5.	NAI - DISHA - New Agent of Information-District level Integrated Services of Haryana for All	Secretariat for Information Technology, Haryana
6.	Food Network (Food NET) — Integrated Food Procurement Information System	Department of Food and Supplies and Secretariat for IT, Haryana

(Contd...)

(Contd...)

7. Transport Regulatory and Roadways Functions Automation	Transport Department, Haryana
8. Integrated State Budget Information System	Finance Department. Haryana
9. Below Poverty Line Survey (BPL) Query System	Department of Rural Development
10. Forms and Procedures Information System	Secretariat for IT, Haryana
11. Centralized File Movement and Tracking Information System (CeFMu,TIS)	Secretariat for IT, Haryana
12. Replicable Suite of Package(Payroll, PIS, Dak-Monitoring, Court Cases and Meetings Management)	Secretariat for IT, Haryana
13. Web Enabled Electrol Rolls (WEER) Information System	Secretariat for IT, Haryana
14. Commercial Taxation Computerization (VAT System)	Excise &Taxation Department, Haryana
15. HaPPIS — Social Welfare Pensions Information System	Department of Social Justice and Empowerment and Secretariat for IT, Haryana
16. Advocate General Office Court Case Information System	Office of Advocate General and Secretariat for IT, Haryana
17. Web Enabled Civil Lists Retrieval System	Secretariat for IT. Haryana
18. Web Enabled Revenue Directory Information Services (DISH)	Secretariat for IT, Haryana and Revenue Department
19. Property and Financial Accounting Management System of HUDA	Town and Country Planning Department and HUDA
20. Web Enabled On-line Electricity Billing System	Power Utility Organization, Haryana
21. BUCAP-Budgeting, Costing, Accounting and Projects Management System	Public Works (Irrigation) Department and Secretariat for IT, Haryana
22. School/Colleges Management Information System	Department of Education, Haryana
23. Rooms Reservation and Restaurant Information System	Haryana Bhawan
24. Integrated Food Procurement Information System	Secretariat for IT, Haryana
25. Land Records Computerization Project (LRCP)	Directorate of Land Records, Revenue Department, Haryana

Source : National database for e-governance projects.

E-Governance Programmes in District Sirsa

District Profile: District Sirsa in located in North-West of

Haryana state, its boundaries touches two states, in North-Punjab and in the West–Rajasthan. District Sirsa was converted to full fledged district on September 01, 1975. It is also located on National Highway No-10(Maharaja Aggressain Marg) 260 km away from Delhi, the capital of India and approximately 250 km away from Chandigarh, the capital of Haryana. Its district headquarter is at Sirsa. There are seven development block in district Sirsa named Sirsa, Baragudda, Rania, Ellenabad, Dabwali, Odhan, Nathusari Choupta.

Sirsa has total population 1116649 (5.28% of Haryana's total population). Its rural population is 823184 (5.47% of Haryana's rural population) and its urban population is 293465 (4.79% of Haryana's urban population. Sex ratio of district Sirsa is 882/1000 is which somehow better as compared to sex ratio of Haryana i.e.861/1000. But its literacy rate 60.55 per cent is low than the literacy rate of Haryana (67.91 %).

Administrative Set-up: District headquarters at Sirsa with mini-secretariat containing offices of Deputy-Commissioner, Police Superintendent, District Education Officer, District Social Welfare Officer, District Employment Officer, etc. There are three sub-divisions named Sirsa, Dabwali, Ellenabad and four tehsil headquarters named Sirsa, Dabwali, Ellenabad, and Rania with two sub-tehsils named Kalanwali and Nathusari Chopta.

Major IT Activities in Sirsa

Name of Project / Application (NIC)	*Location*
Haryana Registration Information System — HARIS	Tehsil Sirsa Tehsil Dabwali Tehsil Rania Tehsil Ellenabad Sub-Tehsil Kalanwali Sub-Tehsil Nathusari Chopta
Haryana Certificate Issuance System	Tehsil Sirsa

(Contd...)

(Contd...)

(HARCIS) at E-Governance Service Centres at Tehsils.	Tehsil Dabwali Tehsil Ellenabad Tehsil Rania
Driving Licence Computerization at E-Governance Service Centres at Subdivision level.	SDO(Civil) Sirsa SDO(Civil) Dabwali SDO(Civil) Ellenabad
Vehicle Registration Computerisation at E-Service Centres at Subdivisions.	SDO(Civil) Sirsa SDO(Civil) Dabwali SDO(Civil) Ellenabad
OTIS — Online Treasury Information System. TDMS — Treasury	Treasury Sirsa Sub-Treasury Dabwali Sub-Treasury Ellenabad Sub-Treasury Rania Sub-Treasury Kalanwali
District and Sessions Court Computerization Suit of 5 Packages - Daily Cause List Judgement Writing BM 10 and BM26/29 Paybill Computerization Statistical Reports Generation	DJ & ADJ Courts at District Court Sirsa
Land Records Computerization	Data Digitization Centre at Panchayat Bhawan Sirsa for Tehsils.
Haryana Pension Processing Information System (HAPPIS)	District Social Welfare Office Sirsa
Passport Application Acceptance System (Webpaas)	DC Office (PLA Branch), Sirsa
Pay Bill Computerization	In regular use at offices of DC Off., Sessions Court, DETC, DD Agriculture, PWD, Public Health, PO ICDS, SDM Sirsa, SDM Dabwali, SDM Ellenabad, Election Office, Zila Sainik Board, etc.
Below Poverty Line Survey (Rural) Computerization	DRDA Sirsa for all Seven Blocks viz, Nathusari Chopta, Sirsa, Dabwali, Baragudha, Ellenabad, Odhan, and Rania
AgmarkNet	Market Committees
Employee Staff Statistics Software (ESS)	District Statistical Office

(Contd...)

(Contd...)

Integrated Child Development Scheme (ICDS)	PO ICDS Office
Rural Habitation Survey of Public Health	Public Health Office
Elections	DC Office
7th All India State Education Survey (AISES) Education Dept.	FoodNet DFSC Office at haryana- food.nic.in
Official WebSite of Distt Sirsa	http:// sirsa.gov.in
Web Enabled MPRs for RD	DRDA at http://rural.nic.in
Web Enabled Rural Soft	DRDA Sirsa at : http://web1.hry.nic.in/rural
Trainings and Demonstrations	Regular Trainings and Demonstrations for District Administration, Departments and Visitors on related Softwares, Internet, E-Mail, etc.
	Traning on E-Governance Applications and related features form time to time NIC acted as coordinator in imparting Computer Training to District Officers/ Officials at Govt. Polytechnics as desired by Worthy FCIT.
Other IT Activities in Offices	District Excise and Taxation Health EO MC (House Tax) Education

Source: NIC office Sirsa.

Hence, it is not possible to measure the performance and effectiveness of all these projects. So we have made a moderate attempt to analyse e-governance process in identified projects at the district level. For this purpose, we have studied following five projects in detail as:

Haryana Pension Processing and Information System

An Overview

'Pension Processing and information System' (HAPPIS) : The system has been developed by NICHSU to monitor all types of pension schemes (Old Age Pension, Widows Pension, National Old Age Pension, Handicapped Pension and Financial Assistance to Destitute Children). The database of pensioners is being computerized. The software has been implemented with much enthusiasm. The application has also been made web enabled (http:/ / socialjustice.chd.nic.in), to provide on-line access of pension disbursement to the beneficiaries and other users.

Salient Features of HAPPIS

The software package follows the prescribed guideline of the Department

Standard codes of villages, tehsils, municipal committees and districts have been used

The package run on a PC installed with Windows 2000 and SQL/ Access The package is Citizen Centric

Up-dating of records is user friendly

Reports for district level and state level offices

Following online reports are generated :

- APR, s (Acquaintance Pension Rolls on monthly basis),
- Information regarding non- receiver of Pension,
- Pension Disbursement States of any beneficiary,
- Category wise Statistical Reports of pensioners,
- Age wise and Age Group wise statistical reports.

Comprehensive search facility.

Information is web enabled.

Database is compatible with other D-Net software package

The package would reduce the paper work and time being taken to compile lists, statements, etc.

Salient Features of Web Site

* Contains information about the various activities of the Department.

Details of NGOs. Budget, Office organization etc.
Dynamic information about disbursement of Pension.
Online MPR from DSWOs.
Online Public Grievances (e- mail).
Electronically Transfer of data from districts to HQ.
Beneficiary's category and pension wise reports.

On Line Treasuries Information System (OTIS)

An Introduction

On-line Treasuries Information System (OTIS) is a secure, workflow automation application for treasuries. The OTIS provide computerization of payments, receipts, budget control with DDOs, linkage with bank branches, information flow to Accountant General, Haryana and Finance Department, On-line query, information flow between Sub-Treasuries and District Treasuries and Directorate of Treasuries and Accounts. The NIC has developed the software, which is being implemented at all Treasuries and Sub-Treasuries in the state (more than 100 locations). This is an online application leading towards e-Governance.

OTIS An Application

Receipt		*Payment*	
Module	For	Module	For
Challan Entry	Banks	Token Entry	Treasuries
Verification	Banks	Bill Passing	Treasuries
Realization	Banks	Cheque Generation	Treasuries
Data Transmission	Banks	Data Transmission	Treasuries
Verification	Treasuries	Payment	Banks
Voucher Preparation	Treasuries	Voucher Preparation	Treasuries

Reports		*Administration*	
Acknowledgement	Banks	User Management	Security
Bank Scroll [Receipt]	Banks	Group Management	Security
Pending Realization	Banks	Installation	Banks & Treasuries
Token Register	Treasuries	Backup	Banks & Treasuries
Expenditure Register	Treasuries	Recovery	Banks & Treasuries
AG Reports	Treasuries	Master Management	Treasuries

OTIS Technical Features

- Security by means of passwords (Biometrics in near future).
- Dynamic Menus (Depending upon the roll of the user).
- Same software with different function.
- Well-integrated work flow application.
- Online help.
- OTIS-Technology
- High-end servers at district treasuries.
- Clients only at Sub-treasuries.
- Client/Server or Client only at Bank end depending upon the workload.
- OTIS developed using Visual Basic 6.0.
- MS-SQL Server 2000 & MS-WINDOWS 2000 Server at Bank District Treasuries end.
- MS-SQL 2000 desktop at Bank and District Treasuries end.
- MS-SQL 2000 desktop at Sub-Treasuries and Banks with low workload.
- MS WINDOWS 2000 Professional at Client side and Sub-treasuries.
- Dialup/online connectivity for data transfer.

OTIS Critical Success Factors

- Availability of correct Heads of Accounts on Challan in Receipt Module.
- Availability of dial-up/Online connectivity between Treasuries and Bank, between Sub-Treasuries and district treasuries, between district treasuries and Directorate of Treasuries and Accounts.
- Availability of Power especially in rural areas.
- Training of Treasuries and Bank officials.
- Availability of computers for each process.

- Approval of cheque system and availability of pre-printed cheques.

Haryana Registration Information System (HARIS)

An Introduction

Haryana Registration Information System facilitates automation of document registration work carried out at tehsil and sub-tehsil levels. The HARIS features includes security checks, online capturing and storing of photos of buyer, seller and witnesses, information of registration fee, printing of registration certificates and various statistical reports. The software provides maintenance of data base and on-line query facilities. The system is being implemented in all tehsils and most of sub-tehsils. The existing registry officials of tehsils and sub-tehsils have been trained and they are operating the system. Encouraging results have been received in terms of revenue maximization, cost minimization and public convenience and satisfaction. NIC has developed software for linking HARIS with land records and now developing automatic updating of record of right (Jamabandi). Up to 40 per cent increase in revenue has been recovered.

Features of HARIS

- To bring transparency in the registration process. To simplify registration procedures. To provide onestop services related to registration.
- To generate MIS reports for monitoring.
- To enhance speed, reliability and consistency of system.
- On-line query on registered deeds.
- Structuring/standardizing the language of deed documents to minimise intermediaries.

- To maintain database of photographs to ensure genuine witnesses executants and claimants.
- Generation of exceptional reports for the purpose, of auditing.
- Maintenance of permanent record of deeds on CD-ROMs.
- Convergence of HARIS with PATIS [PATwaris Information System] Land records.
- Issue of non-encumbrance certificate.

Technicial Features

- User friendly.
- Bi-lingual data entry
- Role based security
- Integration of camera and CD writer in application software.

Critical Success Factors

- Public awareness on benefits of HARIS
- Implementation of HARIS in Hindi
- Training of Sub-Registrar office'staff
- Continuous maintenance and up gradation of systems.

Haryana Land Records Information System (HALRIS)

HALRIS is a work flow application on revenue developed by NIC Haryana State Centre, Chandigarh.

The following are the salient features of HALRIS:

- *Jamabandi Entry and Editing*—The software provides facility to Enter and Edit the Jamabandi Data.
- *Add/Delete Khewat/Khatoni*—Software provide facility to Add/Delete Khewat and Khatoni
- *Intkal Entry and Editing*—Software provides facility to enter and edit an Intkal.
- *Integration with Registration Software*—The HALRIS

software is integrated with HARIS (Haryana Registration Information System).

- Online Maintenance of Jamabandi using the Integrated Mutation Module.
- Maintains the Double View of the Jamabandi i.e., Online Jamabandi and Intermediate Jamabandi.
- Touch Screen Module provides the Nakal and Query Service to General Public with the touch of a finger.
- Bio-Metric User Authentication as some of the crucial modules like sanctioning of mutation requires finger print authentication.
- *Local Language*—Data Entry is through GIST Font.
- *Mutation Processes*—It provides facility to verify mutation by Patwari/Kanungo, Mutation Sanction by Tehsildar and Mutation incorporation.The effects of the mutation automatically goes to the Jamabandi. The provision to revert and delete a mutation has also been provided.
- *Validation Reports*—The software provides the facility for generation printing of the validation reports, based upon which correction to data is made.
- *Issuance of Nakal*—It provides updated compute-rized Nakal of Khewat and Khatoni of Jamabandi and Mutation to the citizen through computer.
- *Online Information using Query*—Provides online information about the land records to the citizens using query system.
- *Web Nakal*—It provides the facility for Web interface for viewing the nakal of various documents, thus a person can sec the details of his land holding using internet.
- *Printing of Jamabandi*—Software provides the facility for processing and printing of the complete Jamabandi.
- *Printing of Index Numbran Khasra* — The software provides the features for printing of Index Numbran Khasra.
- *Storage on CD for Record Maintenance*—Feature for Regular Backup of data on CD from the software is available.

- *Linkage of Mutation Module and Land Records Data*—The Software will pick the data of land records during the registration of agricultural land. Software has the capability to capture the details of mutation from software. This feature is very important part of the linkage.

Election Duty Assignment Software

Election Duty Assignment Software has been developed by NIC Haryana State Centre, Chandigarh to carry out the process in an automated, and transparent manner keeping in view the guidelines framed by Election Department. The software has the following features :

Supported by User Name and Password to avoid unnecessary tempering with Data.

- Locking of database after formation of parties to avoid tempering to database.
- Master Information Creation on the basis of Parliamentary/Assembly Election—
- Information. on Polling Booths and Location and their codification.
- Data Entry of Employees on the following Parameters :
    - Name
    - Designation
    - Qualification
    - Home Assembly .
    - Posting Assembly
    - Address
    - Contact Number
    - Age
    - Basic Pay
    - Eligible for PO/APO/Supervisor etc.

Generation of Various Reports

- Employee Checklist
- Designation wise Checklist
- Detailed Employee Status as per Designation and Pay scale
- List of Departments and List of Offices.
- List of Reserve Staff
- Department-wise Summary Reports and Detailed Reports

Further Provisions for—

- Randomization of Booths
- Searching an Employee from the Database
- Rehearsal Details
- Generate Duties
- Polling Staff Position
- Extra Staff other than Reserve (if Required)
- Duty Orders
- Duty Orders E-Office wise list of Deputed Employees
- Generation of Identity Cards
- Attendance Sheets
- Attendance Certificate
- Sitting Orders
- Formation of Parties
- Randomization of Parties
- Payment of Remuneration
- Codification of Booths
- Decodification of Booths.

Findings of the Survey

To know and analyse the exact impact of e-governance programmes in district administration, we made close and detailed observations of the five e-governance programmes (which are explained above). We arranged discussions and interviews with the officials who are implementing these e-programmes in their respective departments and the beneficiaries of these programmes.

In our study, we found that the district office of National Informatics Centre (NIC) is the hub agency in supporting and assisting technically all the e-governance programmes at district level. The state unit of NIC has an appreciable hand in software programming. A 'programme, "Election Duty Assignment Software" developed by this unit got appreciation everywhere. Due to unique features of this programme and support provided by the NIC Sirsa during the process of election, district administration honoured the district office of NIC with the Certificate of Appreciation for their good job.

Our findings also conclude as:

E-Governance has tremendous opportunities in effective delivery of government services.

Empowerment of Citizens: Right to Information Act and use of IT in governance facilitate citizens to know what and how of government very easily, and quickly.

Success of IT depends upon; culture and attitude of bureaucrats, social support, infrastructure and leadership etc.

Success rate of e-governance programmes differ programme to programme and department to department due to above said variations. There is a big gap in theory and practice of e-governance programmes.

The employees may be classified into pro-IT and not pro-IT.

Use of IT reduce the work-load dramatically, specially manual and written work.

Scarcity of IT trained man-power in most of the offices.

Conclusion

E-government has the potential to transform governance. Governments can advance the agenda on governance reform, transparency and empowerment of the citizens, while making the interaction of the government with other bodies, more meaningful and productive. It is however, not a panacea for all troubles of governance. Reaching the poor and realizing the potential benefits of e-governance is a difficult endeavour. Now it is proper tune to bring changes in mind-set for completely harvesting the advantages of IT.

NOTES AND REFERENCES

1. The Atlantic Monthly, October 1999, *Beyond the Information Revolution* 99.10, volume 284, No. 4, p. 47.
2. Macmillan Dictionary of Information Technology.
3. Information Security- Wikipedia, the free encyclopedia.htm.
4. Mehrotra, P.K., "E-Governance Options and Opportunities" 2001, article presented in 5th Annual National Conference of NEPASI, New Delhi, p. 2.
5. Ministry of Information Technology, GOI.
6. Kochhar Sameer & Dhanjal Gursharan, *"From Governance to E-Governance" Skoch e-Governance Report Card*-2005, p-4.
7. INTOSAI- Standing Committee on IT Audit: "Auditing e- Government, p. 1.
8. *Ibid.*, p. 1.
9. *Ibid.*, p. 1.
10. Rajashekar, H.M., "Efficiency and Transparency of E-Governance in India: A Case Study of Karnataka"—(2002) paper presented at International Conference: *Building Effective E-Governance*, MGSIPAP. Chandigarh.
11. World Bank Report.
12. Egan Jasmeet Kaur, "Implementing e-Service Delivery: Govt. to Citizen 2002, paper presented at International Conference : *"Building Effective E-Governance"*, MGSIPAP. Chandigarh.
13. Hota, P.C. Committee on Civil Service Reforms quoted in www.darpg.nic.in.
14. Mehrotra, P.K., *"E-Governance Options and Opportunities"* 2001, op. cit, p. 2.
15. Budhiraja, Renu, "Electronic Governance—A key Issue in the 21st Century". http:/ *www.mit.gov.in/eq/article 2.htm.*
16. P.M's Independence Day Speech, 15 August, 2002.

21 Restructuring of Rural Credit Co-operative Institutions in India

A Glance

*R.S. Gulia** and *Neera***

The rural credit co-operative institutions (RCCIs), one of the strong arms of rural financial institutions, have made significant strides in delivering credit for agriculture and rural development. Of the total credit disbursed every year, the share of co-operatives is about 49 per cent. With the green revolution and commercialization in Indian agriculture, demand for credit in rural areas increased manifold.

With the onset of the financial sector reforms since the beginning of 1990s, the expectations from co-operatives have been very high. In view of such new expectations, the co-operatives may have to get an altogether a new look in the coming century. What is required to make them relevant in the changing economic setting is rationalization of co-operative structure and dovetailing their functioning with the demands of its clientele[1]. The co-operative movement derived its principles from the Rochdale pioneers[2]. The setting up of early co-operatives was in response to a market failure—that the growers were charging excessive prices.

During the later part of the 19th century, the problem of rural indebtedness became acute and the passing of

* Faculty Member, Department of Political Science, M.D. University, Rohtak, Haryana.

** M.Phil (Gold Medalist), Research Scholar, Department of Political Science, M.D. University, Rohtak, Haryana.

agricultural lands from the hands of the peasants to the money-lenders became a common phenomenon. The system of state loans (*tagavi*) followed by the British fell almost into disuse. Committees and commissions like the Deccan Agriculturists Relief Act, 1879, Land Improvements Loan Act, 1863, Agriculturists Loans Act, 1884 are some of the notable attempts to address rural indebtedness. With the failure of these Acts, Nicholson favoured the European model of co-operatives to be established in India. The Famine Commission, 1901 also enrosed the idea and a bill for the co-operative credit societies was drafted by Edward Law in 1901 with the objectives of assisting farmers, artisans and low paid employees with credit. So, the Co-operative Credit Societies Act was passed on March 25, 1904.[3] However, the practice of extending institutions credit for agriculture can be traced back to 1870 when farmers were provided with such credit by the government during drought years. Initially, experimental credit co-operatives were organized in an effort to break the poverty cycle of small farmers.

In 1912 another legislation was passed for creating non credit co-operatives of producers and consumers and central organizations like co-operative unions, central co-operative banks. In 1919, the responsibility for co-operative legislation was shifted to states and independent co-operative acts were made paving the way for development of co-operative credit system particularly central land mortgage and primary land mortgage banks[4].

Land mortgage banks came into being in 1929. The Royal Commission on Agriculture made a strong plea for government assistance for the development of the co-operative movement. However, the Depression of 1929-30 was a severe blow to the movement when societies collapsed. But, with the establishment of RBI and the Agricultural Credit Department in 1935 gave a fillip to the movement. Till 1947, the King was in favour of promoting multipurpose primary societies in rural areas. During the period 1947-56, co-operatives were re-organized so as to make them instruments of economic development, as the co-operative system was considered more suitable for dispensation of farm credit. Provision of adequate institutional finance for agriculture received proper attention when the All India Rural Credit Survey Committee appointed by the RBI, made pin pointing recommendations on the adoption of integrated scheme of rural credit. The scheme envisaged the strengthening and development of co-operative credit institutions at all.

After independence, a tremendous expansions[5] took place in RCCIs.

Organization and Structure

The short term RCCIs have been organized at three levels, state, district and village. The long term co-operatives are organized at two level-the unitary structure in which state co-operative agricultural and rural development banks operate at state[6] level through their branches and the federal structure in which primary co-operative agricultural and rural development banks (PCARDBs) operate as independent units at the primary level and federate themselves into state co-operative agricultural and rural development banks at the state level.[7]

Primary agricultural co-operative societies are village level co-operative organizations. They are generally mufti purpose and mufti functional. They provide agricultural production credit, sell fertilizers, consumer goods and provide storage facilities and procurement of agricultural commodities.

In the era of liberalization these co-operatives are expected to undertake profitable business to fulfil members' objectives and survive in the open and free market economy.

A Reformative Process

The foundation for building a broader credit infrastructure

for rural credit was laid by the report of the All India Rural Credit Survey, 1954. It stressed that co-operatives had a vital role in channelising credit to the farmers.

However, the All India Rural Credit Survey Committee was set up in 1966 which suggested substantial changes in the co-operative sector like leverage of commercial banks for extending loans to farmers, availability of credit to purchase fertilizer, seeds, pump sets for irrigation in the wake of green revolution, etc.[8]

Despite all these efforts, the flow of credit to rural areas failed to exhibit any appreciable improvement due mainly to the fact that commercial banks did not co-operate to finance the small and marginal farmers while co-operatives lacked resources to meet the expected demand. As a result regional rural banks were set-up in 1975 on the recommendation of the working group led by M. Narasimaham.

Following the recommendations of the Committee to Review Arrangements for Institutional Credit for Agriculture and Rural Development, the National Bank for Agriculture and Rural Development (NABARD) was set-up in 1982. In India microfinance was formally started in 1992 with the NABARD launching the pilot project for linking SHGs with banks. Moreover, the rural infrastructure development fund was established in 1995.[9]

Following the era of liberalization and globalization, the report of the committee on the financial system, 1991 provided a blueprint for carrying out overall financial sector reforms during the 1990s. Furthermore, various committees/working groups/task forces[10] were set-up to look into the operations of co-operatives.

Problems and Challenges

Credit co-operative movement in India, despite its long existence, has not been able to keep pace with contemporary rural financial institutions. They have neither remained member driven enterprises, nor their leadership, in quite a long number of cases, have proved to be professional, transparent, accommodate and functionally effective.

Most of them have been small in size to be economical and viable and a large number of them dormant and moribund. They suffer from infrastructure weaknesses, operational ineffectiveness and structural flaws.

They do not appear to be inspiring confidence in their existing and potential members, depositors and borrowers.

Problems and challenges confronting the co-operative banks are :

Lack of Corporate Governance

Because of no formal system of corporate governance, co-operative banks have become the hot beds of political patronage, unscrupulous financial practices and gross mismanagement. In certain cases there have become private fieldous of individual political and other functionaries sustaining themselves on public money. There are umpteen cases of scams and frauds in co-operative banks. Excessive government control and patronage have become an obstacle to the growth of co-operatives in many ways including their inability to hire professional managers who are badly needed to improve their financial performance. Besides, the government officers deputed to head co-operatives are not accountable and do not have any stake in the co-operatives. There is no transparency in their operations.

The Duality of Control

In the presence of more than one regulatory agency i.e. Registrar, Co-operative Societies on behalf of state government and RBI on behalf of government of India, there is no effective control.

Lack of Freedom and Level Playing Field

The co-operative sector clamouring for freedom from the archaic law, the government, the bureaucracy and the politicians, is yet to be liberated and given the freedom that it needs to compete with the private corporate sector.

Lack of Good Leadership

Due to leadership vacuum, the Chief Executive Officer or Managing Directors are appointed who hijack the co-operatives for self-aggrandizement.

Lack of Appropriate Systems of Financial Management

There are constraints on capital formulation due to laws and regulations preventing the members from obtaining the benefits of surplus retain in co-operative. The regulation governing accounting and audit constitute an another type of constraint to healthy financial management. Further, the auditors in co-operatives are neither professionals nor the representatives of the members[11].

Political Considerations

The states have been treating co-operatives on par with other political institutions where electoral politics play a role. The political class should withdraw from this role.

Lack of Financial Support

In the absence of any other organizational structure which has an outreach of the rural credit co-operatives, all the state governments continue using them for distribution of agricultural inputs and also the PDS, but no financial support is forthcoming for improving their financial health.

As per report a large number of district central co-operative banks had eroded their entire owned funds and also parts of deposits and so many of the state cooperative banks[12]. But nobody appears to be worried about these depositors or farmers who were easier being serviced by them. It is wondered whether the authorities would have shown same indifference, if these were urban depositors.

Restricted Area of Operation

Unlike the commercial banks with a nationwide area of operation, the co-operatives have a very restricted area for raising capital resources.

Absence of Long-term Credit to Farmer

In some of the states like Maharashtra, Orissa, Bihar and Assam, the long term co-operative credit structure has really collapsed with the result that a large number of farmers are being deprived of long term investment credit opportunities which are important for improving the economic well being of the farmers as well as the productivity of agriculture.[13]

High Rate of Interest

A high transaction and risk with a large number of smaller cases and operating in a limited geographical area and sector. The cost of depositors in co-operatives, due to their mix and interest rates, is higher than that of the commercial bank. Add to this smaller loan size and higher risk profile increases the operational cost.

Capital Starvation

The theory of capital starvation applies to co-operatives because there are no residual claims on current or liquidated incomes acting as disincentives for increasing financial stakes. If the design of the co-operatives cannot build in stakes, their revival would only be temporary.

Moreover, the bad governance, political interference, management and tax regulation have turned co-operatives banks into setting targets for scamsters and free loaders and there is an urgent need to reform the existing system of governance. Absence of timely democratic management, vulnerability of political pressure, general lack of earnest action by state government, inability of credit institutions to mobilize deposits and consequent vertical dependence on higher institutions, inadequate margin on loaning operations and high transaction costs disproportionate to the level of business, poor recovery efforts and vitiated recovery climate due to loan/interest waiver schemes, etc.

Arid Area

About 60 per cent of the net sown area has no assured irrigational facilities and agriculture co-operatives to be a high risk activity and a gamble against the monsoon. There is a question mark about the viability of small and marginal farmers particularly in the resource poor dry land area. With not effective risk mitigation system of its position, the credit risk is very high. In the event of drought, the cooperatives wait for the declaration of the area as drought affect by the state government and issue of operational instructions from the corporate office before the branch manager plans some relief to the borrowers. Thus, the initiatives are with the political system and all decisions regarding waiving/write-off/rescheduling of loans, etc. are announced by the political system. Sometimes, the borrowers who have repaying capacity become recalcitrant awaiting some government announcement. In certain regions, the poor quality of appraisal and an anxiety to fix shorter maturity of investment loans particularly lift irrigation schemes have caused problems.

Absence of Crop Insurance

The absence of an effective and efficient system of mitigating the sufferings of the farmers due to crop or market failure by insurance product has also resulted in poor recoveries.

Red-tape in Co-operative Banks

In rural banks what the client hears most often is 'Phir aao' and 'paper bhee nahin hai'. The repeated visits mean cash expenses involved in visits to the branch and also loss of wages/work in the fields.

Declining Profitability in Agriculture

Profitability in agriculture had declined sharply by 14 per cent during the 1990s, squeezing the already low level of margins. Among the crops, where the margins have been badly affected are cotton and most of coarse cereals. To add to the problem, many small and marginal farmers have attempted the move towards commercial agriculture from a very vulnerable position of a meager asset base, extremely limited knowledge of technology and market and a weak support system, occasionally leading to suicides in certain areas.

Lackluster Attitude of Commercial Banks

The rural credit could not get the attention from the commercial banks particularly after 1994s — the era of global economy, even after the directions of RBI to achieve a target of 18 per cent of the net bank credit for lending to agriculture in 1989, it is a petty that commercial banks did not pay any heed to it so far even after 17 years.[14]

Climatic Problems, etc.

Any climatic aberration or adverse market swing land the

co-operative banks of district or village level into serious financial problems without prompt support from the state government, thus, any of these institutions over the time have become financially very weak or sick.

Despite the efforts which NABARD is putting to increase the supply of rural credit manifold through the co-operative credit institutions, the fact is that the overall share of agricultural credit in the overall economy is declining-which is understandable because the growth in the manufacturing and service sectors far outstrips the growth in agriculture sector.

As per the survey of the *Hindustan Times* in July 2005, it is found that about 46 million earners i.e. 70 per cent still borrow from money lender as having no access to co-operative credit institution or commercial banks. The quantum of governments loans is only one per cent, co-operative banks 6 per cent, Public Sector bank -10 per cent, self help group-1 per cent, other 12 per cent and money lenders -70 per cent (about Rs.66,909 crores).

Interestingly 50 per cent of the customer borrowing from money-lenders belongs to rich state including Andhra Pradesh, Karnataka, Tamil Nadu, Maharashtra and Gujarat. 71 per cent of them are farmers and wage labourers.[15]

On the other hand as per recent World Bank report, more than 87 per cent of the India's poor have no access to a formal source[16] and depend on money-lenders who charge them interest rates varying from 48 to 120 per cent.

The Planning Commission has also admitted in its mid-term-appraisal of the Tenth Five Year Plan that only 4 crores farm households out of 10 crores have access to the institutional credit. However, as per RBI estimates, only 31 per cent population has access to the banking services, lowest in Bihar and highest in Punjab whereas 94 per cent of the British population have their bank accounts.[17]

The rural borrowers have to pay 45 per cent of their loan amount in bribes to official dealing with them in co-operatives.

It takes an average of 33 weeks to get a loan approved from co-operatives in rural areas.[18]

Thus, since their birth in 1904, co-operative societies in India have traversed a long and arduous path. Notwithstanding of their achievements and phenomenal growth in many parts of India, they are still beset with several financial, organizational and management constrain and problems cited above in the new era characterized by deregulation, delicensing, liberalization, privatization and globalization. How to cope with these problems and challenges and survive and grow the in new era-is a question to be pondered over.

A Stratagy for Revamping of Co-operatives

Despite their overwhelming presence in the rural sector, co-operatives suffer from a variety of organizational, managerial, administrative and financial problems. Consequently, they are not able to reach out at all segments of rural society, especially the poor and meet their demands and aspirations.

In view of this, there is need for an all party political consensus at the national level for doing away with all such populous measures to ensure that politicians and other vested interests for their self-aggrandizement do not misuse co-operatives.

Revival of co-operatives is a must for a variety of reasons like;

- A wide network existing in rural India with an enormous number of 545 thousand co-operatives of various types at different levels with membership of nearly 230 million, it is one of the longest in the world. It has covered 100 per cent villages and 75 per cent of rural households.[19]
- Are the alternative institutions to neutralize the ills of economic and financial sector reforms to protect

and enhance livelihood. In other words, there is no alternative to co-operative.

Time is now ripe that the Government of India and RBI should initiate concrete restructuring steps for putting the system in order so that banking system is really enabled to play its catalytic and developmental role on the one hand and state government in whose jurisdiction the subject of agriculture falls demonstrate their total commitment to the development of this sector on the other.

While multi-agency approach to rural credit delivery system is a must for a country of our size and diversified socio-economic environment, there is immediate need for:

- Re-engineering the system through the implementation of well studied and conceived recommendations of earlier expert committees;
- Improving operational efficiency of the rural credit system to make the system vibrant and responding to the changing requirements taking place inside India and in the global economy; and
- Removing the regulatory rigidities.

The common reservations against a credit programme for the poor are:

- Credit alone is useless unless packaged with training, marketing, transportation facilities, technology, education, etc.
- Credit to the poor is counter-productive as it imposes the burden of loans on the poor who have no repaying capacity.
- The consumption and social needs are so pressing that any loan will be diverted from production requirements.
- Chronic poverty has a crippling effect on the mind and aspirations of the poor and this shackles the poor to lower levels of living.

- The rural power-structure is too powerful and entrenched to allow such a credit programme for poverty alleviation to succeed.
- By encouraging the poor to take up independent professions, a shortage in wage labour will be created. This results in higher wages, increasing the cost of agricultural production.
- Credit programmes for the poor will be highly inflationary and cause imbalances in the rural economy.
- By extending credit to women, the traditional place of women in the family will be disturbed.
- Credit helps the poor only temporarily and does not achieve an equitable restructuring of production relations.
- Success of credit programmes depend on wider national economic policy issues. If the term of trade for food and cash crops between rural and urban areas are based against the rural poor, credit programmes will have limited impact.

According to James J. Wadsworth[20] RBS Agricultural Economist, the basic elements of such a strategy to restructure the co-operatives are as follows:

- Unification through mergers, consolidation, and acquisition;
- Contraction through selling assets, and closing loss making facilities and discontinuing products or services;
- Setting up joint-business ventures with other co-operatives, or other legal business entities;
- Entering into agreements or working relationship, pact, or strategic alliance with other successful co-operatives;
- Expansion through purchasing of assets, or business

units, building new facilities, expanding existing facilities, and acquiring outside businesses; and
- Revamping through upgrading or modifying operations, services, functions or organizational structure.

Apart from such efforts, others can be as under:

- Constitution of self-help groups to solve the twin problem of restricted availability of credit to weaker sections and non-viability of institutions.
- Autonomous co-operatives[21] on the lines of Andhra Pradesh where the Registrar is only a registering and regulatory authority and can't intervene in the functioning of newly formed mutually aided co-operatives.
- The short-term and long-term co-operatives should be integrated on the levels of Andhra Pradesh.
- De-layering the co-operative structure is the need of the hour to bring down the transaction cost.
- Credit for the poor households is the real problem. To solve this problem self-help groups be constituted to protect the poor from the money-lenders.
- More local recruitment and improved working conditions in rural areas as the urban-oriented staff is reluctant to work there.
- The rural banking is required to handle credit extension work, scheme appraised work in connection with farm and non-farm investments and the production of different crops, monitoring and recovery of loans spread over villages apart from having a basic knowledge of agriculture and rural development.
- Primary co-operative development fund should be established.
- Professionalism in co-operatives should be promoted by providing training to primary managing commit-

tee members in productive lending, projectisation accountability business planning, etc.

- Politics-free cooperative leadership by barring active politicians from their management.
- There should be depositors' representative on the primary and district level managing committees on the lines of Kerala.
- Co-operative should be allowed to offer all types of financial services on the lines of commercial banks such as money transfer through drafts/MT etc.
- Crop insurance products have not worked well because loss assessment is complex due to fragmentation of land holdings. The methodology has relied on crop cutting experiments using large geographic as a base. Costs do not justify imaging technology[22]. Therefore, the risk triggers have to be unbundled and subsidies have to be targeted at the institutional level. If this is not addressed we may find co-operatives left with clients that are not serviced by commercial banks and intrinsically vulnerable.
- Co-operative bodies should not be government driven but people's driven on the lines of Maharashtra.
- Re-capitalization/rehabilitation package be declared on the pattern of direct financing by the Centre to the commercial banks[23] to enable them tide over their problem of non-performing assets.
- The responsibility may be shared by the Centre and states on 60:40 basis and the co-operatives be immuned completely to share any such responsibility.[24]
- Control over co-operatives credit society be made by a single agency instead of multi-agency.
- Process of reforms be made stringent on the lines of commercial banking sector[25].
- Co-operatives be de-politicized and de-bureaucratized[26].

- There is needed a holistic and multi-faceted strategy to revamp the cooperative banks such as;
  - Improved governance and leadership development
  - Better system of Audit.
  - Induction of professionals into the management and keep the politicians out.
  - Delineating the roles of RBI and NABARD.

Since the introduction of the new economic policy package, the rural financial system is undergoing important changes. The Expert Committee on Rural Credit, 2001 highlighted some basic issues of concern like:

(i) Poorest of the poor are left out of the formal credit system who comprise weaker sections, marginal farmers and women.
(ii) Off farm activities and rural enterprises are not adequately financed by the credit institutions.
(iii) The linkages with research, extension, input supply, marketing and processing are weak.
(iv) The legal and regulatory mechanism are inadequate, giving rise to non-financially viable institutions.
(v) Changes in the livelihood pattern, land holding input and activity mix as greater use of fertilizer, preference for high value crops are fuelling a shift to new financial intermediaries.

To address these issues the Committee recommended in order to finance the assetless poor, small farmers and tenants :

(i) New financial agencies or grouping such as SHGs and non-financial companies be established.
(ii) Subsidy should go to the groups which may be free to choose its activities.
(iii) Contract farming.
(iv) Conversion of crop loans into term loans.

In order to finance the dry-land farming and on-crop activities:

(i) Methods of fixing scales of finance be recast.
(ii) Watershed development should be promoted
(iii) Links between credit and marketing be improved.

In order to finance non farm sector:

(i) Bridge loans may be provided.
(ii) Capital structure be strengthened
(iii) Renovation such as artisan credit card be issued
(iv) Beztter loan recovery mechanism,

The financial institutions should also have role in financing private investment in infrastructure building such as irrigation structures and devices, minor projects like wells and tank.

The National Policy on Co-operatives 2002, seeks to achieve[27]:

- Ensuring the functioning of co-operatives based on basic co-operative values and principles as enshrined in the declaration of the International Co-operative Alliance Congress, 1995.
- Revitalization of the co-operative structure particularly in the sector of agricultural credit;
- Reduction of regional imbalances through provision of support measures by the Central government/state government, particularly in the under-developed and cooperatively undeveloped states/regions;
- Strengthening the co-operative education and training and human resource development for professionalisation of the management of the co-operatives;
- Greater participation of members in the management of co-operatives and promoting the concept of user members;
- Amendment/removal of members in the manage-

ment of co-operative laws providing for the restrictive regulatory regime;

- Evolving a system of integrated co-operative structure by entrusting the federations predominantly the role of promotion, guidance, information system, etc. towards their affiliate members and potential members;
- Evolving a system of inbuilt mechanism in co-operative legislation to ensure timely conduct of general body meetings, elections and audit of cooperative societies;
- Ensuring that the benefits of the co-operatives' endeavour reach the poor sections of the society and encouraging the participation of such sections and women in management of cooperatives;
- Strengthening the Co-operative Credit Institutions the government is to provide the required resources for recapitalized co-operative banks as per recommendations of Jagdish Kapoor Committee, such as:
- A Model act be framed at the central level in order to bring unifirmity in states act.
- At grassroots level, the primaries should be revitalized.
- The district co-operative banks and state cooperative banks be merged.
- The long and short term structures be integrated on the lines of Andhra Pradesh.
- Human resource development through proper recruitment and training.
- Proper legal norms for better recoveries and improved disbursals. Provision of an Annual Rural Credit Conference.
- Strategy for the effective functioning of co-operative banks[28].
- There is need for the apex level banks to play an important role in the development of different tiers in the system and necessarily achieve and inject into

human resources, the managerial, organizational and financial capabilities to face the future challenges.

- They have also to bestow greater attention on specialization and diversification in loan business, non-fund business, efficient financial intermediation, risk management and reduction in non-performing assets at each tier in the structure.
- They should play effective role as supervisors of the lower tiers and ensure efficient internal control system in each tier and timelines of the internal inspections and external audits which should reflect on the quality of management and operations of the institutions.
- It is desirable that the training programmes encompass skill upgradation and aptitude development in full measure. It is necessary to keep the staff sufficiently motivated through periodic job rotation, job enrichment and recognition of performance. training should address the capacity building of the banker such that a rural banker not only acquires the knowledge of banking parse, banking laws and practices but also acquires various skills.
- Effective communication ability is another quality which a rural banker has to possess so that he could deal with the rural clientele and earn their confidence.
- Allowing Agricultural and Rural Development Banks (ARDBs) to function as full fledged banks would enable them to mop up rural savings effectively, build up strong resource base and reduce dependence on external financial support. This will help these banks provide banking facilities in competition with other banking and financial institutions; have wider coverage and outreach for the co-operative sector; increase their investment avenues and utilize their experience and expertise in investment credit in the competitive markets. This would also reduce

structural weaknesses and constraints in the growth of ARDBs.

- Increasing borrowing membership and volume of business are essential steps to improve the profitability of cooperatives.
- Power of supersession of the Boards of Directors should not vest in the state government alone but it should be done very sparingly and that too in consultation with NABARD.
- Government should not appoint its officers as Chief Executive Officers in the event of supersession of Boards but CEO should be a person with suitable banking qualification, experience and expertise. Boards, if superceded, should be restored within six months at the maximum.
- To remove overlapping of controls and endow functional autonomy and operational freedom to co-operatives, specific plans should be developed which should redefine the relationships clearly the roles and responsibilities and areas of regulation through delegation of powers among state government, RBI, NABARD and Apex.
- Diversification of business products at all levels in co-operative credit institutions is the prime need. Banks should upgrade their services and technology to provide instant, efficient and affordable services to members/customers. Diversified avenues may include, inter alia, housing loans, consumer loans, consortium financing, financing of service sector, distribution of insurance products, etc.
- Natural calamities often impact upon loan delinquency and poor repayment. An institutional mechanism to ensure uninterrupted credit flow to affected farmers needs to be devised.
- In the present context, cooperative banks must realize the need for operational viability and subsequent

financial sustainability in their operations. They will have to necessarily work out the costs of operations realistically and scientifically which include cost of raising funds, transaction and risk cost, reasonable provision to meet exigencies and eventualities and then arrive at interest rate to be charged to members on their loans. Besides, interest on members' deposit should be market related and not arbitrarily higher than commercial banks.

- Non-remunerative business like participation in public distribution system should be dispensed with.
- The banks should include other informal sectors in the list of potential borrowers.
- Loan delivery system should be made more transparent, easy and simple.
- The cash credit concept should also be liberally made available to the farmers.

Strategy for Successful Operation of Primary Agricultural Co-operatives (PACs)

The following are the basis initiatives enable successful operations of PAC's :

(1) Sensitive leadership style: Even though, they have been honest, innovative, risk taking, sensitive to member needs, they must have open mind and effective developmental approach in the new era. They must improve their work systems, management and administrative process, business operational system.

(2) Education and training facilities to be offered to the PAC's members and Management Committee members.

(3) Recovery of loans must be made more efficient and effective.

(4) PACs must aim at higher business turnover with good margin of surplus.
(5) Active participation of all members in the business transactions must be enhanced.
(6) Active participation of members in the management and administration of co-operative efforts.
(7) Degasification of business activities in the light of profitability and viability.
(8) Use of proper information system.
(9) Improvement of lending policies and procedures.
(10) Appointment of professional managers to run the business affairs of PACs.
(11) PAC's must develop viable business development plans.

"Class Banking" and "Mass Banking" Mode

Against the above background the Integrated Rural Development Programme (IRDP), the ambitious subsidy linked credit programme of the Government of India targeted for the poorest of the poor was the biggest micro-credit programme in our country and in the world as well. The programme, however, could not achieve the desired objective of poverty alleviation and is often criticized for contaminating the loan portfolios of banks wish Non-Performing Assets (i.e. Non-income yielding loans which warranted writing off).

Inspite of all these noble efforts, as well as the vast banking network comprising 1,50,000 retail rural outlets, the disadvantaged sections of the society could not access financial services from the formal financial system and they had to depend on the information system for meeting their credit need.

The All India Debt and Investment Survey, 1991, reports that approximately 24 per cent of the rural households accessed debt either from formal or informal source. And, of these, 36 per cent had to still depend on informal credit channels, relatives etc. for meeting their needs.

In fact, by the late eighties, the poor came to be recognized as 'unbankable' and there appeared a tendency to blame the poor for the mounting NPAs in the rural bank branches. It was the paradoxical case of finding fault with the customers (the poor) for the inadequacies of the product (subsidized project loans for asset creation).

The less than desired impact of credit flow to the poor could perhaps be attributed to the following factors:

- Target-oriented approach in reaching out to the poor,
- Inability of the formal system to understand the credit needs of the poor,
- Overemphasis on 'asset creation' and absence of any adequate system for meeting emergent credit needs of the poor,
- Emphasis on security and collateral security,
- Excessive paper work and procedural complexity.

There was, therefore, the need for a fresh approach for making available institutional credit to the poor.

The Paradigm Shift

Now, the microfinance approach[29] has engendered a new relationship between the banks and the poor. A relationship which is based on sound business principles and which enables the poor to approach banks as 'customers' and not as 'beneficiaries'. It is with this approach that the SHG-Bank Linkage Programme was initiated in 1992 by the National Bank for Agriculture and Rural Development which marks a watershed in the history of rural banking in India.

A decade of SHG-Bank linkage has finally set at rest the question about 'bank ability' of the poor. The banks have reported 95 per cent on-time repayment by SHGs across the country; and, they have reported nil NPAs. Nothing short of a miracle when compared to earlier interventions. What is the "mantra" of this miracle?

The *mantra* is banking through groups. The essential features of the approach is to provide financial services through the groups of individuals, formed their in joint liability or co-obligation mode. The other dimensions of the microfinance approach are:

- Saving/thrift precedes credit
- Credit is linked with saving/thrift
- Absence of subsidies
- Group plays an important role in credit appraisal, monitoring and recovery
- Installing proper human resource planning and development systems
- Since the government is to keep the interest rates on agriculture on low side, the need for providing adequate cheaper funds/interest subsidy to the co-operatives needs to be looked at carefully and urgently.
- It would be worth while for the government to study the cost structure of the co-operatives, develop appropriate cost norms for rural banking and extend suitable support where the costs are higher inspite of efficient working.
- Co-operatives should be autonomous, self-governed, member-managed institutions
- Legal reform to ensure that co-operatives work as self-reliant, mutually aided autonomous institutions
- Preparation of co-operatives to clean up, starting with an assessment based on accounting norms applied to the financial sector.
- Separate rural banking cadre to ensure full attention for the rural sector and motivate personnel who opt for this cadre, besides providing them with career prospects.

- Primary co-operative credit societies should have direct access to NABARD finance.
- In order to encourage the banks to provide micro-finance to the rural poor, the ceiling on interest rates be removed in order to expand the micro-credit market.
- Multi-laterals, donors, NGOs, private sector led institutions and government should collectively promote micro-finance as a serious part of the financial sector and as an instrument of poverty alleviation.[30]
- Legal and institutional reforms should be introduced.
- Prompt measures to improve their quality of management are need of the time.
- Financial restructuring be started by bringing the primary agricultural co-operative societies to an acceptable level of financial health through cleansing of their balance-sheets and strengthening their capital base[31].
- One time settlement offers be made by the state governments to settle recovery of loans from chronic defaulters.
- Credit and marketing functions be integrated to provide better management and efficiency.
- Co-operatives be brought under the purview of Reserve Bank of India.
- A new regulatory body be formed for co-operatives.
- Elections of co-operatives be held regularly to make them democratic and self reliant.
- To provide complete freedom to such co-operative credit institution in running their affairs, which do not take any financial aid from the government and make them powerful instrument of rural credit.[32]
- Imbalances in the distribution of loans to farmers and artisans when 75 per cent such loans confined only to 7-8 states and the poor states got only 25 per cent.

Such distribution be made balanced and be spread over to poor states also.

- The Kisan Credit cards became popular and the feasibility of finances in rural areas gives many more options to the farmer.
- The introduction of contract farming for export commodities or for use by processors with links to established brands given the farmer a choice, as well as binds him to quality parameters which are transparent.
- Basic needs of the rural sector like land reforms, development of land and irrigation, marketing and transportation infrastructure, etc. be taken into consideration.
- And credit is an important part of these. However, the other urgent needs like public investment in agriculture sector, especially in irrigation are to emphasize much. Even credit will not be able to play its part in the long run, if investments are not made in developing rural infrastructure.
- So, it is now time for the state to fully withdraw from the co-operative sector. This does not mean the state has to withdraw from the function of facilitating access to financial services for the poor and vulnerable, but that it has to recognize that partner of co-operatives is not the only route through which this could happen.

NOTES AND REFERENCES

1. KJS. Satyasai, KC Badatya, Restructuring Rural Credit Co-operative Institutions, *Economic and Political Weekly*, January 29, 2000, pp. 307-30.
2. M.S. Sriram. Reviving Co-operatives Credit Institutions: Implementation Issues, *Economic and Political Weekly*, January 28, 2006, pp. 298-300.
3. P.N. Sankaran, Indian Co-operative Movement : Retrospect and Prospect, *Kurukshetra*, Vol. 52, No. 12, October 2004.

4. Rakesh Mohan, Agricultural Credit in India: Status, Issues and Future Agenda, *Economic and Political Weekly*, March 18, 2006, pp.1013-23.
5. The RBI set up the All India Rural Credit Survey Committee in 1954 which recommended for reorganization and strengthening of primary co-operative societies and district and state level co-operative banks. In 1963, the RBI set-up a Agricultural Refinance Corporation and in 1975 it was reconstituted as Agricultural Refinance and Development Corporation, mainly to finance the land development bank.
6. This includes the states of Bihar, UP, Maharashtra, Gujarat, Tripura, Jammu and Kashmir etc.
7. The states of Tamil Nadu, Karnataka, Rajasthan, M.P. are in this category.
8. Rakesh Mohan, *ibid.*
9. Ibid.
10. They include the High-level Committee on Agricultural Credit through Commercial Banks, 1998 Task Force, 1999, Expert Committee on Rural Credit, 2001, The Working Groups, 2002, to suggest amendment in the Regional Rural Banks Act, 1976, Advisory Committee on Flow of Credit to Agriculture and Related Activities from Bank System, 2004, Task Force on Revival of Rural Co-operative Credit Institutions, 2005, etc., ibid.
11. Kartar Singh, Survival and Growth of Co-operatives and Cooperative Banks: A Strategy, *Kurukshetra*, Vo1.52, No. 12, October 2004, pp. 13-15.
12. Balasaheb Vikhe Patil, Rural Banking: Problems of Localized Banking Institutions, *Economic and Political Weekly*, March 19, 2005, pp.1224-28.
13. Ibid
14. Edgar Parnell, *Reinventing the Co-operative Enterprise for 21st century*, Plinkett Foundation, long Hansboirouoh. Oxford, UK.
15. *The Hindustan Times*, New Delhi, July 27, 2005
16. *The Tribune*, Chandigarh, December 11, 2005
17. Ibid
18. Ibid
19. A.R. Patel, *Rural Credit Delivery System, Kurukshetra*, November 2002
20. J.James, Wadsworth, Co-operative Restructuring, 1989-98, Badeground Material prepared by the Institute of Rural Management, Anand.
21. See a lecture delivered by J.G. Craig on December 7-11, 1992, Institute of Rural Management, Anand.
22. Tara, S. Nair, Rural Financial Intermediation and Commercial Banks : Review of Recent Trends, *Economic and Political Weekly*, January 29, 2000.
23. In 2001, there arose a debate between the Finance Minister and Agriculture Minister of India over the issue of recapitalization of cooperative banks in a meeting of Planning Commission. The Agriculture Minister was of the view that the Central Government

should do for recapitalization and the Planning Commission and some Chief Ministers supported his views. However, the Prime Minister kept sum on the issue, *The Economics Times*, New Delhi, September 14, 2005.

The Central Government doled out Rs.20,000 crores to the commercial banks in 2003. *The Tribune*, Chandigarh, January 6, 2003.

24 .The Vaidyanathan Panel proposed the formula of 53:31:16 i.e. 16% by the co-operatives. Ibid.

25. The Prime Minister suggested such things to the Chief Ministers of different states; *The Times of India*, New Delhi, August 26, 2001.
26. Ibid.
27. P.R. Dubhashi, National Policy on Cooperatives: A Critique, *The Cooperative*, August 2001.
28. N.Muralydharan Balaswami, District Central Co-operative Bank in Agricultural Finance and Recovery, *Indian Co-operative Review*, Vol. XXII, No.3, 1985
29. See *Kurukshetra*, Vol. 52, No.4, February 2004
30. As per suggestions of World Bank, 2005.
31. See recommendations of the Vadayanathem Committee, 2005
32. As stated by the Finance Minister, P. Chidambaram in a NABARD functions of September 13, 2005 in New Delhi, *The Economic Times*, New Delhi, September 14, 2005.

Also see

- Devades Bharoh, *Co-operative Banking and Economic Development*, New Delhi; Deep and Deep, 1998.
- S. Nakkiram, *Wintfred A John, Co-operative Banking in India* Coimbature: Rainbow, 1988
- MOA/GOA, National Policy on Co-operatives, Department of Agriculture and Co-operative, Ministry of Agriculture, Government of India, New Delhi, 2002.

22 Effective Management of Drought at District Level

An Overview

Satyawan and *Anju**

It is a well-known fact that natural disasters strike countries, both developed and developing, causing enormous destruction and creating human sufferings and producing negative impacts on national economies. Due to diverse geo-climatic conditions prevalent in different parts of the globe, different types of natural disasters like floods, droughts, earthquakes, cyclones, landslides, and volcanoes, etc. strike according to the vulnerability of the area. India is considered as the world's most disaster prone country. It has witnessed devastating natural disasters in recent past like droughts, floods, cyclones, earthquakes, landslides, etc.

With its vast territory, large population and unique geoclimatic conditions, Indian sub-continent is exposed to natural catastrophes traditionally. Even today the natural hazards like floods, cyclones, droughts and earthquakes are not rare or unusual phenomenon in the country. While the vulnerability varies from region to region, a large part of the country is exposed to such natural hazards, which often turn into disasters causing significant disruption of socio-economic life of communities leading to loss of life and property.

The shortfall in raining cause droughts or drought like situation in various parts of the country. The country has

* Lecturers, Ch. Devi Lal University, Sirsa, Haryana.

faced some severe earthquakes causing widespread damage to the life and property. India has a coastline of about 8000 km, which is prone to very severe cyclonic formations in the Arabian Sea and Bay of Bengal. Another major problem faced by the country is in the form of landslides and avalanches. Concerned with the impact of natural disasters in the background of the United Nations' resolution, and realizing that the preparedness and prevention are integral components of the development process, the governments at the central and state levels are gradually evolving strategies, policies and programmes for natural disaster mitigations, preparedness and prevention.

Indian subcontinent is among the world's most disaster prone areas.

- 54 per cent of land vulnerable to earthquakes
- 8 per cent of land vulnerable to cyclones
- 5 per cent of land vulnerable to floods
- 16 per cent of land vulnerable to droughts

Parched and cracked lands, dried up streams, ponds, tube wells and even hand pumps, people trudging miles on end in search of drinking water, with their cattle dead and their crops destroyed, farmers turn labourers and labourers are forced to bag, deaths due to starvation comes the next. Is a tragic yet a familiar picture of Indians? This all is because a precious resource that is water is once again being wasted, polluted, mismanaged and allowed to runoff. This is an act, which is played out year after year with almost chilling regularity.

It is not that India has a resource crunch—it rains about 350 million hectare annually. India is in an enviable position with respect to her water resources. The country is literally crisscrossed with 14 major, 44 medium and 55 minor rivers. In addition the vast network of ponds and other water harvesting systems bring essential element to India's people. But only 15 per cent of water resource is tapped and rest is allowed to flow down to the sea.

Drought in simple terms is the dryness due to deficient rainfall or shortage of water for an extended period—a season, a year or several years over a particular region. It can be defined according to *meteorological, hydrological* and *agricultural* criteria.

Any substantial, prolonged deficit of rainfall qualifies as meteorological drought. In India, the southwest monsoon describes the meteorological drought. The monsoon rainfall above 19 per cent of the normal value is termed as excess rain. When the rainfall departure is within 19 per cent it is known as normal rain, below 19 per cent it is deficient rain and scanty if the rainfall is between 59 per cent. There is no consensus over the threshold of the deficit or the minimum duration of the lack of the precipitation that makes a dry spell an official drought. The term drought hinges on the societal expectations and public perceptions that available water is too meager to sustain normal activities. Thus, the meteorological drought is only a representation of the rainfall distribution pattern and statistics.

The *hydrological drought* is the manifestation of critically low ground-water tables and noticeable reduced river and stream flow. It involves the water availability and the off-take rates in normal requirement i.e. domestic, agricultural and industrial usages.

The *agricultural drought* refers to extended dry spell in which the lack of rainfall or the water source results in insufficient moisture in the root zone of the soil causing adverse effects on cultivated vegetation. The agricultural drought is the impact of meteorological and hydrological droughts on the crop yields. It is the agricultural drought that affects socio-economically the most and causes serious disruption to the nation's food supply.

Drought may occur at any place and time, causing from mild annoyance to deaths through famine. The severity depends on the intensity of rainfall deficiency, duration of dry spell, size of the affected area and the extent of available water resources such as irrigation facilities. To describe the severity, an index called "Palmer Drought Severity Index' is the index ranges between +6 (very much wetter than normal) to - 6 (extremely severe drought). The index measures the relative dryness of local weather within successive time intervals. It accounts for the differences between the actual precipitation and the amount normally expected to sustain evapo-transpiration, run-off and moisture storage in a given climate and location.

Historically, the country has been grappling with droughts very frequently during the last sixty years India has experienced more than fifteen droughts out of which the 1987 drought was the worst which affected almost half of the country.

Table 22.1: The major droughts of the last five decades are as follows:

Year	*% area affected in the country*	*Category*
1951	33.2	Moderate
1952	25.8	Slight
1965	42.9	Moderate
1966	32.3	Moderate
1968	20.6	Slight
1969	19.9	Slight
1971	13.3	Slight
1972	44.4	Severe
1974	29.3	Moderate
1979	39.4	Moderate
1982	33.1	Moderate
1985	30.1	Moderate
1986	19.0	Slight
1987	49.2	Severe

Factors Promoting Droughts

In all, about 16 per cent area of the country is drought prone. The regions most prone to drought are the arid, semi arid and dry sub-humid areas. The major factors responsible for the droughts in India are:

- Deficient rainfall
- Demographic patterns

- Poor water management strategy
- Indiscriminate exploitation of the ground-water by the industries and the agricultural sectors
- Soil erosion
- Large scale deforestation for various purposes
- The meteorological causes of drought vary according to the climate of the affected region.

Two major points emerge from the recent write-ups on the subject:

(i) Drought is more of a man-made disaster resulting from total mismanagement of our water resources, and

(ii) The debate over the issue revolves round two extreme positions. The first propagates that big dams and irrigation projects are badly needed to solve the present water crises and the second searches for answers in our traditional rainwater harvesting techniques for domestic and agricultural purposes. India has a rich tradition of sustainable water harvesting systems from the ages.

Remnants of such systems are still found in several places all over the India.

- Rajasthan: Tankas
- Thar desert: Kunds
- Kutch : Virdas
- Ladhak: Small tanks called as ZING to collect snow water in daytime
- Meghalaya: Interconnected Bamboo pipes to make channels.

The deficiencies in the modern water system can be removed to a great extent by resuscitating these ancient Indian water management techniques.

Rain Water Harvesting (RWH)

The principle of collecting and using precipitation from a catchment surface.

Why Rain Water Harvesting

- Surface water is inadequate to meet our demand and we have to depend on groundwater.
- Due to rapid urbanization the infiltration of rain water into the subsoil has decreased and hence recharging of ground-water has diminished.

Objectives of RWH

- To reduce runoff
- To store excess water for subsequent times
- To maintain ground-water table

Rainwater Harvesting Techniques

Two main types

- Storage of rainwater in impoundments (underground tanks, ponds, chech dams, etc.) for further use,
- Recharge to ground-water, with the help of Pits, Trenches, Dug wells, Hand-pumps, Recharge Wells, Recharge shafts, Spreading techniques, etc.

Impacts of Drought

Droughts devastate crops and usher in difficult times leading to famines, malnutrition, epidemics, forced migration, economic destabilization, loss of lives and social conflicts. The primary effects of drought mainly stem from lack of water. However, the secondary effects follow resulting form the primary effects. The primary effects are loss of water for drinking and hygienic use, loss of crops, livestocks and other animals. The impacts of drought cannot be assessed on the basis of economical loss alone. The social and the ecological/ environmental damages are irreversible so that their impacts remain lorever.

Prediction and Management

Disasters have been mankind's constant companion since time immemorial. Natural disasters continue to strike unabated and without notice. The previous decade, International Decade for Natural Disaster Reduction (1990-2000), was dedicated to promoting solutions to reduce risk from natural hazards. The decade, on the contrary, ended with more deaths from more disasters, involving greater economic losses and more human dislocation and suffering. It was then realized by the international community that the dedication of a decade to the core issue could not be expected to solve the repercussions of centuries of mismanagement arid of passive fatalism before the vagaries of nature.

Though it is not possible to completely avoid the natural disasters, but the sufferings can be minimized by creating proper awareness of the likely disasters and its impact by developing a suitable warning system, disaster preparedness and management of disasters through application of information technology tools. The changing trends have opened up a large number of scientific and technological resources and skills to reduce disaster risk.

GIS and Remote Sensing can be used in drought relief management such as early warnings of drought conditions will help to plan out the strategies to organise relief work. Satellite data may be used to target potential ground-water sites for taking up well-digging programmes. Satellite data provides valuable tools for evaluating areas subject to desertification. Film transparencies, photographs and digital data can be used for the purpose of locating, assessing and monitoring deterioration of natural conditions in a given area. The National Agricultural Drought Assessment and Management System (NADAMS) has been developed by the Department of Space for the Department of Agriculture and

Cooperation, and is primarily based on monitoring of vegetation status through National Oceanic and Atmospheric Administration (NOAA), Advanced Very High Resolution (AVHR) data. The drought assessment is based on a comparative evaluation of satellite observed green vegetation cover (both area and greenness) of a district in any specific time period, with that of any similar period in previous years.

Drought is a "Creeping" or slow onset natural hazard, which develops over a period of months and even years and spreads over a extensive area. Factors like water use and availability of additional water resources need to be closely monitored. The length of the warning time is not well defined and is highly subjective to a region. Metrological and agricultural indicators together with remote sensing observations are relied upon for early warning of drought.

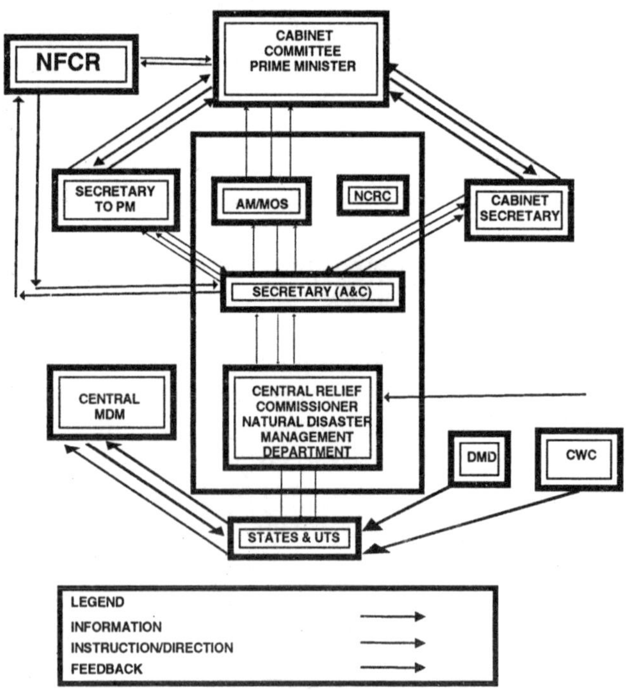

Fig. 22.1 : Natural Hazards–The Interaction Pattern in the Government

The present government policy for drought relief has evolved over a period of time, based on long experiences of drought management in the country. Ministry of Agriculture, Government of India is the nodal ministry for drought management in the country. The onus of declaring a district drought effected lies completely on the state. The district collector makes an assessment and if more than fifty percent of the crops are found damaged the district is declared drought effected. The report is then sent to the states' revenue department.

Once drought is declared...

- Revenue collection for the region is suspended.
- Interest on loans is waived.
- Loan recovery is either stalled or staggered for a certain period.
- Food for work programmes are started.
- Cash relief is distributed to all farmers.
- Assistance is given for crop damage, damage to animal husbandry, fodder, etc.

National level efforts are made for immediate relief to victims. Funds are dispensed out of the Calamity Relief Fund (CRF), National Fund for Calamity Relief (NFCR). Most of the disaster prone states have a relief commissioner responsible for emergency preparedness. At district level the district collectors are responsible for preparing emergency response plans for directing, supervising, coordinating and monitoring relief measures.

Keeping in view the long-term needs of drought prone areas various development programmes have been launched by Government of India. These include :

- Desert Development Programme (DDP)
- Drought Prone Area Programme (DPAP)

- Food for Work Programme (FWP)
- National Rural Employment Programme (NREP)
- Rural Landless Employment Guarantee Programme (RLEGP)
- Integrated Rural Development Programme (IRDP)
- Accelerated Rural Water Supply Programme (ARWSP)

The state governments are autonomous in organizing relief operations in the event of natural disaster and a long-term preparedness/rehabilitation measures. The state governments efforts are supplemented by Central Government. There is a State Crisis Management Group (SCMC) under the Chairmanship of Chief Secretary/Relief Commissioner to take into consideration the infrastructure and guidance received, from time to time, from Government of India and formulates action plans for dealing with different natural disasters. There is a State Level Control Room set-up whenever a disaster situation develops. States are further divided into districts, each headed by the District Collector (also known as the District Magistrate or Deputy Commissioner), who is the focal point at the district level for directing, supervising and monitoring relief measures for disaster and for preparation of district level plans. The Collector exercises coordinating and supervisory powers over functionaries of all the departments at the district level. The relief measures are reviewed by the District Relief Committee consisting of official and no-official members, including local legislators and members of parliament. In the wake of Natural disasters, a Control Room is set-up in the district for day-to-day monitoring of the rescue and relief operations on a continuing basis. The Collector/Deputy Commissioner maintains close liaison with the Central Government authorities in the districts, namely, Army, Air Force and Navy, Ministry of Water Resources, etc., who supplement the effort of the district administration in the rescue and relies' operation, They also co-ordinate all voluntary efforts by mobilizing the non-government organizations capable of working in such situations.

Fig. 22.2 : District/Local Level Disaster Management Structure

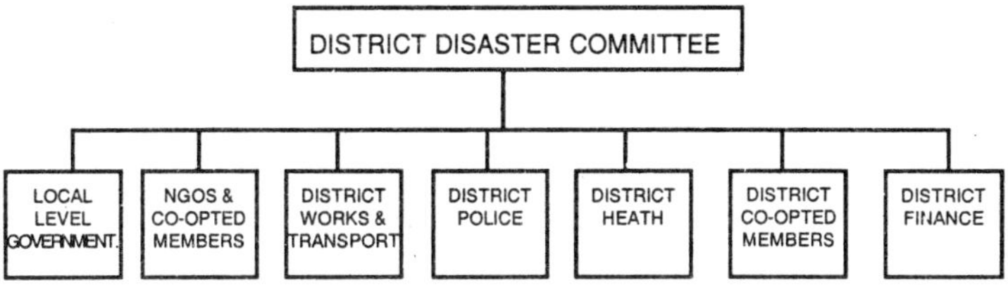

Table 22.2 : The major programmes under this category are:

Ministry of Agriculture	(i)	National Watershed Development Project for Rainfed Areas
	(ii)	Watershed Development Projects in Shifting Cultivation areas
	(iii)	Reclamation of Alkali Soils
Ministry of Rural Development	(i)	Integrated Wasteland Development Project
	(ii)	Drought Prone Areas Programme
	(iii)	Desert Development Programme
Ministry of Environment and Forest	(i)	Integrated Afforestation and Eco-Development Project
	(ii)	Area Oriented Fuel Wood and Fodder Project
	(iii)	Grant in Aid Scheme for Afforestation and Tree Planting
Planning Commission	(i)	Western Ghat Development Programmes

On the basis of lessons learnt from 1987 and other droughts in the country, the Government of India revised its guidelines in 1989 on drought management. The current policy emphasizes more on mitigation and preventive measures. The relief measures have been integrated with the development in the new approach. The government has identified areas prone to droughts, which are being continually treated under various programmes, implemented by ministry of rural development, ministry of agriculture, ministry of water resources, ministry of environment and forest and planning commission. These programmes along with preventing and mitigating drought also help in developing the wasteland of the country.

The situation of the drought are best tackled by a common approach of watershed management, which aims at overall development of the region along with measures for mitigation of droughts. The results of these programmes have been very encouraging and enthusiastic.

In this era of advanced satellites and other remote sensing techniques, the impacts of disasters in general can be reduced considerably through awareness knowledge and optimum use of technologies with a focus on cultivation of "Culture of Prevention".

The strategy designed for preventing and mitigating the natural disaster such as drought should take into account the following points:

(1) Bottom – Up – Approach.
(2) The approach can not be uniform for all the places
(3) The technique should be based on indigenous know-how because that has evolved over centuries in a given economic and ecological setting
(4) Peoples movement.
(5) Simple technologies so that farmers and villagers can adopt it.
(6) Low cost, so that resource poor people can adopt and replicate with minimum external support.
(7) In Indian setting the rainfall is limited (i.e. 3-4 months) and the technology should answer the challenge of how to relocate water in time so that water received during monsoon becomes available in the entire year.
(8) It is time we should modify our traditional systems of water harvesting into the modern systems to get maximum benefits.

(9) The deficiencies in the modern water distribution systems can be removed to a great extent by resuscitating the ancient Indian water management traditions. The modern must assimilate the merits of the traditional. An amalgamation of old and new means of progress would solve the problem to a considerable extent.

It has been observed in India that after every disaster both people and administration talk much about organization and problems of disaster management. But with the restoration of normalcy both tend to forget the gravity of preparedness and orientation. In any form of management, the organization structure plays vital role. In disaster management the cooperation between government and people is a key factor. Therefore, the organizational structure should be so designed that the government agencies and common people can support and cooperate each other. Table 22.3 provides a skeletal view of five-tier disaster management organization.

Table 22.3 : Organization Structure for Disaster Management

Tire	*Organization Type*		*Level Constitution*
I	National Disaster Management Council (NDMC)	National	Prime Minister and the Council of Ministers, Leader of the Opposition five experts on Disaster Management
II	State Disaster Management Council (SDMC)	State	Chief Minister and Council of Ministers, Leader of the Opposition, Two experts on Disaster Management, General Officer Commanding for that region, one expert each from voluntary sector, Red Cross and UNISEF.
III	District Disaster Management Council (DDMC)	District	Collector, Superintendent of Police, Executive Engineers for PWD, Electrical, PHD, Irrigation Tele-phones and National Highways, District Agriculture Officer, Chief District Medical Officer, one senior most

(Contd...)

(Contd...)

			elected people's representative of the district two members each from voluntary service organization, senior and experienced citizens of the district.
IV	Block Panchayat Disaster Control Council (PDCC)	Block	Sarpanch and his Executive Members, Block Development Officer, two members from voluntary service organizations, Officer in-charge of the Police. Stations of the region, Doctor in-charge of the PHC, two senior citizens of the Panchayat.
V	Village Disaster Control Council (VDCC)	Village	Two experienced senior citizen of the village, two women members, five young executives (not above the age of 45 or below 25 years), two members each from SC & ST and other minority segments from the active village club or voluntary organization.

Each tier should have its own fund to be utilized for disaster management. Under no circumstances this fund should be transferred to any other fund or be utilized for any purpose other than disaster management.

(A) *Disaster Control Force (DCF):* Both central and state government should constitute a specialized task force titled "Disaster Control Force".

(B) *District Disaster Control Team (DDCT):* At district level, the state government should empower the district collector to enroll civilian volunteers from different registered and active voluntary organizations, NCC, NSS, Scouts and Guides and other organizations to constitute an active DDCT. The members of DDCT should be trained. A consolidated remunration should be given to the volunteers.

These need to be urgently considered for evolving a national policy keeping in view of the Government of India's commitment to the Yokohama Strategy for Natural Disaster Reduction :

(1) The first and the foremost is to restructure the National Policy on disaster management reflecting the holistic approach involving *prevention, mitigation* and *preparedness* in *pre-disaster phase* with appropriate additional funding, alongwith the so far existent policy of the *postdisaster relief and rehabilitation* under crisis management.

(2) *Creation of awareness* for disaster reduction is urgently needed amongst policy makers, decision-makers, administrators, professionals (architects, engineers and others at various levels) financial institutions (banks, insurance, house financing institutions) and NGOs, and voluntary organisations.

(3) *Creating awareness for improving preparedness amongst the communities*, using media, school education, and the network of the building centre.

(4) *Appropriate amendments* in the legislative and regulatory instruments (state laws, master plans, development area plan rules, building regulations and byelaws of local bodies) alongwith *strengthening of the enforcement mechanisms* at different levels.

(5) *Capacity building at local and regional levels* for undertaking rapid-assessment surveys and investigations of the nature and extent of damage in post disaster situations.

(6) *Conducting micro-zonation surveys of large areas* falling in the disaster prone regions and preparing appropriate preparedness and mitigation plans on an urgent basis.

(7) *To create a suitable institutional mechanism at national/state level to advise and help the existing disaster relief set up in formulation and updating of short and long-range action plans* for the preparedness, mitigation and prevention of natural disasters. (The mechanisms suggested are establishment of a National Scientific and Technical Committee at Central level and Natural Disaster Mitigation Centres at State levels).

(8) To promote the study of natural disaster prevention, mitigation and preparedness as *subjects in architecture and engineering* curricula.

(9) *To create detailed database* on hazard occurrences, damage caused to buildings and infrastructure and the economic losses suffered and ensure its accessibility to interested researchers for effective analysis of costs of disasters and benefits of mitigative actions.

REFERENCES

Bose, S. and Saxena N.; Drought : The Indian Scenario, *Employment News*, May 2000, vol. XXV, no. 9, pp. 1-2.

Dhameja, A.; Coping with Droughts, *Employment News*, June 2000, vol. XXIV, no. 11, pp. 1, 3.

Khan, H.J.; Drought A Man Made Scourge, *Science Reporter*, June 2000, pp. 10-15.

Pattanaik, P.K., A Blue Print for Effective Management of Natural Disasters, *Yojana*, July 2000, pp. 19-25.

Sabri, M.A.; Cyclones and Disaster Management, *Kurukshetra*, May 2000, pp. 33-36.

Satendra, Droughts, *Employment News*, August 2002, vol. XXVII, no. 18, pp. 2.

Index